CREATIVE CENTERS AND HOMES

Volumes in this Series

Volume I. RATIONALE FOR CHILD CARE SERVICES: PROGRAMS VS. POLITICS

Volume II. MODEL PROGRAMS AND THEIR COMPONENTS

Volume III. CREATIVE CENTERS AND HOMES

Volume IV. SPECIAL NEEDS AND SERVICES

Early Education Series

Child Care: A Comprehensive Guide, Vols. 1–4
Auerbach, S., Ph.D. (Ed.)

Day Care: Problems, Process and Prospects
Peters, D.L., Ph.D., (Ed.)

Day Care and Early Education Magazine

Headstart: A Tragi-Comedy with Epilogue
Payne, J.S., Ed., Mercer, C.D., M.S., Payne, R.A. and Davison, R.G., B.A.

Let's Play and Learn
Hartman, H.

Sparks: Activities to Help Children Learn at Home
Belton, S., M.A. and Terbough, C., M.A.

Home Visitor's Kit:
Training and Practitioner Materials for Paraprofessionals in Family Settings
Gotts, E., Ph.D.

Enhancing Self-Concept in Early Childhood: Theory and Practice
Samuels, Shirley, C., Ed.D.

CREATIVE CENTERS AND HOMES

Infant Care, Planning and Developing Family Day Care, and
Approaches to Designing and Creating the Child's Environment

VOLUME THREE
in the series
CHILD CARE:
A COMPREHENSIVE GUIDE

Edited by
Stevanne Auerbach, Ph.D.
with
James A. Rivaldo

Foreword by
Edward Zigler, Ph.D.
Yale University

HUMAN SCIENCES PRESS
72 Fifth Avenue   3 Henrietta Street
NEW YORK, NY 10011 ● LONDON, WC2E 8LU

Library of Congress Catalog Number 78-7401

ISBN: 0-87705-275-1

Copyright © 1978 by Stevanne Auerbach

All rights reserved. No part of this work may be reproduced or utilized in any form or by any means, electronic or mechanical, including photocopying, microfilm and recording, or by any information storage and retrieval system without permission in writing from the publisher.

HUMAN SCIENCES PRESS
72 Fifth Avenue
New York, New York 10011

Printed in the United States of America
89 987654321

Library of Congress Cataloging in Publication Data

Auerbach, Stevanne.
    Creative centers and homes.

    (Their Child care—a comprehensive guide; v. 3)
      Bibliography: p.
      Includes index.
      1. Day care centers—United States—Addresses, essays, lectures. 2. Infants—Care and hygiene—Addresses, essays, lectures. I. Rivaldo, James A., joint author. II. Title.
HV741.A94 vol. 3 [HV854]   362.7 08   78-7401
ISBN 0-87705-275-1

PREFACE TO VOLUME III

In approaching child care as a developmental service to all families, we recognize that the need begins with the care of the very young child and will depend on the specific situation of the individual family. Many parents must return to work or school when their child is an infant. For many young families, organized services are not available or are not geared to the specific needs of the young family. Some reasons for this are the high costs of offering quality infant care, confusion about the deleterious effects of parent-child separation, and resulting parental indecision. As the result, we see in each community the shortage of good care for infants and very young children.

Perhaps with the systematic approach suggested by many in this series, the government in cooperation with state and local communities will find a way to provide a variety of services that supports the needs of families with infants. Warm, responsive environments will be created with a well-trained staff and the adequate funding necessary to develop flexible, long-range developmental services. The views and experiences of the authors in this volume are intended to assist the reader in assessing what the components of these services should be.

This volume continues the theme of this series in viewing child care as an integral and vital comprehensive service for all families. We began in the first volume with politics, history, and needs, reviewed outstanding programs in Volume II, and now focus on the specific services required. Among these are the earliest age at which to begin child care, the location and extent of services to be offered, the important aspects of quality controls, and the actual design of the environment for young children.

The author's viewpoints and suggestions provide an important contribution to analyzing the nature of the services and the quality of the physical spaces for child care programs.

We hope the reader will find this information pertinent and thought-provoking to their own situations. In the next volume more programmatic issues are included to expand the areas under consideration in this series.

S. A.

CONTENTS

Preface	STEVANNE AUERBACH	v
Foreword	EDWARD P. ZIGLER	ix
Introduction		xv

1. Infant Day Care: Fads, Facts, and Fancies   BETTYE M. CALDWELL   1

2. Infant Day Care in the Black Community: Boon or Boondoggle?   GLORIA J. POWELL   15

3. An Alternative for Infants with Special Needs   JUDITH LEWIS   39

4. Family Day Care: One Alternative   JUNE SOLNIT SALE   60

5. Family Day Care: The Humanistic Side   LORRAINE B. WALLACH and MARIA W. PIERS   75

6. Reaching Family Day Care Homes   BERTHA ADDISON   83

7. Developing Quality for Family
   Day Care   MARGARET ANN BROSTROM   93
8. Licensing Child Care   EDNA H. HUGHES   108
9. Registration of Family Day Care
   Homes in Massachusetts   LINDA McCAULEY   123
10. Suggestions for Designing a
    Children's Center   FRED OSMON   137
11. Creating Interior Spaces for
    Child Care   VALERIE ANIXTER
    and ALYSON KUHN   163
12. Designing Stimulating
    Environments for
    Children   GLORIA M. WEISSBERG   184
13. Creating Environments
    for Play   JAY BECKWITH   215

Appendix   239
Bibliography   258
Index   265

FOREWORD

REFLECTIONS AND NEEDS IN CHILD CARE*

In dealing with current problems of the American family, a government responsive to family needs certainly must come to grips with the issue of day care for the children of America's working mothers. Good quality day care was given the number one priority at the 1970 White House Conference on Children. An example of the magnitude of this problem can be seen in a needs assessment carried out to develop a state plan for children in Texas: 60% of those queried spontaneously listed day care for their children as their most pressing need. Thus day care is a problem of immense proportions and one whose solution is not attainable overnight. What the nation really needs is a 20-year plan for a child care system that would involve realistic increments in public and private funding, as the development of facilities and increase in trained personnel war-

*Excerpted from testimony at hearings on "American Families: Trends and Pressures," Committee on Labor and Public Welfare, U.S. Senate Subcommittee on Children and Youth.

rants. While I think that the real solution to the day care problem can come only from such careful long-term planning, there are several things that can be done immediately to improve the day care situation in our nation.

Approximately one billion dollars were spent in 1972 by the federal and state governments for child care, with the bulk of this money going to two programs: Head Start, administered by the Office of Child Development (OCD), and Title IV (of the Social Security Act), administered by the Community Services Agency within the Social and Rehabilitation Service of the U.S. Department of Health, Education, and Welfare. It should be noted that approximately one-third of the Head Start monies is being spent for day care for working mothers. There has been no real coordination between these two sizable programs, and the rules, regulations, and philosophies of each of the two programs are at odds with those of the other. Were these two programs combined and operated by a single agency, some order as well as new economics could be brought to the child care effort which the federal government is already funding. Indeed, such a combined program would finally give the nation at least an embryonic national child care system providing parents with a variety of child care services, including the all-important service of day care for working mothers. Such a unified system could be held responsible for ensuring the quality of child care that is necessary if children are not to be harmed by programs mounted and funded by the federal government. I think that Head Start has been sensitive to the quality issue while the Title IV program has not.

When we think of day care we often think of centers serving 30 or more children. This accounts for only a small percentage of the day care funded through Title IV. A much larger percentage of these funds is paid by local welfare agencies to family day care homes which typically serve six or fewer children. Some of these homes are good, but others are ghastly, and thus we are witnessing federal funds being spent to place children in circumstances detrimental to their development. If combining the Title IV and Head Start programs into an organized and unified child care system seems to be too demanding a task, then I would suggest that at least we direct our attention to the problem of implementing and enforcing some minimum standards for every kind of day care that is subsidized by federal funds. Such a set of enforceable and realistic standards was developed under my direction at OCD. These standards were then sent to the Office of Management and Budget and, to the best of my knowledge, have never again surfaced. Until such standards are promulgated and enforced, children will continue to experience the horrors documented in the National Council of Jewish Women's report by Mary Keyserling, *Windows on Day Care*.

Even within the present framework, day care can be improved and made more available. Family day care can be of good quality and should continue over the years to be an important component of the total day care picture. It is necessary to provide day care mothers with training and general support by those equipped to give it. There are already commonsensible, practical models of how this can be done. One good example is the Pacific Oaks model in which family day care homes are tied into a network with a central training and technical support facility.

The present day care picture also suffers from a serious lopsidedness in that concern is almost totally limited to the preschool child. The fact of the matter is that two-thirds of the children in this nation who require day care are of school age and need adult supervision before and after school and during vacations. Because of our slowness in developing day care models for school-age children and in inducing schools and other institutions to employ such models, we are now witnessing the national tragedy of over a million latchkey children, cared for by no one, and probably another million are being cared for by siblings who are themselves too young to assume such responsibilities. The human cost of this situation to families and to the nation as a whole is great indeed. Although there is growing concern over increasing juvenile delinquency, few have forcefully pointed out the relation between the growing phenomenon of young children socializing with one another and the rise in juvenile delinquency. If this nation is interested in preventing delinquency rather than in punishing it, a major component of such an attempt should be an expanded school-age day care program.

Another child care problem that can and should be dealt with immediately is the need for personnel. Our nation simply does not have an adequate cadre of appropriately trained individuals to care for even the present number of children in our child care systems. The development of such a cadre should have top priority and should consist in large part of personnel whose salaries can be met without making day care costs astronomical. OCD moved forcefully into this area by creating a new child care profession in America—the Child Development Associate. The national implementation of the Child Development Associate concept is now in the hands of a consortium consisting of major early childhood education associations and associations representing a variety of consumer and child advocacy groups. A key feature of this new thrust is that accreditation and certification are granted on the basis of demonstrated competency rather than on completion of academic programs. However, if this program is ever to produce enough child care workers, it will require the infusion of some new federal money, probably in the neighborhood of 50 million dollars. This is a relatively small amount when one thinks of the annual billion dollars now being spent, much of which is buying poor day care primarily because well-trained people who can be employed at a reasonable cost are simply not available.

Let me conclude by saying that it is my conviction that we can spend the money that we already have at our disposal more effectively. We certainly know how to do much more than we are presently doing. We can agree that every child of a working mother has a right to a day care environment conducive to his optimal growth, and that every working mother has a right to the peace of mind that the existence of such an environment for her child provides. We can agree that the family is the most important determinant of a child's development, and that our society must do everything it can to support family life. Perhaps we cannot reasonably expect major new commitments at this point, but we can and should demand a renewed commitment to the proposition that families are indeed important and that it is the federal government's role to reduce the stresses and to meet the problems confronting families. Such a renewed commitment would at least constitute a first step in developing a real family policy for America.

INTRODUCTION

The first volume in this series, *Child Care: A Comprehensive Guide,* introduces the history of child care and the political issues in child care programs. Volume two reviews various communities' experiences in starting child care programs and focuses on a central component of quality comprehensive programs.

This, the third volume, begins with an examination of perhaps the most controversial issue in child care, the earliest age at which a child should enter a program. Three of the authors in this volume evaluate the experiences of various infant care programs and focus on the special requirements of these programs.

The core of Volume three deals with family day care homes, a system of child care intermediate between private in-home care and child care centers. In addition to describing various family day care programs, this volume discusses the procedures and problems in certifying and regulating family day care homes.

Volume three concludes with suggestions by experts of ways to design interior and exterior environments for maximum stimulation, enrichment, and efficiency in child care programs.

Bettye M. Caldwell offers data on the effects of infant child care on young children. Although limited by the small number of children currently involved in infant programs and available for long-range study, her report nonetheless concludes confidently that fears of the consequences of maternal deprivation are unjustified in quality infant care programs, and that considerable benefits to the child and parents may indeed result.

Gloria J. Powell examines the special needs of black children in infant care programs and stresses that such programs will succeed only if they avoid the mistaken assumptions about black family life that have caused public education to fail so conspicuously in serving black children. Instead of concentrating on the supposed inadequacies of black family life, infant care programs should recognize and use to good advantage the cultural strengths of the black family.

Judith Lewis describes the program of the San Francisco Family Developmental Center, in which high-school-aged mothers and fathers receive credit for work with their own children in the Center. High-school-age parents bring very special problems and conflicts to child care programs, and the Family Developmental Center provides unique services to the emotional and educational needs of these parents.

The general public views the issue of child care as a clear-cut choice between children living at home with their mothers or attending a child care center similar to an elementary school or nursery school. Much of the debate on child care issues turns on questions of whether an institutionalized environment can ever approximate the warm, nurturing security of the ideal family environment. Likewise, much of the criticism of child care programs focuses on the depersonalization and lack of individual attention paid to children and their families in child care centers.

One often-overlooked possibility for providing convenient, affordable, quality child care in a homelike environment is the family day care home. With a degree of social service regulation and funding and the availability of outside resources and training for providers, family day care homes have enormous potential for granting much needed relief for the child care shortage, as well as for being a source of personal fulfillment and income for the family day care providers, who ordinarily might not join the labor force.

Family day care homes have suffered from a lack of communication and the lack of resource pooling among themselves. Usually the fees paid by parents provide for little more than a baby-sitting service with few or no developmental opportunities for the children. The family day care providers usually lack formal training in child development and rely more on their personal experience and intuition as mothers. However, once they become involved, many providers seek continuing education to upgrade their skills and to improve their qualifications.

Although most communities license family day care homes, the licensing procedures often serve only to limit the number of such homes and to discourage unlicensed homes from seeking assistance from the community.

An entire section of this volume is devoted to family day care homes because, despite their prevalence in many communities, their enormous potential for meeting the criteria of comprehensive quality child care programs has not received the recognition it deserves.

June Solnit Sale discusses the efforts of the Community Family Day Care Project, which explored an existing network of licensed and unlicensed child care resources delivering a variety of services to a diverse group of children. Ms. Sale describes the educational, affective, and social components of the program, operated by women of varied ethnic and economic backgrounds, and she discusses the creation of a self-help organization aimed at enhancing the status and importance of family day care mothers.

Lorraine B. Wallach and Maria W. Piers assert that family day care settings vary widely and present difficulties in regulation, but the key to effective service to children in a family care home is the care giver. Their paper discusses the requisites of a family day care home and the necessary attributes of the care giver.

Bertha Addison describes her efforts as a member of a project for the Far West Laboratory for Educational Research and Development to reach family day care homes and to introduce, through the Parent-Child Toy Lending Library, a training program with developmental components to these homes.

Edna Hughes examines the theory and purpose of licensing and the role of the government in setting standards to safeguard the public interest in child care. She describes the interrelationships among various government regulatory agencies responsible for dealing with the various components of comprehensive child care systems, and she draws attention to the many areas of overlap, conflict, and confusion. The blurring of distinctions between licensing and regulation is the source of much of this confusion, and Ms. Hughes spells out the difference.

Margaret Ann Brostrom outlines the procedures followed for licensing family day care homes in California and focuses on the experiences of The Neighborhood Day Care Program of San Mateo County in establishing a community family day care home system.

Linda McCauley relates the experiences Massachusetts had in regulating family day care. Licensing proved too restrictive and time-consuming and often served to limit, rather than to expand, the availability of child care. Massachusetts has devised a more satisfactory system to establish basic standards of quality—a system of registration and guidance that enables day care homes first to establish themselves, then to demonstrate their credentials in follow-up examinations and evaluation, rather than in rigorous prelicensing procedures.

Few aspects of a child care program bear more directly on its eventual success than does the environment in which its daily activities take place. Young children are sensitively attuned to their environment and readily adopt the mood suggested by the colors, decorations, displays of their work, objects of interest, and play equipment found there. A bright, cheerful environment contributes substantially to a child's vitality and sense of belonging. A drab, institutional environment does little to stimulate the natural curiosity, imagination, and feelings of security a small child needs.

The physical organization of the child care center's facilities likewise organizes the activities that take place there. Thoughtfully designed and well-organized facilities enable activities to flow smoothly, freeing the staff to devote greater attention to the children rather than to housekeeping.

Different types of child care programs operate more efficiently and effectively in differently designed facilities. For example, programs emphasizing free choice of activity by the children require that the children have ready access to different activity centers, each of which functions independently of the surrounding areas. Programs stressing more structure and greater teacher involvement require a setting that encourages children to focus their attention on group instruction. Whatever the philosophy of the child care program, careful thought must be given to its specific physical requirements. The contributors to this volume present relevant considerations for designing the interiors and outside play areas of day care centers.

Fred Osmon, in excerpts from his book, *Patterns for Designing a Children's Center,* presents perhaps the most complete guide to all the major considerations in designing or remodeling a child care center. Without involving himself in the debates about program content, Mr. Osmon provides a comprehensive body of information that can be applied to almost any child care program.

Valerie Annixter and Allison Kuhn suggest novel and inexpensive ideas for creating an exciting and stimulating environment for young children. Emphasizing typical problems and situations faced by child care people working on limited budgets, Ms. Annixter and Ms. Kuhn bring to light the seemingly small details that make enormous differences in the effectiveness of child care programs.

Gloria Weissberg, a talented designer, focuses on each of the different areas in a typical children's center and suggests creative, important, and inexpensive ways to maximize their utility and enjoyment by young children. Her accompanying illustrations graphically depict the potentials for the imaginative use of space.

Jay Beckwith brings a playful spirit to his exposition of a philosophy of children's playgrounds. Voicing his dissatisfaction with typical commerically manufactured play equipment, Mr. Beckwith challenges child care people and parents alike to apply their imaginations and creative energy to creating playgrounds built of everyday materials in unexpected configurations. The sense of play involved in creating Mr. Beckwith's spontaneous playgrounds finds later expression in the enthusiasm with which children use them.

CONTRIBUTORS TO VOLUME III

BERTHA ADDISON has served as Coordinator of the Day Care Training Program of the Far West Laboratory for Educational Research and Development, and of the Richmond, California, Model Cities Day Care Program. She has focused her efforts on the Parent-Child Toy Lending Library and has published several articles on its use as a developmental education tool.

VALERIE ANIXTER became interested in day care as a result of her own experiences in locating child care arrangements for her two children. A former teacher in a Marin County day school and in her own home, Ms. Anixter has served on a committee for designing and constructing playgrounds.

JAY BECKWITH, an independent planner-builder of schools, parks, and day care centers, has designed innovative playgrounds throughout California, and primarily in the San Francisco Bay Area. Combining a degree in fine arts and graduate study in child development, Mr. Beckwith has described his work in a substantial book, *Playground,* published by the San Francisco Book Company and Houghton-Mifflin. The De Young Museum of Art in San Francisco featured a one-man show of facilities installed by this creative new designer. Jay Beckwith conducts workshops in planning and building community playgrounds.

MARGARET ANN BROSTROM is Director of the Neighborhood Day Care Program sponsored by the Family Service Agency of San Mateo County, California. Previously she taught at Bing Nursery School, the child study laboratory school at Stanford University. Ms. Brostrom's experience includes several years as a parent with her four children in a Parent Participation Nursery School, President of the Peninsula Council of Parent Participation Nursery Schools, and President of the California Council of Parent Participation Nursery Schools. She also served on the Child Care Task Force for the city of Palo Alto, California.

BETTYE M. CALDWELL, PhD. has served as Director of the Children's Center at Syracuse University, and has combined research and teaching as Professor of Elementary Education at the University of Arkansas and Director of the Center for Early Development and Education in Little Rock, Arkansas. The Center is a comprehensive educational child care facility for infants, preschoolers, and elementary school children. It is jointly sponsored by the University of Arkansas and the Little Rock School District and is housed in an elementary school. In addition, Dr. Caldwell is the editor of Volume III of the *Review of Child Development Research* and was until recently the editor of *Child Development*. She also serves on many national committees concerned with either developing or evaluating programs for children.

EDNA H. HUGHES, until her recent retirement, served as a specialist in day care and residential care licensing in the Office of Child Development in Washington, D.C. She is currently creating a national organization for improved standards for child care. Her previous experience included several years as a consultant on public welfare services with the Child Welfare League of America, 8 years as the State Director of Child Welfare Services in the Tennessee Department of Public Welfare, child welfare casework for the State of Tennessee, and 9 years teaching mainly high school in the Tennessee public schools.

ALYSON KUHN has had a wide variety of experiences with preschool children. She and a friend operated their own nursery school, Pint-Sized Playhouse, near Irvine, California. She has also taught in a Montessori kindergarten and prekindergarten program, and has worked with a laboratory preschool affiliated with the University of California at Irvine.

JUDITH LEWIS, Project Director of the Family Developmental Center, has worked in the area of infant development since 1960, when as Staff Psychologist for the Philadelphia Child Guidance Clinic she participated in the revision of the Bayley Scales of Mental and Motor Development as part of a nationwide research study. She subsequently taught infant assessment and worked in the field of infant research as Pediatric Psychologist and Assistant in Pediatrics at the Johns Hopkins University and Hospital. She has worked as Research Psychologist for the National Institute of Mental Health and as a Research Psychologist for the Research Foundation of Children's Hospital of the District of Columbia.

LINDA MCCAULEY joined the staff of the Department of Public Welfare as a family day care licenser in 1970, when Massachusetts first began licensing family day care homes. In 1973, when the Office for Children was created and delegated licensing responsibility, she became the coordinator of the state's family day care licensing program, and subsequently planned and implemented the Massachusetts model of registration. She is currently doing graduate work in early childhood education at Tufts University.

FRED OSMON has an architectural practice in Cave Creek, Carefree, Arizona, and teaches in the Department of Architecture at Arizona State University. Previously he had an architectural practice in Oakland, California, and taught at the University of California at Berkeley. His building projects include the Far West Laboratory for Educational Research and Development in San Francisco and the Migrant Camp Children's Centers discussed in his article. He is the author of *Patterns for Designing Children's Centers,* published by Educational Facilities Laboratories, New York.

MARIA W. PIERS, Ph.D., is Dean of the Erickson Institute for Early Education. Formerly she was a member of the faculty of the University of Illinois, Jane Addams School of Social Service, and a lecturer in child development at the University of Chicago.

GLORIA J. POWELL, M.D. is Assistant Professor of Psychiatry at the UCLA Center for the Health Services. She is on the clinical staff of the Martin Luther King Jr. Hospital, Consultant to the Johnny Tilman Child Care Center, and Director of the Parent-Child Learning Foundation. She is the author of *Black Monday's Children—A Study of the Effects of School Desegregation on Self-Concepts of Southern Children,* published by Appleton-Century-Crofts.

JUNE SOLNIT SALE has been involved with young children and their families in the Los Angeles area as a nursery school teacher, as an administrator of Head Start programs, and as a member of the faculty of Pacific Oaks College. She received her M.S.W. degree in community organization from UCLA. Ms. Sale was the Director of the

Community Family Day Care Project for Pacific Oaks and is currently Codirector of the Day Care Consultation and Media Project at Pacific Oaks.

LORRAINE B. WALLACH is the Codirector of the Erickson Institute for Early Education, Chicago. Ms. Wallach has also been active as a director of Head Start programs in Chicago and as a consultant to national child care programs.

GLORIA MARSHAK WEISSBERG, interior designer, space planner, and furniture designer, received her masters degrees in education from Columbia University and in design education from the New York School of Interior Design. Formerly associated with Emily Malino for 8 years, she is now President of Gloria Weissberg, Inc., in Washington, D.C. Ms. Weissberg's design and space planning projects have included schools, hospitals, offices, residential environments, and psychiatric hospitals. She has also founded the Organization for the Research of Environmental Education and served as a consultant on environmental planning with the U.S. Department of Health, Education, and Welfare.

Chapter One

INFANT DAY CARE: FADS, FACTS, AND FANCIES

Bettye M. Caldwell

There can be little doubt that day care, until recently an outcast of the child welfare field, has become the belle of the ball. Persons like the author, who only a few years ago were castigated for advocating at least an open mind about group experience for infants, now suddenly find themselves running the risk of being trampled by stampeding advocates of more day care for ever younger children.

INFANT DAY CARE—A NEW FAD

The tendency to succumb to fads has always characterized advances in the realms of both ideas and programs in Western society. But fads are short-lived unless the knowledge upon which they must rest can manage to keep pace with the public fancy.

Elardo, R., & Pagan, Betty (Eds.). *Perspectives on infant day care.* Southern Association on Children Under Six.

REASONS FOR RELUCTANCE TO ESTABLISH INFANT PROGRAMS

There are at least three important reasons why infant day care was denounced for so long. First, day care involved separating a child from its mother for a significant part of the child's waking hours. For a long time many people felt that such separation meant the same thing as the prolonged absence of a mother—that short-term daily separations had the same psychological impact as prolonged maternal deprivation. It was easy to document the harmful consequences of prolonged maternal deprivation, particularly if it occurred during the first 3 years of life. Thus as long as maternal-infant *separation* (such as that when a mother works) was thought of as automatically signifying maternal *deprivation,* any kind of program for the child under 3 was discouraged, but particularly those that involved putting infants in groups.

A second reason for the reluctance to establish infant day care was a very real concern about health hazards associated with bringing large numbers of young children together. If one reflects on how recently the scourges of polio and measles disappeared as threats to the well-being of infants, one can easily realize that the timing of the fad for infant day care is not coincidental. It simply could not have happened until significant advances in medical science greatly reduced the threat of serious illness associated with significant exposure of infants to one another.

A third reason for the reluctance to develop infant day care is eminently practical—the high cost of quality care for very young children. To avoid the hazards found when large numbers of infants were cared for by few adults, whose efforts could not be enhanced by attractive play materials because of budgetary limitations, one had to plan on a large expenditure per child. Not only would one have to allow for more employees in a center that cared for infants, but one would have to think in terms of more costly equipment—cribs as opposed to cots, and so on. Thus, in addition to the fear that infant day care would produce the clinical syndrome of maternal deprivation, there were ample reasons for a paucity of infant day care programs.

BASES FOR PROGRAM DEVELOPMENT

In spite of these forces which kept infant day care programs to a minimum, there were equally powerful forces that helped move us to the point where we stand now. In the first place, the need for infant day care continued to mount no matter how vigorously various social and public agencies tried to discourage it. Women with infants and young children entered the work force in ever greater numbers, and social censure for such entry diminished. Obviously every mother who worked had to find some type of day care for her very young children. But in addition to the sheer number of women entering the work force, the conscience of the women's liberation movement began to intrude into the consciousness of many people. If we were to let our actions go beyond our rhetoric in support of women's right to fulfill their own talents and potentialities, then the society as a whole had to give some attention to wholesome ways of providing care for very young children.

Still another factor related to the need for more facilities came from the significant increase in the number of children born to young unwed mothers who did not wish to place the babies for adoption and who did not wish to discontinue their own schooling. If the young mothers were to return to school, facilities for the care of their infants obviously had to be made available. Thus, whatever the official professional and scientific attitude toward infant day care, the need in the society increased exponentially in a 5-year period from about 1965 to 1970.

There were other forces at work that were to some extent unrelated to the social need for more and better day care. This incentive came with the recognition of the tremendous importance of the first few years of life in pacing cognitive and emotional development. Research evidence accumulated to suggest that during the first 3 years of life children needed an optimal level of social and intellectual stimulation in order to normalize their general development. A number of pioneers, particularly Hunt (1961), Bruner (1960), and Bloom (1964), began to point out that we largely left the environment of the human infant to chance, instead of planning as we plan the environments of children who reach 6 years of age. On the basis of data which suggested that the period before age 3 or 4 might indeed be more important than the years to follow, many people began to look for a forum through which this early period could be enriched—and they saw in day care such a setting.

Coupled with this commitment to the importance of the early years was a research-based awareness of the fact that many children, especially children of the poor, were being forced to spend their early years under conditions that could only be considered barren and depriving rather than enriching and fulfilling. It was perhaps because of this new awareness that day care for the very young received its final acceptance, because children from economically disadvantaged families are very likely to have mothers who work and are therefore especially in need of day care. Thus it appeared that infant day care for such children could both provide a much needed social service and at the same time offer the kinds of support for development that the child might otherwise not receive.

EARLY PROGRAM DEVELOPMENT

In about the mid 1960s, insightful persons in the Children's Bureau of the Department of Health, Education, and Welfare recognized all of these factors which appeared to be suggesting that infant day care could serve a useful purpose. Accordingly, the Research Department of the Children's Bureau began to support a number of research and development centers that offered infant day care. Three of the first projects of this sort in this country are the Children's Center in Syracuse, New York, the Frank Porter Graham Child Development Center in Chapel Hill, North Carolina, and the Demonstration Nursery Center for Infants and Toddlers at the University of North Carolina in Greensboro. Each of these centers, in operation for at least 5 years, has enough experience upon which to make recommendations to persons who are interested in beginning program operation.

Shortly after these early demonstration projects began, the Parent-Child Center Program, a component of Head Start, was launched in 36 cities throughout the nation. Although these programs in general concentrate on the parent-child dyad rather than on the child as an individual, many Parent-Child Centers offer infant day care. Also, many hospitals throughout the country have begun to utilize some of their space to offer infant day care as a means of encouraging nurses to return to work and are thus helping to remedy the acute nursing shortage. Finally, this author would have to mention her program in Little Rock, which began in 1969—the Center for Early Development and Education. Although our center has a balanced concern for the development of children from early infancy through age 12, the infant care program is a major component of the total project.

THE EFFECTS OF INFANT DAY CARE

Because the research-based projects described above have been established for only a few years, it is difficult to assemble a large amount of research evidence to demonstrate the effects of infant day care. The oldest children who have participated in these projects are only now reaching public school age. Thus we cannot hope to offer any long-term data demonstrating effects associated with infant day care. However several centers have been in operation long enough to suggest some leads about the effects of such programs.

INTELLECTUAL DEVELOPMENT

Although most people who operate infant day care would immediately deny that their primary concern is the effect of their program on the intellectual development of their children, all the programs have at least looked for the effects of day care on this aspect of development. One reason for this is that the old literature on maternal deprivation tended to stress the deleterious intellectual consequences of such experiences for very young children. For example, Ainsworth (1962) suggested that if maternal deprivation were prolonged and extended and began before the child was 18 months of age, one could assert almost without qualification that there would be negative consequences that would be virtually irreversible. Another reason for always checking on this aspect of development is simply that there are more instruments available for such tests than for looking at the effects of the experience on other aspects of development.

The literature dealing with the effects of infant day care on intellectual development can be summarized by saying that, in general, children either are not harmed by the experience or tend to show substantial gains. The author's own data from the Syracuse project can be cited as typical of the results that have been found to date. Recently, data were presented on 86 children who had entered day care before age 3 and had remained in the Syracuse program for at least 6 months (Caldwell, 1971). These children were compared to a control group of 34 children from comparable socioeconomic settings but who had not had any day care experience. Depending upon their age at entry into the program, children were tested either on the Cattell Infant Intelligence Scale or the Stanford-Binet Intelligence Test. For the subsequent evaluations, all children were tested on the Stanford-Binet. The children who had been in day care gained an average of 17 points on the intelligence tests, whereas the average change in the control group of children was a decline of about 6 points. This 23-point difference between the two groups was highly significant statistically.

An early report from the Greensboro project (Keister, 1970) did not report significant cognitive gains associated with the day care experience. This fact is mentioned not to imply any superiority of the one program over the other, but rather to emphasize an important point about the effects of early enrichment upon children from different kinds of environments. The children enrolled in the Greensboro project were mainly from middle-class, intact families which could be expected to provide quality environments for their infants at home. The Syracuse sample, on the other hand, consisted primarily of infants from extremely deprived families or from middle-class families in which there was often an impressive incidence of social pathology. Thus for many children in the Syracuse project, the day care environment probably played a major role in helping to bring the children's development up to a level that it could be expected to reach in an optimal environment. In short, the disparity between the home and the day care environment for the Greensboro sample was probably much less than it was for the Syracuse sample. It is this discrepancy between home and day care environments that probably accounts for the significant increases in the Syracuse sample.

SOCIAL AND EMOTIONAL DEVELOPMENT

We must all be vitally interested in the effects of day care on the social and emotional development of young children, for no one in the field wishes to be involved in an experience that would have negative consequences. We need a great deal more data about how a young child internalizes the social experiences inherent in early group activities and integrates them with his other significant developmental tasks.

In this regard, Bowlby (1958, 1969), Ainsworth (1969), and others have suggested that primary maternal attachment is an essential foundation for all subsequent social attachments that a child will form. Thus no matter how much day care might benefit a child in the intellectual aspects of development, one would not want to encourage such an experience if it were to weaken the child's primary tie to his own mother. In one of our studies (Caldwell, Wright, Honig, and Tannenbaum, 1970), we examined the effects of early day care on the attachment of children to their mothers and the reciprocal attachment of the mothers to their children.

Eighteen mother-child pairs who had been day care patrons since before the children were 1 year old were compared with 23 mother-child pairs in which the mother had remained the principal care giver of the child throughout the first 2.5 years. When all the children were approximately 30 months old, they were brought individually to a neutral setting (not the day care center, which would have given the day care infants a slight advantage), and the interaction between each mother and her child was observed. Additionally, the mother was interviewed about her techniques of handling the child and for her appraisal of the child's overall development. The interview-observation for each pair lasted about 3 hours.

The findings from this study should be very reassuring to all who are involved in infant day care. The toddlers who had been in day care since early infancy were rated to be as attached to their mothers as were the toddlers who had never been in day care. There were differences between the groups, however, in terms of the breadth of attachment. The day care toddlers were rated as more outgoing and friendly and more interested in persons other than the mother than were the home-reared children. Similar findings had been reported by Schaffer and Emerson (1964) for a sample of infants in Glasgow, Scotland: Those infants who had been exposed to more people during infancy tended to be friendlier and more interested in such people than did infants who had spent a more sheltered infancy and had not been in contact with other people.

But what about the attachment of the mothers for their children? Did infant day care tend to weaken the mother's attachment to her own child? Not insofar as we could detect. This finding of essentially no difference between the two groups of mothers supports what many people have reported on the basis of their clinical observations—namely, that the progress a child makes in a day care setting can serve to enhance the relationship between the mother and the child by helping to establish more positive attitudes on the part of mothers toward their children.

Another study conducted in Syracuse is relevant at this point. This study by Braun and Caldwell (1972) dealt with psychiatric ratings made of all the 3- and 4-year-old children in the Syracuse project who had enrolled either before or after age 3—the point which usually serves as a dividing line between infant day care and early child care. All the 3 and 4-year-olds were observed by a child psychiatrist for the better part of a week and were rated on a 5-point scale which ranged from "well adjusted" to "very poorly adjusted." Most of the children received ratings indicating a favorable level of emotional adjustment. Only one child in the whole group received the lowest rating. When the children who had entered before age 3 were compared to those who entered after age 3, there were no differences in the proportions receiving high or low ratings. Early enrollment in day care did not seem to be associated in any way with a preponderance of emotional problems during the 3- to 4-year period.

It is hoped that the many other centers conducting infant day programs will concentrate during the next few years on the social and emotional correlates of participation in early group programs. We very desperately need more data in this area.

HEALTH

All programs, even those not conducted in medical settings or with close liaison with medical personnel, need to keep careful records of the incidence of minor and major illnesses of children participating in infant day care. Studies indicate that participation in group programs during infancy need not be accompanied by a significant increase in minor and major illnesses. Because we are now conducting programs all over the country, we very much need to make every effort to collect some of the same kinds of information that Dr. Frank Loda and his colleagues have meticulously gathered, to determine whether the Chapel Hill finding of essentially no increase in illnesses associated with day care is indeed characteristic of the whole country.

EFFECTS ON PARENTS

In this area it is difficult to separate fact from fancy, because relatively few of the early programs have included a formal evaluation of the effects of the program on participating parents. As we all know, parent involvement in day care is difficult to achieve. It is not hard to understand this, because working mothers must double their efforts with their homes, their children, and their husbands to keep the total routine functioning smoothly. And alas, women, like other living creatures, do get tired.

Most of the existing infant care programs have attempted at least an informal evaluation of the effects of their program on participating parents. Usually parental reactions are highly positive. Infant care directors have reported that parents sometimes complain that the center does not open early enough or does not stay open late enough, or might object to the behavior of a particular staff member, or complain about fees or other regulations. However, in general they are usually enthusiastic about how the program is helping their children and how it has helped them to become more aware of the abilities of young children. It is this author's conviction that infant day care will have an important indirect effect on parents, which in turn will further benefit the children. Simply stated, most parents interact happily with their children when the children please them. And parents one and all are invariably pleased when their children develop well. If infant day care succeeds in its goal of helping young children to develop optimally, then it will indirectly help to set in motion more favorable patterns of social interaction between the parents and the children.

THE COST OF INFANT DAY CARE

Whenever I talk about infant day care I am invariably asked how much it costs. To be more specific, I am usually asked something like, "How much does one have to have in order to run a quality program for young children?" Fortunately or unfortunately, I have never faced up to the question of minimal cost per child per year when one strips away all the developmental services which we like to see associated with infant day care, but which perhaps are not essential to the operation of a quality program per se. In my own work in infant day care, I have had to be almost equally concerned with research in child development and with training personnel to be involved in other infant care programs. When the program is comprehensive in that way, cost per child will not accurately reflect the minimal cost figures.

In the Children's Bureau Research and Demonstration programs, the cost per child per year has ranged from $2400 to $8000. Obviously, if the latter figure is more common, few children will ever experience infant day care. Fortunately, such is not the case, and the median cost per child in the programs is closer to the lower than to the higher end of the range.

I feel that we all need the benefit of experience from private day care operators, who have learned how to be economical and efficient in their operations, before we will have any reasonable figures of cost per child per year. It is, after all, from such persons and such programs that the greatest bulk of day care is offered in this country. We need these private programs, as well as the experiences of their operators.

One major difficulty in estimating the cost of the quality day care is the difficulty inherent in defining "quality infant day care" operationally. Today a key word in the field of evaluation is "accountability." People who operate programs are expected to specify their objectives and to demonstrate that their programs do indeed accomplish these objectives. Translated into the type of criterion that we generally use—the developmental test—this means that we might be offering to increase the developmental level of the participating children on the average by 10 points the first year, 4 points the second, 2 points the third, and so on. Yet, of course, many of us would cringe at the thought that this is what we are really trying to do. We are involved in infant day care to try to create settings in which little children can develop well and can be happy. Can we ourselves ever tolerate any attempt to translate that goal into so many points on a developmental test?

While we shudder at the thought, we must also give serious attention to other ways of coming to grips with this unpleasant but necessary question. Until we have adequate resources to meet every social need, every service offered to families and children must be able to justify its claim on the public resources. I am convinced that infant day care will be able to do that, but we cannot justify it merely on the basis of statements of belief. We must come to grips with the question of how we can meaningfully and persuasively demonstrate the positive benefits associated with such an experience.

SUGGESTED EXTENSION ACTIVITIES OF THIS PAPER

The reader is encouraged to think about some of the questions raised in this introductory discussion. To what extent is the current fad for infant day care based upon facts about human development and to what extent is it based upon our current whimsical fancies? What are the policy issues with which we must grapple before we can extend such programs? How can we make sure that our plans are representative of the families we will be dealing with and not merely our own ideas? And as we move forward, how can we select and train people who will most effectively play a role in the endeavor? However we shall not deal altogether with such world-shaking issues, because we are equally concerned with how we can manage the long day with little children. How can we monitor the progress of our infants and young children in the absence of extensive evaluation programs? And, even more basic, how do we get started if we want to begin an infant day care program?

REFERENCES

Ainsworth, M. D. S. *Reversible and irreversible effects of maternal deprivation on intellectual development.* Child Welfare League of America, 1962, pp. 42–62.

Ainsworth, M. D. S. Object relations, dependency, and attachment: A theoretical review of the infant-mother relationship. *Child Development,* 1969, 969–1025.

Bloom, B. S. *Stability and change in human characteristics.* New York: Wiley, 1964.

Bowlby, J. The nature of the child's tie to his mother. *International Journal of Psychoanalysis*, 1958, *39*, 350–373.

Braun, S. J. and Caldwell, B. M. Emotional adjustment of children in day care who enrolled prior to or after the age of three. *Early Child Development and Care*, 1972, *2*, 13–21.

Braun, S. J., & Caldwell, B. M. Social adjustment of children in day care who enrolled prior to or after the age of three. *Early Child Development and Care*, 1972, *2*, 13–21, 29–35.

Bruner, J. S. *The process of education.* Cambridge, Mass.: Harvard University Press, 1960.

Caldwell, B. M. Impact of interest in early cognitive stimulation. In H. E. Rie (Ed.), *Perspectives in child psychopathology*. Chicago: Aldine-Atherton, 1971, 293–334.

Honig, A. S., Caldwell, B. M., & Tannenbaum, J. Patterns of information processing used by and with young children in a nursery school setting. *Child Development*, 1970, *41*, 1045–1065.

Hunt, J. M. *Intelligence and experience.* New York: Ronald Press, 1961.

Keister, M. E. *"The good life" for infants and toddlers.* Washington: National Association for the Education of Young Children, 1970.

Loda, F. A., Glezen, W. P., and Clyde, W. A. Jr. Respiratory Disease in Group Day Care. *Pediatrics*, *49* (March 1972) 428–437.

Schaffer, H. R., & Emerson, P. E. The development of social attachments in infancy. *Monographs of the Society for Research in Child Development*, 1964, *29*, (3, Whole No. 94), 1–77.

Chapter Two

INFANT DAY CARE IN THE BLACK COMMUNITY: BOON OR BOONDOGGLE?

Gloria J. Powell, M.D.

In 1968 I set out to do a study of the psychological impact of school desegregation on the people most vitally involved—the black children themselves (Powell, 1973a). Out of that study emerged not only data on the psychological effects of school desegregation, but more importantly data on what a black child needs to overcome in spite of the vicissitudes of racism, poverty, and indifference. The discovery was that black southern children who remained in all-black schools in cohesive black communities not only fare better than their black counterparts in a desegregated southern school, but also fare better than (a) white southern children in segregated and desegregated schools, and (b) white and black northern students in segregated and desegregated schools (Powell, 1973b). In short, black people had a way of life that was enhancing the development of their children, and before it could be looked at and understood, it was cast aside (Sowell, 1974).

It is from that experience that I write, as well as from my experience as a black health professional who works with black children and their families, both in the United States and in Africa, as a black parent who has had to bird-dog the educational system to minimize the noxious effects for my children, and as a black woman who came through the system, but saw many who were kept out and many who got trapped within.

My concern about infant day care is the same as my concern about school desegregation: So often we institute social change for "the good of humanity," but when the social good that we expected becomes a social nightmare, we become frightened and helpless and have no insight into how to turn the process around. School desegregation is not the only social good that has become a social nightmare. Public school education, in toto, with all its initial hopes and promises, has become so problematic that some feel that it should be scrapped and rebuilt (Jencks, 1971; Silberman, 1970). Somehow our best intentions get programmed for failure, and having seen so many programmed failures in the black community—compensatory education, Head Start, foster parent programs—I have become a very cautious advocate, realizing that all too often the way to hell is paved with just as many good intentions as bad.

Fortunately, in most instances when programs for good become disastrous for those for whom they were designed to benefit, the people have been old enough to cry out. But in the case of infant day care, who will be the spokesman? Many infant day care advocates hasten to reassure me of all the guidelines that have been written by various professional groups to set standards, policies, and guidelines to be adhered to in order to prevent misuse or malpractice, but my response is that our country's record on commitment to black children has been worse than abominable. I can only agree with the message of Dr. Andrew Billingsley (1970) to the Black Children Development Education Center.

> Given the anti-black attitudes of the dominant political forces in this country and the reactionary attitudes of

some prominent social scientists, the extensive research, surveys, tests, analyses, and the programming both being planned and now taking place in our black communities, all point to a very critical and dangerous period for our most valuable institution, the Black Family.

Much of the diabolitical attention being given to black families is focused on the black child who is somehow to be removed from the damaging influence of his "fractured, disorganized family." There are thus underway ominous schemes and programs to make him "more docile," "more malleable," "less aggressive," "more socialized," "less violence prone," etc. At the same time he, along with his parents and other blacks, is being pronounced as possibly having "defective genes" and an inferior intelligence and are contributing to a "defective gene pool."

... That's my speech, it says the black child is the center of our concern. We who are black cannot think about our children without thinking about our families. We cannot think about black children and black families without thinking about the black community. (p. 57)

Herein lie my concerns and my biases, which I state openly and frankly. The task confronting me throughout the remainder of this paper is twofold: (a) Given this perspective as frankly and openly stated in the preceding paragraphs, what are the facts about infant day care? (b) When we add it all up, what are the benefits and what are the dangers of infant day care in the black community?

PUTTING THE FACTS TOGETHER

The data to be analyzed in assessing the benefits and dangers come from several sources. We need to review the relationship to date of the U.S. government and the black child. Has it been a beneficial one for the black child? If so, how and why? If it has not, why not and how detrimental? Second, we need to review the data on the needs of infants. What are the variables for healthy growth and development for infants? How much do we know about their needs and where are the gaps in our knowledge? Third, we need to take a look at the needs and even the rights of parents. What are the concepts of parenting? What constitutes adequate parenting and what impedes it? A fourth consideration must be a review of the black family—its current status, its strengths, and yes, even its weaknesses. And of course the analysis would not be complete without some review of the current status of day care. How well is it doing? What are some of the problems that are emerging, and how well are they being resolved?

THE U.S. GOVERNMENT AND THE BLACK CHILD

The commitment of this nation to the well-being of the black child is eloquently stated by Dr. Rodney N. Powell in his paper, "Poverty—The Greatest Handicapping Condition in Childhood" (1970).

> Since 1909, at the time of the first White House Conference on Children and Youth and each succeeding decade of the 20th Century, the United States has held a great national conference devoted to its children, their circumstances, and their prospects. In no way do I wish to impugn either the origin, or the stated goals and objectives or the contributions to the well-being of the children of America that resulted from these conferences. I merely wish to state unequivocally that since 1909, every 10 years, the White House Conference repeats the same urgency, the same recommendations, put in the jargon of the time, followed by almost the same inaction, the magical thinking, that somehow America's great strength, its children, free of handicapping conditions, will be emerged, resplendent in the American dream. . . . All of this to me reads like a dreary

litany of hope, disillusionment, frustration and finally despair because, unfortunately, the White House Conferences on Children and Youth have been purely that, "white."

Dr. Powell continues to present the health statistics as they relate to nonwhite children. A brief review of them here speaks to the lack of this country's commitment to the health of its minority children. Although the infant mortality rate has dropped significantly for all people from the beginning of the century to the present time, the fact remains that the mortality rate for the nonwhite infant is triple that for the white infant. The maternal mortality rate is four times higher for the nonwhite mother than the white mother, and indeed, the combined perinatal and maternal mortality rates have actually increased for the nonwhite population relative to the white population. In summary, Birch reports that "it appears that the non-white infant is subject to an excessive continuum of risks reflected at its extremes by perinatal, neo-natal, and infant death in the survivors by reduced functional potential" (Birch & Gussow 1970). In short, we need a much greater commitment to the health of minority children in this country.

Perhaps we score higher in educational services. The Report of Equality of Educational Opportunities reveals that a minority child enters the public educational system 1 year behind his white counterpart and finishes 13 years later, 4 years behind. We have only to read Jencks, Wilcox, Kvaraceus, Silberman, Kozal, Jones, Green, and Clark, to name a few to hear the theme more recently reiterated in a collection of current articles from the *Harvard Educational Review* (Challenging the Myths: The Schools, the Blacks, and the Poor). That theme is that institutional racism in the public schools inhibits equality of educational opportunity, compensatory education programs notwithstanding.

As we move on to economic status, we could review the Department of Labor statistics on unemployment and underemployment. However, when we look at family size and income, we know that 15 million children in the United States live in abject poverty, with less than $3000 per year for a family of four. This figure represents 9 million poor white children or 15% of the total white population, and 6 million nonwhite children or 60% of the total nonwhite population. Then if we review the Nixon "Work-fare" program initiated in 1970, there is no doubt that our nation's commitment lies not with children and families, but with the pocketbooks and the status quo of the Negro-phobic, not-so-silent, middle American white majority. The message was clear: Let's get those lazy mothers off welfare and find any kind of job for them, promise to take care of their children in kennels, and save our money for the privileged few.

In summary, the verdict has already been rendered by the Joint Commission on Mental Health.

> This nation, the richest of all world powers, has no unified national commitment to its children and youth. The claim that we are a child-centered society, that we look to our young as tomorrow's leaders, is a myth. Our words are made meaningless by our actions—by our lack of national, community, and personal investment in maintaining the healthy development of our young, by the miniscule amount of economic resources spent in developing our young, by our tendency to rely on a proliferation of simple, one-factor, short-term and inexpensive remedies and services. As a tragic consequence, we have in our midst millions of ill-fed, ill-housed, ill-educated, and discontented youngsters and almost 10,-100,000 under age 25 who are in need of help from mental health workers. Some means must be devised to delegate clear responsibility and authority to ensure the well-being of our young. (p. 24)

Naively, perhaps, and cynically for certain, I ask only one question: If this, the richest of all nations could not "get it together" to provide quality health care for black children or quality education, not to mention significant economic opportunities to enhance the quality of life of black families, how do we know that it will get it together to provide quality services for day care facilities for black children? In the face of the morbid facts presented in the previous paragraphs, I cannot have faith, trust, and hope. I can only wonder if it is just another bag of tricks, more white carpetbagging in the black community, or just sheer boondoggling. However not all the facts are in: Let's take a look at the needs of children and parents in the black community and how day care can begin to meet those needs.

THE NEEDS AND RIGHTS OF BLACK INFANTS

Many children are lost from public and professional surveillance from birth until their entry into school. It is during these lost years from birth to age 3 that development is extremely rapid and malleable for all children, whatever their color. The inadequacies of prenatal and postnatal care, especially for nonwhite groups, have a high correlation to the incidence of infant mortality and morbidity, prematurity, birth defects, mental defects, and mental retardation, and they contribute significantly to many neuropsychiatric problems in black children. Yet our health and educational services are most deficient for this early age group. The present system identifies children for such services after age 6, when it is often too late for effective intervention.

Continuity of medical care for infants and children does not exist for at least 40% of the white middle class, 75% of minority group middle class, and 90% of minority group lower class (Mindlin & Densen, 1970). The Joint Commission on Mental Health for Children estimates that 35% of apparently normal children of self-sustaining families show behavioral difficulties as early as age 4. The prevalence is even higher among poor children and since 6 million or 60% of nonwhite children are poor, we can assume that they too are not escaping the neuropsychiatric consequences of poverty. The children who run the greatest risk for psychosocial, educational, and health problems are the nonwhite (namely the black), the central city ghetto dweller and the rural dweller, those in large families or families with one parent, and those in families headed by a parent or parents of low educational achievement.

The Joint Commission on Mental Health for Children (JCMHC) proclaimed in its report that "if we are to optimize the mental health of our young and if we are to develop our human resources, every infant must be granted" (p. 38) the following rights.

1. The right to be wanted
2. The right to be born healthy
3. The right to live in a healthy environment
4. The right to satisfaction of basic needs
5. The right to continuous loving care
6. The right to acquire the intellectual and emotional skills necessary to achieve individual aspirations and to cope effectively in our society
7. The right to receive care and treatment through facilities which are appropriate to their needs and which keep them as closely as possible within their normal social setting

As we put the facts together, we know that very few black infants have these rights fulfilled. The questions which we must now address ourselves to are (a) does the black community need infant day care programs, and (b) how will infant day care help promote these basic rights for black children?

Insofar as the black child is at higher risk for educational, neuropsychiatric, and physical disorders because of a variety of social, economic, and health reasons, and insofar as prevention and early intervention measures are most essential and effective if undertaken during the optimal stages of development (birth to 3 years of age), the black community needs quality infant day care if it is to help promote the basic rights of black infants which are currently denied. The question of how it will help should be answered and evaluated in great detail and with great care.

Caldwell, Richard, et al. (1968) have provided an answer or at least have pointed the way in answering how, and they have provided a model for a day care program for the very young as "an opportunity for primary prevention," and hence another step toward the promotion of the seven basic rights of infants as outlined by The Joint Commission of Mental Health for Children.

In 1964 "the pressing clamor from working mothers for better child care facilities for their children" resulted in the establishment of a Children's Center at Syracuse University by Caldwell and Richmond. "The broad aim of the program was to create an environment which would foster optimal cognitive, social, and emotional development in young children from disadvantaged families. With the establishment of such a service for infants and toddlers of working mothers, was the intent to and the recognition of a possible model for the creation and dispersal of community support systems to sustain optimal growth patterns in young children." It should be understood that the Syracuse program was a pilot program and that it was part of a large-scale research program concerned with infant learning and patterns of social care. That the center accomplished its goals has been well documented. The promising results of their program has far-reaching implications for community planning for the care of children. In short, what the Syracuse model says is that if it is well planned, well implemented, and continuously evaluated, day care for the very young can be an opportunity for primary prevention.

However, Caldwell and Smith (1970) offer the following caution.

> These findings do not guarantee that a socio-emotional deficit would never be associated with infant day care. In the strict statistical sense, we can generalize only to samples participating in similar programs. As such programs are so scarce in America, the generalizability of the findings is sharply restricted. What they do show is that one can have infants in quality day care without having jeopardized the child's primary emotional attachment to his mother. In the present program, great pains were taken to avoid this jeopardy. For example, no infants were taken into the program prior to the age of six months, by which time rudimentary forms of attachment have developed. In point of fact, most children who enter the program during infancy do so around one year of age. Also, the program is one which offers a generous adult-child ratio and which features in abundance the kinds of behavior shown to be associated with strength of attachment (intensity of response, sensitivity to child's needs, and general competence as adults). (p. 411)

It is important to highlight an important aspect of the Syracuse program—that it excluded children under 6 months of age. Indeed, most of the children who entered the program were around 1 year of age. It is interesting to note that there are already day care centers in the black community that admit children under 6 months of age, erroneously extrapolating from the Syracuse data to justify such programs.

Consequently, any discussion of the rights and needs of infants would be incomplete without some airing of (a) the issue of maternal attachment and deprivation, and (b) the issue of individual vs. group care of children. In 1960 the Child Welfare League of America published a pamphlet entitled "Standards for Day Care Service," which reiterated the prevailing professional stance that (a) the very young child should be cared for in his own home by his own mother, and (b) communities must support the mother's role with financial assistance, homemaker assistance, and counseling. They stated definitively that "if children under three must be cared for outside their own homes, they should have individual care in a family and should not be in groups or group facilities" (Child Welfare League, 1960). By 1966 the organization had taken a more modified but very cautious and, in my opinion, very responsible stance (Boguslawski, 1966).

> Experience has shown, however, that children so young (under three) are generally not ready for group living. They are not mature enough to play with other children; they need a highly personalized individual relationship with an adult and can suffer if they do not have it. Some research-demonstration centers now in operation are providing group care for children of this age; these centers have a high ratio of staff to children and a continuing evaluation by psychologists, psychiatrists, and social workers. It is too soon to know whether the optimum conditions will be found under which infants can be cared for in groups without damage to their personality development. For the present, family day care is considered the best supplementary-care resources for children under three. (p. 22)

We must remember that there was and, might I add, still is reason for such a cautious stance. We must not forget so easily the work of René Spitz with infants in institutional settings who experienced "failure to thrive" and anaclitic depression, many of whom died in spite of the good physical care they received (Spitz, 1945). Nor can we easily forget the Provence and Lipton study of infants in institutions, which further elucidated the nature of the deprivation experienced by infants in institutions (Provence & Lipton, 1962). Should we also discard the studies of Yarrow (1961),

Bowlby (1958, 1954), and Ainsworth (1973)—to name a few who contributed greatly to our understanding of infant attachment and maternal deprivation? Caldwell's answer (1970) is provocative.

> The implicit equation of infant day care with institutionalization should be put to rest. Infant day care *may* be like institutionalization, but it does not *have* to be. Day care and institutional care have only one major feature in common: children in groups. Characteristics of institutional children that day care children do not share—prolonged family separation, a sameness of experience, absence of identity, isolation from the outside world, often no significant interpersonal relationship—undoubtedly far outweigh the one characteristic that the groups have in common. (p. 398)

Unfortunately, there is no guarantee that infant day care will not be merely institutionalized care. We did away with infant institutions and substituted foster home care for deserted and orphaned newborns, but an assessment of foster home care does not yield optimal development of children. Our social welfare system was to oversee foster home care, but somehow there was nobody to watch the watchers. The 1954 Supreme Court mandated school desegregation, but an assessment of how black children are faring in these hostile, often degrading situations is only another chapter in the history of man's inhumanity to man (Powell, 1973a; 1973b). Neither the Supreme Court nor the Department of Health, Education, and Welfare watched to protect the black children in desegregated schools from the nonviolent but hostile acts of white teachers.

The question is who watches the watchers, and the answer *must* be the establishment of a vocal, consistent, aggressive, determined, and dedicated child advocacy system. Infant day care will remain noninstutionalized to the degree that the caretakers are cognizant of each child's innate characteristics and individuality. "The child's needs vary according to his stage of development, his individuality, and his previous experience. These variations do not allow us to talk about a specific amount of care as being adequate for all children. What is adequate for one child may be not nearly adequate for another" (Provence, 1968).

In other words, like penicillin, infant day care cannot be prescribed for any and every infant. A total assessment of the infant and his family should be completed before admission. However all too often, especially for poor black families, community resources are so scarce that other more feasible alternatives are not available. So an infant may be placed in an infant day care program not because it is best for him and his family, but because it is the lesser of two evils. Consequently, if an infant day care program is to function at its highest quality level, it must have ancillary health, educational, and social welfare support systems, which brings us full circle, back to our country and its commitments and priorities. Thus far the evidence is not stacked in favor of the children.

More often than not, most programs are short-term, short-sighted, single-variable approaches which may or may not help in the short-run and are meaningless in terms of alleviating problems in the long-run. There has yet to be devised in this country a comprehensive family-centered care system. There has yet to be created a system whereby a child and his family can enter one door and have his health, educational, economic, and social needs met. Can infant day care be that one door, or will it be just another welfare service poorly coordinated with the families' other needs?

The Syracuse program attempted to provide many, but not all, of the ancillary support systems needed. So often we institute programs ostensibly "for the greater good," but when "the good" is not realized, the finger is pointed again at the minority child. That child is innately inferior and that is why the "social good" did not result. Never does it occur to us that perhaps the programs were not adapted to meet the needs of the black children and families for whom they were designed, or that the needs were not adequately assessed in terms of providing realistic, more comprehensive solutions.

So once again what was to be a boon for the black community is perceived by them as another boondoggle—"the [white] 'man' has programmed us for failure again," another program was created to fail. The community perceives the program failure as a boondoggle because they can't really believe that such knowledgeable people—the university, the county health department, or some other "do-good" organization—could possibly have been so unperceptive. Infant day care can be a boon to the black community if it is the first step toward comprehensive programs for children and their families. It may be just another boondoggle if it is just another short-sighted, single-variable approach to a multifaceted problem. It can become a boon if there is some insightful assessment of the needs and rights of black parents and families, as well as the immediate needs of infants.

THE NEEDS AND RIGHTS OF BLACK PARENTS AND FAMILIES

The emotional and attitudinal climate into which a child is born has its beginnings long before his arrival. The mother's fantasies about babies and motherhood, the marital relationship, the experience of the mother during pregnancy, labor, and delivery all play a role in her functioning as a mother. Out of the interaction between the mother and infant, the ego and mental organization of the infant begins to develop.

Bingham Dai (1953) has pointed out that there are two major problems of personality development among black children: (a) problems that are inherent in the primary group or family situation which are common for both blacks and whites; and (b) problems that are more or less peculiar to black children because of the class-caste position their elders occupy in this society and the consequences of such a position. The modern family is subjected to unique stresses and strains. However, even when socioeconomic status is held constant, the stresses imposed upon a black family are qualitatively different from those on a white family in a number of ways. The black family is much more likely than the white family to be on the lowest economic rung, and a small percentage of blacks are more than one generation removed from abject poverty. As a result, most black children inherit a family that is economically insecure. It has been stated repeatedly that because of this economic caste-class status, the black slum child is far more liable to experience an unstable home than a white slum child (Harrington, 1963).

A great deal has been written about the black family, and indeed there have been some heated discussions generated over the issue. The reader is referred to the discussion of the subject by Frazier (1966), Rainwater (1966), Moynihan (1965) and others. Most studies have focused on the disorganization and pathology of black families and their children. The social welfare literature and the sociological and psychological studies focus on the inadequacies and maladjustments of black families and black children, e.g., juvenile delinquency, gangs, poor academic performance, illegitimacy, low IQ scores, unemployment, and suicide. Nowhere are we told about those children and families who have overcome the vicissitudes of poverty and racism. We maintain that only when we begin to look at some of the strengths and adequate coping styles of black families will we be able to devise meaningful and effective intervention and prevention programs.

In 1971 the National Urban League recognized the need to examine the strengths of black families as a way of understanding and thus ameliorating some of the pressing social problems. To that end, it issued a position statement on black families based on the work of Dr. Andrew Billingsley, as well as a report on the strengths of black families (Hill, 1972). The report of the National Urban League identified and substantively supported five strengths of black families: (a) adaptability of family roles, (b) strong kinship bonds, (c) strong work orientation, (d) strong religious orientation, and (e) strong achievement orientation. The Urban League's report relied on national data collected by the Census Bureau and the Labor Department, Health, Education, and Welfare, to name a few. In addition, the report focused on four major questions which are germane to our discussion of infant day care in the black community (Hill, 1972).

1. What are the historical, contemporary, and emerging situations of black family life in America?
2. What are the patterns of functioning which these families have evolved?
3. What is the relationship between family structures and family functioning?
4. What is the relationship between the operation of the political, economic, and social forces of the larger society on the one hand, and the structure and functioning of black families on the other? (p. xii)

Other black scholars are continuing to focus on the strengths of black families and the gaps in our understanding of black family life (Ladner, 1971; Willie, 1970; Staples, 1971; Billingsley, 1968). Particular attention is given to the seeming preponderance of one-parent families among blacks. Lewis noted in his study of child-rearing practices among low-income black families that there is "a wide variety in the styles of individuals and families," and that all low-income, female-based, black households are *not* destructively organized and do not always support a disintegrated way of life (Lewis, 1967). Thus the work of notable black scholars stresses the importance of assessing the functioning patterns of different kinds of families, rather than making erroneous assumptions based on moral judgments.

Likewise, Baratz and Baratz in their discussion of early childhood intervention programs such as Head Start, again stress the distortion of the social pathology model in interpreting the behavior of the black ghetto mother. When intervention programs are mounted based on such social science distortions, then such goals as "altering the child's home environment," or "improving his language and cognitive skills," and particularly changing the patterns of child rearing within the black home are not only "unrealistic in terms of current linguistic and anthropological data, but at worst ethnocentric and racist" (Baratz & Baratz, 1973).

> Finally, we do not question such programs when they are described as opportunities to screen youngsters for possible physical disorders, even though follow-up treatment of such diagnostic screening is often unavailable.... [However] the theoretical base of the deficit model employed by Head Start programs denies obvious strengths within the (black) community and may inadvertently advocate the annihilation of a cultural system which is barely considered or understood by most social scientists." (p. 112).

We destroyed Southern black schools, which for decades produced most of our black leaders and professionals, before we understood the worth of what we annihilated and before we could reproduce it in our intervention models (Sowell, 1974). And we are in danger of perpetuating that kind of cultural destruction with our piecemeal approach to day care planning in the black community.

THE PROMISES OF DAY CARE

Are we saying that there is no poverty or pathology in the black community? That there are no black families for whom day care services for children are needed? Day care can be an asset if it is planned with a mind to enhancing parent and family support systems, as well as maintaining those cultural systems that have traditionally been supportive for the black family. A variety of child care systems need to be offered to meet the diversity of needs of the individual children and their families. Day care facilities for young children must be part of a comprehensive health and social service delivery system. We cannot be so naive as to think that putting a child in a new building with lots of gadgets can prevent his "cognitive demise."

In our particular community, teenage pregnancies present a major problem (Note 1). With the rising cost of living and increased pressure for employment, many of these children are not easily absorbed into the extended family. Consequently, the pregnant adolescent is confronted with the care of a young child while trying to finish her education. We must remember that not all black communities are alike. Harlem may be different from Watts, and both Harlem and Watts may be quite different from North Minneapolis or New Orleans. These regional variables in black community life have been explored elsewhere by the author (Powell, 1970, 1973a; 1973b). These unique regional variables should be considered in any program development, for example, the broad expanse of Los Angeles vs. the compactness of Southside Chicago; the migration pattern of blacks to California vs. their migration to New York City; the wide range of economic groups in Roxbury vs. the isolation of poor blacks in Watts from the middle-class blacks living outside the area.

The field of child development is expanding, as is our knowledge about the psychology of parenthood (Benedict & Anthony, 1970). The innate and individual differences of children means that the parent-child interactional model is not one-sided; the child contributes to the interactional dyad. More and more parents are looking toward the community for support for their parent roles, not only in the black community, but in all communities. The need for parent re-education is pressing in on *all* American families.

Within black poverty communities, day care and child care facilities can be utilized to disseminate new knowledge about child development, because parent education materials have traditionally been programmed for white middle-class families. They can also become the focal point for child advocacy groups composed of concerned parents, and hence, for pressure groups for needed reforms in our educational system and our juvenile court system. In short, day care is needed to supplement, but not to displace the black family's support system.

SOME OF THE PROBLEMS

Earlier in this chapter we alluded to some of the problems of infant day care in the black community vis-à-vis the social system within which the black family must function —for example, racism, poverty, and indifference. However there are very specific aspects of infant day care which must be noted if the needs of children and families are going to be met in a way that is psychologically and culturally enhancing. We should also note and, one hopes, avoid some of the pitfalls that ofttimes go unnoticed in our haste and eagerness to begin and to help.

In a review of programs for infants and small children both in the U.S. and other countries, Dr. Richmond pointed out some general characteristics of many such programs as well as attitudes toward infant care (Note 2). Particularly in the U.S. there seems to be great disapproval of group care of infants if mothers are not working or involved in some "productive activity." The parents' need for time alone away from young children is only acceptable for the affluent. Hence many of the day care programs in black communities are provided for children only if their parents are working.

A second important factor pointed out by Dr. Richmond is the widespread assumption that if a person has had training in some area of teaching, nursing, etc., he doesn't need any special training for infant care. "Other than experimental programs, most child care environments are adult oriented." The environments are developed to be attractive for the adult, but it is seldom viewed from the infant's point of view.

The third aspect of infant program to be noted is the tendency for most programs to provide either warm interpersonal relations or encouragement of curiosity and motor skills, but rarely both.

Although much lip service is given to the concept of the individuality of each child and recognition of his innate characteristics and special needs, it is easier to have one program to which all children are expected to adhere. Often there is not enough money for adequate staffing to have individual programs or schedules. Or the absenteeism among the staff, who themselves often are community people with family problems, is so high that for most of the week the number of children per staff member is excessively high and a "multiple mothering" phenomenon begins to occur.

These kinds of problems are common not only to infant programs in the black community, but also to such programs in many other communities. However these problems, coupled with those unique to the black community, could negate many of the promises (outlined in a previous section) that infant day care could offer to black families.

In the long run the promises of day care can begin to outweigh the problems only to the degree that the staff of the center is knowledgeable about the growth and development of children and the cultural nuances of black family life; are ready and willing to involve parents in a meaningful way within the center; and try to coordinate center activities with other resources within the community. To the extent that the infant day care program can be an advocate for the child and his family, it can be a real asset to the black community and the black families that it serves. To the extent that such coordination and problem solving does not occur, then we must remember, to quote my grandmother, "as the twig is bent, so grows the tree."

REFERENCES

Ainsworth, M. D. S. The development of infant-mother attachment. In B. Caldwell & H. Ricohi (Eds.), *Review of child development research.* Chicago: University of Chicago Press, 1973.

Baratz, S. & Baratz, J. C. Early childhood intervention: The social science base of institutional racism. *Harvard Educational Review. Challenging the Myths: The Schools, The Blacks, and The Poor,* Reprint Series No. 5, 1973.

Benedict, T., & Anthony, E. J. (Eds.): *Parenthood: Its psychology and psychopathology.* Boston: Little, Brown, and Co, 1970.

Billingsley, A. *Black families in white America.* Englewood Cliffs, New Jersey: Prentice-Hall, 1968.

Billingsley, A. Address to the Child Development from a Black Perspective Conference. Sponsored by the Black Child Development Education Center, Washington, D.C., June 10–13, 1970.

Birch, H., & Gussow, J. D. *Disadvantaged children: Health, nutrition, and school failure.* New York: Grune & Stratton, 1970.

Boguslawski, D. B. *Guide for establishing and operating day care centers for young children.* New York: Child Welfare League of America, 1966.

Bowlby, J. The nature of the child's tie to his mother. *International Journal of Psychoanalysis.* 1958, *39,* 350–373.

Bowlby, J. *Attachment,* vol. 1. New York: Basic Books, 1969.

Caldwell, B., Wright, M., Honig, A., & Tannenbaum, J. Infant daycare and attachment. *American Journal of Orthopsychiatry,* 1970, *40,* 397–412.

Caldwell, B., & Smith, L. Daycare for the very young— Prime opportunity for primary prevention. *American Journal of Public Health,* 1970, *60,* 690.

Caldwell, B. M., & Richmond, J. B. The children's center in Syracuse, New York. In L. L. Dittman (Ed.), *Early child care.* New York: Atherton Press, 1968, 326–358.

Child Welfare League of America. *Standards for day care service.* New York: Child Welfare League of America, 1960.

Clark, K. Clash of culture in the classroom. *Integrated Education,* 1963, *1,* 9–14.

Dai, B. Problems of personality development among negro children. In C. Kluckhohn, H. A. Murray (Eds.), *Persoanlity in nature, society, and culture.* New York: Knopf, 1953.

Frazier, E. F. *The negro family in the United States.* Chicago: University of Chicago Press, 1966.

Green, R. L. (Ed.). *Racial crisis in American education.* Chicago: Follett Publishing Co., 1970.

Harrington, M. *The other America: Poverty in the United States.* New York: Macmillan, 1963.

Harvard Educational Review. Challenging the Myths: The Schools, The Blacks, and The Poor. Reprint Series, No. 5, 1973.

Hill, R. B. *The strengths of black families,* New York: Emerson Hall Publishers, 1972.

Jencks, C. *Inequality: A reassessment of the effect of family and schooling in America. Harvard Educational Review,* 1971.

Jencks, C. Inequality in retrospect. *Harvard Educational Review. Perspectives on Inequality.* 1972.

Jones, R. Racism, mental health, and the schools. In C. V. Willie, B. Brown, & B. Kramer (Eds.) *Racism and Mental*

Health. Pittsburgh: University of Pittsburgh Press, 1973.

Kozol, J. *Death at an early age.* New York: Bantam Books, 1968.

Ladner, J. A. *Tomorrow's tomorrow: The black woman.* Garden City, New York: Doubleday, 1971.

Lewis, H. *Culture, class, and poverty,* Washington Health and Welfare Council of the National Capital Area, Project CROSS-TELL, 1967.

Moynihan, D. P. *The Negro family: The call for national action.* Washington: U.S. Department of Labor, 1965.

Powell, G. J. *Black Monday's children: The psychological impact of school desegregation on southern children.* New York: Appleton-Century-Croft, 1973.

Powell, G. J. Self-Concept in White and Black Children. In C. V. Willie, B. Brown, & B. Kramer (Eds.), *Racism and Mental Health.* Pittsburgh: University of Pittsburgh Press, 1973. (b)

Powell, R. Research for social change. Presented at the 15th Annual Student Research Day Lecture, Meharry Medical College, Nashville, Tennessee, April 21, 1971.

Powell, R. N. Poverty: The greatest handicapping condition in childhood. Presented at the Conference on Earlier Recognition of Handicapping Conditions in Children. University of California at Berkeley, May, 1970.

Provence, S., & Lipton, R. C. *Infants in institutions.* New York: International Universities Press, 1962.

Provence, S. The Yale child study center project. In L. Dittman (Ed.), *Early child care.* New York: Atherton Press, 1968.

Rainwater, L. Crucible of identity: The Negro lower class family. In T. Parsons & K. Clark (Eds.), *The Negro American.* Boston: Houghton-Mifflin, 1966.

Report of the Joint Committee on Mental Health of Children. Crisis in Child Mental Health: Health Challenge in the 1970's. N.Y.: Harper and Row, 1969.

Silberman, C. *Crisis in the classroom: The remaking of American education.* New York: Random House, 1970.

Sowell, T. Black excellence: The case of Dunbar high school. *The Public Interest,* Fall, 1974.

Spitz, R. Anaclitic depression. *Psychoanalytic Child Study,* 1946, *2,* 313–342.

Staples, R. *The black family: Essays and studies.* Belmont, California: Wadsworth, 1971.

Willie, C. V. *The family life of black people.* Columbus, Ohio: Charles E. Merrill, 1970.

NOTES

1. The author was formerly Associate Professor of Psychiatry at the Martin Luther King Hospital in South Central Los Angeles and is presently Consultant to the Johnny Tillman Child Care Center and the Special Nursery at Martin Luther King Hospital.
2. Julius B. Richmond, M.D. Personal communication, 1970.

Chapter Three

AN ALTERNATIVE FOR INFANTS WITH SPECIAL NEEDS

Judith Lewis

Although a large body of research-based knowledge concerning infant development has become available to professionals over the past decade, implementation to the education of the nation's youngest citizens has been minuscule and fragmented. The public in general remains unsophisticated about the emotional and cognitive needs of their young children and about the ways that they can help them to learn and develop. Lack of child development knowledge and outdated child-rearing practices, which hinder the optimal development of many young children, can be expected to prevail until public policies and funds offer alternatives for positive change.

During recent years the concept of the family has changed as our society has changed. Because of the wide variety of life styles today, options are needed to strengthen the family unit and to provide for needs that

The work described in this chapter was supported in part by Grant No. OCD-CB-17 from the Office of Child Development and by Grant No. G007500329 from the Office of Education. Additional support was received from the San Francisco Unified School District.

vary over a wide spectrum. Dr. Urie Bronfenbrenner of Cornell University has repeatedly called attention to the pervasive and growing need for ecological intervention—radical changes in the immediate environment of families—so that life can be maintained and the family can function as a child-rearing system. Adequate health care, nutrition, housing, and employment are all considered to be important components of this recommendation (Bronfenbrenner, 1974, 1976).

One of every six children under the age of 18 lives in a single parent home (Moore, 1977). One of every five babies is now being born to a teenager, at a rate approaching 617,000 each year. A growing number of the mothers are under 16 years of age (Forbush, 1976), and the chances are six in ten that they will have another child while they are still of school age (Webb, 1973). Few are able to finish their schooling because they cannot afford to pay for child care services. Few child care centers exist, whether profit or nonprofit, for children who are under 2 ½ years of age. By the time their children reach that age, these young mothers will have lost their motivation for school and will be trapped in the welfare system.

An alternate solution to this problem is to provide the new parent with child care services along with career counseling and education for parenthood from the time of the baby's birth until educational and vocational goals can be reached. It is difficult, however, to persuade funding bodies such as legislatures and school boards to look beyond their current budgetary binds to the consequences of ignoring these issues. Failure to give serious attention to the issues associated with adolescent parenthood and the educational and emotional needs of children during their first 3 years results in many problems for the child, his family, and the school system as well as the taxpayers as the years pass.

Because of the lack of emphasis given to the developmental needs of infants, no one really knows how many of them require intervention and special educational and therapeutic programs because of developmental delays due to congenital handicaps or environmental conditions. The latter may include lack of appropriate emotional contacts and cognitive stimulation, or outright neglect and abuse. The federal government has mandated that the states must search out and serve such children from birth through the school years, but unless some substantial change occurs, we can probably expect that very young handicapped children will be the last among this age range to receive services, just as young children in general are considered to be low priorities for educational dollars.

In light of the existing climate of the nation, our group has been exceedingly fortunate to have been granted funds for a continuous 6-year period to develop, expand, and demonstrate a model program for normal and handicapped infants and their families.

SERVICES AND GOALS

The Family Developmental Center (FDC) of the Family Service Agency of San Francisco assists infants and their parents by providing day care, infant and parent education, and support services through two innovative programs for families with special needs—the School Age Parent and Infant Program, and the Infant Special Education Project. Located in the Far West Center for Educational Development at 1855 Folsom Street, the Center is a well-designed and well-staffed complex with a spacious nursery, outdoor play area, kitchen, offices, and rooms for observation, naps, and individualized activities. Its visibility and accessibility to the educational community of the state and the nation have resulted in accommodation of over a thousand visitors a year. Supervised field placements have been made available to hundreds of students from high school to postgraduate levels to expand their knowledge of infant development, teaching strategies, and therapeutic techniques. Representatives of most of the area's day care centers and special education programs serving young children have attended training sessions at the Center aimed at upgrading the quality of programming in general and in expanding services to young handicapped children. A weekly half-hour television program, "Baby World," produced over Cable Channel 8 each week, utilizes the participation of parents and infants as well as staff to provide public education about infant development.

The Center was originally funded by the Office of Child Development during 1971–1975 as a research and demonstration project serving school-age parents. Its success in helping these young people to complete educational and vocational goals and in helping their children demonstrate high levels of development in cognitive, physical, social, and emotional areas resulted in continued funding for twenty families by the San Francisco Unified School District. Teenage parents who attend District Schools are eligible for free services, which include educational day care as well as job and career counseling.

A demonstration grant from the Bureau of Education for the Handicapped provides free assistance to 16 infants with handicaps or developmental difficulties, for whom early education may mean a reduction or prevention of learning problems. Parents have a choice between a home teacher for 1 hour per week or a mainstreamed day care program 5 days a week.

All of the infants served by the Center receive periodic developmental assessments and an individualized program of educational activities. Each infant in the day care component is assigned to a particular teacher, and a ratio of no more than four infants to one teacher is maintained. The ages of the children served range from 2 weeks to 3 years; most of them are less than 2 years old. The children share the same space and are not segregated according to age or handicapping condition.

The Family Developmental Center has eight broad goals.

1. To help infants attain their full potential for social, emotional, physical, and cognitive growth through an individualized, developmentally oriented therapeutic program based upon comprehensive and continuing evaluation of each child's development; to concurrently prevent or lessen learning disabilities and retardation in handicapped and/or high risk infants.

2. To provide a program for the parents which is supportive, educational, and individualized to meet their particular needs; to help them to be more effective agents for the positive growth, development, and self-concept of their child by helping them to understand their individual needs.

3. To provide a demonstration model of mainstreamed services to young children with components designed for replication, including assistance and training for others in order to encourage the expansion and improve the quality of such services.

4. To enable school-age parents to continue and complete their high school education so as to have a wider range of options for further education, vocational training or employment.

5. To decrease dependence of parents upon the public assistance system by encouraging, focusing, and facilitating progress toward educational and vocational goals, in order to broaden their vocational potential and enhance their autonomy and self-esteem to the benefit of themselves, their children, and the family unit.

6. To provide specialized preservice and in-service training for the teachers which will enable them to carry out a comprehensive multidisciplinary program and relate in an individual way to each child's ongoing and changing developmental, social, and physical needs, to promote optimal development.

7. To coordinate services with other agencies to make certain that the city's available resources are optimally used.

8. To demonstrate the program and to disseminate information about it to the general public and to special groups.

SCHOOL-AGE PARENTS' PROGRAM

Participants are accepted into the School-Age Parents' Program according to the mother's eligibility. She must be under the age of 21 years, be enrolled in a program of the San Francisco Unified School District, and need regular care for a child from 2 weeks to 2 years of age at the time of enrollment. She must enroll in a 5-hour per week Center field placement, for which she receives five units of school credit. One hour each week is spent participating in a parent group meeting and the other 4 are spent in individual meetings with staff and in nursery-related activities. These include meeting with the head teacher to review her child's stimulation program, caring for her child and carrying out suggested activities with him and with other children, helping with housekeeping tasks, participating in the periodic developmental testing of her child, and discussing the child's health with the nurse. Parents may receive personal counseling by arrangement and may seek out other resource staff and consultants for discussion of particular issues. A designated staff member is available for educational, career, and job counseling.

All services are provided at no cost to the participant, but a high level of performance is required. Child and parent attendance and parent group participation must be maintained within a range of 75% to 100%. The mother must also attend school regularly and maintain passing marks. Each participant's performance record is reviewed at the end of each school semester, and participation is renewed if the parent has demonstrated the motivation to maintain her eligibility.

Although high performance is expected from the parent, the program is structured to assist her to maintain successful participation. When problems become evident, they are discussed by the supervisory and resource staff at weekly program review meetings, and intervention strategies are devised and monitored. Because of its success-oriented structure, the program has almost no turnover of participants during a school semester. Group attendance generally averages around 90%. Good attendance increases the quality, consistency, and effects of program participation by both children and parents. Monies spent by the funding source thus have a maximal impact. Before such a structure was evolved over time, experience showed that many teenagers tested the system and participated at whatever minimal level was allowed.

More than 200 mothers have participated in our program and most have come to us with a basic knowledge of the physical aspects of infant care; many of them have lived at home and have had parents or older siblings as role models. It is the emotional and cognitive processes accompanying the period of adolescence that need to be understood, because they are often incompatible with behaviors that are generally considered to be associated with positive cognitive and emotional growth in young children. The early adolescent is often limited in her capacity to recognize or relate to her child's needs as being different from her own, because she is still operating within a concrete level of cognition or is in the throes of upheavel and change, as is seen in the groping and experimentation that accompany the transition from concrete to formal operations (Piaget & Inhelder, 1958). From this developmental point of view, the focus of intervention should be on a young parent's general emotional and cognitive growth. The way that we structure our thoughts parallels the way that we structure our relationships with others; the developmental trend is in the direction of increasing differentiation. As the young mother grows cognitively, she becomes able to perceive situations from the viewpoint of others, including her baby's. Parent effectiveness increases as an adolescent moves from egocentrism in her relationship with her child to reciprocity.

To experience this kind of growth, the adolescent must be involved in a situation in which she has an opportunity to become aware of her own thoughts and feelings and to expand upon them through interaction with others. She must have the opportunity to experience other points of view and to question her own. This is accomplished in the FDC program through methods which have been incorporated into the weekly parent group and which have been described in an FDC publication, *Growing With Your Baby: A Facilitator's Manual* (Lyman, 1975). These methods include promoting discussion of moral dilemmas; fantasizing about future possibilities for the infant and self with a retracing of methods for attaining them; carrying out value clarification exercises involving practice in abstracting from a particular situation; thinking about alternatives and reflecting on the self; and role playing as an opportunity to experiment with experiencing another's point of view—an experience which often leads to new unconscious thought processes that reinforce reciprocity in relationships.

The uniqueness of this approach to education for parents is that it focuses on a mother's growth as a total person. Successful implementation requires that the group leader be able to elicit real emotional involvement on the part of the group members. *Growing With Your Baby: A Facilitator's Manual* is designed to help her do this. Others have generally approached adolescent parent education by using a linear model which assumes that learning occurs simply as fact is added to fact. It has been our experience that most very young parents will not be receptive to new information unless it is somehow made personally relevent, and that no real learning will take place unless they are encouraged to question their own belief systems in a nonthreatening way through interaction with others.

INFANT SPECIAL EDUCATION PROJECT

Participants in the Infant Special Education Project are accepted according to the infant's eligibility for the program as well as the parent's expressed need for the services. The infant must be between 2 weeks and 18 months of age at the time of admission, and must be diagnosed by his doctor as being retarded, hard of hearing, visually handicapped, emotionally disturbed, or crippled. Health-impaired infants requiring special education and related services because of conditions such as genetic abnormalities, prematurity, drug withdrawal, various conditions associated with central nervous system involvement, and/or undiagnosed developmental delays, are also accepted.

Parents must be willing to participate in the diagnostic and evaluative components of the program, which include periodic developmental testing of the infant and their evaluation of the program elements. Participants in the Center's day care program must agree to bring the child to the Center on a regular daily basis and to participate in periodic parent group sessions.

Each child enrolled in the program is evaluated by a multidisciplinary team which includes an infant development specialist, a physician, a nurse, an occupational or physical therapist, and a social worker. These staff members exchange impressions and recommendations which are then communicated to the parent and the assigned teacher, who incorporates their suggestions into the child's individualized educational and therapeutic program.

After the determination of infant eligibility and the assessment of parent needs, infants are entered into the Home or Center Program as openings permit. The Home Program is usually chosen by parents who are able to be at home during their child's infancy because they do not go to school or work. Most of these parents have transportation problems or several other young children at home, which makes it difficult for them to attend any Center-based program. Some feel that their infants are too young or too health-impaired for the Center program. By the time the baby reaches the age of 12 to 18 months, they often begin to feel that group experience would be good for him, and that they are ready to return to work or school themselves. For some of these families, an early home-based program followed by transition to a Center-based program is optimally suited to family needs. The flexibility created by the combination of home and Center components is regarded as very desirable.

For both home and Center participants, the focus is on individualized programs suited to the needs of both the infant and the parent. Differences in staff-parent-infant involvement between the home and the Center components require different approaches to implementing the infant's program. The full day, 5-day a week day care program allows the teacher to be the primary teacher of the child, while parents participate in carrying out stimulation activities in the evenings, on weekends, and during their daily participation at the Center. In the home program, staff contact with the infant is limited to 1 to 1½ hours per week. The parent must therefore be considered the primary teacher, while the Project staff contributes with some direct teaching of the infant and with encouragement of the parent's teaching skills. Effective assistance to the infant's development must be carried out with and through the parent; intervention must be carefully suited to individual parents.

Many factors can limit the effectiveness of a parent as a teacher of a handicapped infant. For many parents, the period of infancy is the time of initial adjustment to the baby's handicap and potential. The process of denial, anger, grieving, acceptance, and information gathering which many parents go through is a critical one with long-term impact on the infant-parent relationship. It may be hard for the parent to teach or even to interact comfortably with the infant until some level of acceptance is accomplished. In other cases there may be instead a lack of concern with the baby's delays, either because of a lack of information about early development or because of low expectations based upon the parent's own life experiences. Some parents may need assistance only in discovering appropriate materials and activities to supplement their intuitive teaching skills. Others may lack a basic healthy parent-infant relationship on which all other interactions must be based.

The period of infancy is a critical one in which the basic parent-infant relationship is established. For a handicapped infant, this relationship may be even more needed and more vulnerable. An important goal, then, is to help parents to grow as parents, particularly during this early critical period. The actual home visit often consists of a great deal of modeling of appropriate behaviors and feedback to the parent about the significance of the child's responses. The initial activities that are demonstrated may be chosen so that the infant will succeed easily, to allow for positive comments and perhaps for some corresponding positive feelings by the parent. For those parents who are overwhelmed by their concern with the handicap, early home visits may concentrate on direct support to the parents to increase their information about the handicap and the child's potential and to help the parent to understand and work through their feelings about it. The primary goal of the home program is to help the infant attain optimal development by helping the parent to develop emotionally and cognitively through enjoyment of the baby, feedback and modeling, reinforcement of good parenting skills, support, information, and written suggestions when appropriate.

As in the Center program, additional resources are available to home-based families. Special resource staff may make consultation visits with the Coordinator. Social workers are available for counseling and for helping families secure needed financial assistance. The Center's toy lending library makes interesting materials available for all infants. Families are assisted in obtaining supplementary services, such as early hearing evaluations and genetic counseling.

Good emotional development of the infant is valued as well as optimal mental and physical development. In the home such development frequently involves helping the parent to be aware of the emotional impact of a handicapped infant on other siblings. Concern with emotional development may also raise issues related to the impact of a handicapped infant on marital relationships. Whenever possible, these concerns are referred to the social worker or outside counseling resources so that the home visitor can continue in the educational role.

Coordination with other agencies and community resources involved with the family is a frequent activity in both home and Center programs. A public health nurse, hospital staff member, or Protective Service worker is frequently invited to make a joint home visit to observe a developmental assessment, special consultation, or teaching activities. Agency coordination may also involve meetings with other professionals to determine the best way to avoid overlapping services, to reinforce each other's goals for the infant and parent, or to establish jointly an effective approach to a specific problem.

CENTER PROGRAM FOR CHILDREN

Participants who choose the day care service are usually offered the full day educational program. (Occasionally two families are able to arrange schedules so that one full day slot is shared by two children who attend the Center at different times.) Children are brought to the Center by their parents between 7:30 and 9:30 A.M. and may stay until

4:30 or 5:00 P.M. Most children spend 8 to 9 hours in the Center, Monday through Friday. Breakfast, a morning snack, lunch, and an afternoon snack are served, and infants are fed according to individual schedules. Good nutrition is emphasized and weekly menus are posted. Parents communicate with the child's teacher about special instructions and leave written instructions if medication is recommended by the nurse. Sick children with noncontagious illnesses are cared for by their regular teacher in the usual setting.

The Center program for children is based on the following assumptions.

1. Homostasis of a baby's organic systems must be established so that his energy can be directed toward learning (Maslow, 1954).

2. Attachment to one primary care giver is vital: The care giver then becomes a developmental agent, an active participant in the learning process (Bowlby, 1969).

3. The establishment of basic trust is an essential component in providing for the child's safety and emotional security (Erikson, 1950).

4. The program for any one particular child should be totally individualized to meet his special needs within the limits of the overall necessities of the program (Lewis, Latzko, Klinefeld, Lyman, & Lodge, 1975).

5. Each child must be encouraged to learn to cope and to master his environment in an active way (White, 1965).

6. The concepts of consistency and regularity in the environment, reinforcement of the child's positive functioning, and stimulation appropriate to the individual child are essential (Maslow, 1954).

7. A multitude of materials should be available to the child so that he can learn from interacting with objects (Piaget, 1975).

8. A toddler needs to have his feelings of power and initiative respected. He should have help and guidance in

learning to control his feelings, while being given the latitude to express these feelings (Erikson, 1950; Bach & Goldberg, 1974).

9. Teachers need to be encouraged to invent, devise, and improve methods to accomplish goals for the children (Piaget, 1975).

Children are assigned to one care giver/teacher for the length of their stay. In this way an attachment is formed and learning becomes clearly associated with the relationship between teacher and baby. The teacher and parent also form a relationship which will facilitate the parent's development as an agent for growth in the baby's life.

Since the Center program is totally individualized to accommodate the unique needs of each child, there is no regular schedule of activities. Although consistency and regularity are maintained in the environment, the sleep and feeding schedules are flexible enough to allow the teacher the time to work individually with each of the four children assigned to her, and to take advantage of optimal times for learning when the child is alert and receptive.

The teacher works within the overall goals of a written educational program which is available in the nursery for her own reference, for the parents' use, and as a guide for substitute teachers and students on field placements. The "stimulation program" consists of activities appropriate to the unique response of each child and devised to accomplish specified short-term goals. The program is reviewed and revised every 2 weeks by the teacher and is checked periodically by the program director.

In order to closely monitor each child's progress every 2 weeks and to help focus on short-term goals so that suggested activities will be optimally effective, a tool developed by the Center staff, called the "Sequences of Development," is used. Nine subscales assess sensory responsiveness, gross motor skills, fine motor skills, exploration and competence, body image, self-concept and confidence, social relatedness, gestural imitation, perceptuo-cognitive development (with subscales of objective constancy and development of schemas relating to objects), and language.

Curriculum activities to accompany the goals are derived from many sources including *Baby Learning Through Baby Play* (Gordon, 1970); *Child Learning Through Child's Play* (Gordon, Guinagh, & Jester, 1972); *Teach Your Baby* (Painter, 1971); *Infant Curriculum: The Bromley-Health Guide to the Care of Infants in Groups* (Tronick & Greenfield, 1973); *Teaching the Mentally Retarded Child* (Barnard & Powell, 1972); *The Karnes Early Language Activities* (Karnes 1972); *The Portage Guide to Early Education* (Bluma, Shearer, Frohman, & Hilliard, 1976); *How to Keep Your Child Fit from Birth to Six* (Prudden, 1964); *Handling the Young Cerebral Palsied Child at Home* (Finnie, 1975); *The Preschool Special Education Project Curriculum Manual* Rochester, New York, (Jordan, 1972); and *Curriculum Guide, Hearing Impaired Children—Birth to Three Years—And Their Parents* (Northcott, 1972).

As new curriculum materials become available, they will be reviewed and added to the Center's resource library when appropriate. Suggestions that relate specifically to a child's special motor and language needs are provided by the consulting occupational and physical therapists and the language pathologist. Finally, and most importantly, the teachers draw on their own knowledge and experience in devising activities that will have high motivational value to each child. We have found that the use of many curriculum sources encourages teachers to incorporate a maximal degree of flexibility and creativity into their planning.

The Bayley Scales of Infant Development are the primary tool by which each child's development is evaluated. Handicapped children are assessed at entrance and at 3-month intervals, whereas the other children are tested at 6-month intervals. Performance and progress are reviewed across nine areas of development, according to a profile devised by Lodge (1973).

The program for the babies is conducted in an environment in which there is optimal opportunity for development. Growth of cognitive and personal skills are both considered important in helping the children to develop their potential and in assisting the handicapped children to compensate for and/or overcome their handicaps. A large central nursery is broken into homelike areas with rugs, couches, rocking chairs, bean bags, indoor play equipment, and low dividers. A wide variety of toys and books is kept easily accessible for the child to choose and use. A kitchen, bathroom, sleeping room, and two activity rooms adjoin the central nursery. One activity room is arranged for quiet and soothing play with a rug, couch, waterbed, and book corner. The other contains cabinets with a multitude of materials which are used in learning activities and messy play. The room contains a water table which is also used for oatmeal play, an easel and low tables for painting, a record player, puzzles, formboards, formboxes, pegboards, logos, sorting materials, clay, and many other materials.

A large, grassy, lattice-enclosed outdoor play area is easily accessible from the nursery. This yard holds a large partitioned sandbox and a specially designed structure with ramp and steps, enclosed platforms of different heights, barrels, and a slide. The yard also contains balance beams, swings, and a hammock. The Center is located in a warm belt of the city and the day is arranged so that the children spend part of every mild day outdoors.

After lunch, many of the children nap. Since individual schedules are honored, this is a time when teachers can work individually with children who are awake. It is also a time that teachers can use for record keeping, program planning, and conferences with the program director.

While a few of the mothers spend their daily field placement hour participating in morning activities, most are present in the nursery between 3:30 P.M. and 4:30 P.M. Upon arrival, they become primarily responsible for their child. In addition to general care and stimulation activities, they help with assigned tasks which help to keep the nursery clean, safe, and organized. The afternoon head teacher coordinates and supervises their participation in the nursery.

Visitors usually observe the program from 10 A.M. to 12 A.M. so that they can see the teachers working individually with children, and can watch during free play, outdoor play, snacktime, and lunchtime.

TEACHER SELECTION AND TRAINING

Methods of staff selection, training, and evaluation have been studied over a 6-year period, as well as educational and experience requirements and job roles. While particular screening techniques have been found to be somewhat useful, (Lewis et al., 1975), no method approached the effectiveness of on-the-job observation. For this reason, new teachers are required to have worked as substitutes.

Teachers are required to have a minimal educational background of an A.A. degree in child development, psychology, or early childhood education, with 2 years of experience with the age group being served, or a B.A. degree with some experience in working as a substitute at the Center. They must demonstrate competency in areas of knowledge, program planning, and program implementation, according to criterion-referenced standards before the end of a 6-month probationary period. Knowledge must be demonstrated for a minimum of 10 field-tested teacher training units, which deal with teaching and caring for normal and handicapped infants and in relating to their parents. Teachers must also demonstrate consistent competence in planning their children's entire programs independently within the planning time provided; goals and activities to accomplish them must be reviewed and updated every 2 weeks.

Good staff morale and cooperation are especially important in an infant program. Infants sense the tensions in the persons who care for them, and toddlers imitate the behaviors of significant adults. Work with young children is both physically and emotionally demanding, and work with disinterested or neglecting parents can be frustrating and depressing. Regular in-service training sessions and weekly staff meetings help to ensure common goals, continuing enthusiasm, and open lines of communication between all staff members. Staff development plans are individualized according to periodic needs assessments and are accomplished through methods which include group training, individualized tutoring, independent study, workshops, and conferences. Developmental agents are most effective when their own developmental needs are met.

SUMMARY

The Family Developmental Center has developed a model program for infants with special needs and for their parents. Work with almost 300 families over 6 years has emphasized services to teenage parents and high risk and handicapped children from ethnic backgrounds that include black, Latino, Filipino, native American, Caucasian, Vietnamese, Chinese, and Puerto Rican. Welfare level families and low-income, single-parent families have been the predominate group served. The program emphasizes the individualization of infant and parent programming and offers families mainstreamed educational and therapeutic day care or an alternate home visit program, as well as a number of support services. School-age parents receive school credit for participating in a work/study program at the Center each day.

Ongoing evaluation of children, parents, and staff has demonstrated progress toward established goals. A number of publications concerning the Center's model, research, and program evaluation are available from FDC and the ERIC Clearinghouse on Early Childhood Education. Among these are a facilitator's manual for running a personal-growth-oriented teenage parent's group (Lyman, 1975) and a guidebook for the operation of infant and toddler centers (Latzko, 1975). A section on infant and toddler resources developed for dissemination by FDC as part of a grant from the Bureau of Education for the Handicapped (Note 1) is included in the Appendix in this volume (Latzko, 1977).

REFERENCES

Bach, G., & Goldberg, H. *Creative aggression.* New York: Avon Books, 1974.

Barnard, K. & Powell, M. L. *Teaching the mentally retarded child.* St. Louis: C. U. Mosby Co., 1972.

Bluma, S. M., Shearer, M. S., Frohman, A. B., & Hilliard, J. *Portage guide to early education.* The Portage Project, Portage, Wisconsin: Cooperative Educational Service Agency, 1976.

Bowlby, J. *Attachment and loss,* vols. I & II. New York: Basic Books, 1969.

Bronfenbrenner, U. Is early intervention effective? *Day Care and Early Education,* 1974, *2*.

Bronfenbrenner, U. Research on the effects of day care on child development. Appendix A in *Toward a National Policy for Children and Families.* Report of the Advisory Committee on Child Development. Washington, D.C.: National Academy of Sciences/National Research Council, 1976.

Erikson, E. *Childhood and society.* New York: W. W. Norton, 1950.

Finnie, N. *Handling the young cerebral palsied child at home.* New York: E. P. Dutton, 1975.

Forbush, J. *National Alliance Concerned with School Age Parents.* Brochure, 1976–1977.

Gordon, I. J. *Baby learning through baby play.* New York: St. Martin's Press, 1970.

Gordon, I. J., Guinagh, B., & Jester, R. E. *Child learning through child's play.* New York: St. Martin's Press, 1972.

Jordan, E. C. *The preschool special education project curriculum manual.* Rochester, New York: 1972.

Karnes, M. B. *The Karnes early language activities.* Champaign, Illinois: GEM, 1975.

Latzko, T. *Some practical aspects of operating an infant and toddler center.* San Francisco: Family Developmental Center, 1975 (ERIC: ED 121–415).

Latzko, T. *Resources for infant educators.* San Francisco: Family Developmental Center, 1977.

Lewis, J., Latzko, T., Kleinfeld, P., Lyman, P., & Lodge, A. *Family developmental center: A demonstration project. Final Report.* San Francisco: Family Developmental Center, 1975 (ERIC: ED 121–412).

Lodge, A. Innovations in the assessment of infant behavior. Presented at a meeting of the Western Psychological Association, Anaheim, California, April 1973.

Lyman, P. *Growing with your baby: A facilitator's manual.* San Francisco: Family Developmental Center, 1975 (ERIC: ED 121–413).

Maslow, A. *Motivation and personality.* New York: Harper, 1954.

Moore, P. (Ed.). N.A.S. panel urges income aid for children and families. *A.P.A. Monitor,* January 1977.

Northcott, W. H. *Curriculum guide, Hearing impaired children—birth to three years—and their parents.* Washington: The Alexander Graham Bell Association for the Deaf, 1972.

Painter, G. *Teach your baby.* New York: Simon & Schuster, 1971.

Piaget, J. Piaget takes a teacher's look. *Learning,* 1975.

Piaget, J., & Inhelder, B. *The growth of logical thinking from childhood to adolescence.* New York: Basic Books, 1958.

Prudden, B. *How to keep your child fit from birth to six.* New York: Harper & Row, 1964.

Tronick, E., Greenfield, P. M. *Infant curriculum: The Bromley-health guide to the care of infants in groups.* New York: Media Projects Incorporated, 1973.

Webb, H. J. Pregnant schoolgirls and pregnant teachers: The policy problem school districts can sidestep no longer. *The American School Borad Journal,* March, 1973.

White, R. A. Competence and the psychosexual stages of development. *Nebraska Symposium on Motivation,* 1965.

NOTE

1. "Resources for Infant Educators" was developed for dissemination under Grant No. G007500329 from the Office of Education.

Chapter Four

FAMILY DAY CARE: ONE ALTERNATIVE

June Solnit Sale

The largest existing network of out-of-home care for infants and children in the United States has consistently been either ignored or maligned (Grotberg, 1971; Keysering, 1972; Willner, 1970; 1971). That network is family day care. This child care service provides 78% of the out-of-home nonrelative care for children under 12 years of age in the United States (Ruderman, 1968, p. 212). It may well be that lack of careful analysis by social scientists has protected the spontaneity, humanness, and lack of institutional flavor found in family day care. This system of child care is low status; it is concerned with children of all socioeconomic classes, races, and cultures; it defies licensing procedures; and it is successfully meeting the needs of many working parents and their children.

There may be good reasons why investigators have ignored it. Dubos (1965) has pointed out that social scientists investigate that in which they are interested or with

---

Article first appeared in *American Journal of Orthopsychiatry*, Vol 43 No 1, January 1973 and is reprinted here with permission.

which they have grave concern. Using the medical model, social scientists often become involved in programs that deal with malfunctioning. From our exploration of this ubiquitous social system in a varied socioeconomic and racial area of Pasadena, California, we are pleased to report no malfunction. On the contrary, family day care is alive and well. From our experience with 22 family day care mothers, we have found that the potential of this child care network is great. We have also found that family day care is an existing system that can and does provide excellent child development services for many children and their families.

The Community Family Day Care Project was initiated in August 1970 by Pacific Oaks College in order to test the growing belief that group day care is the best way to provide care for children of working parents. Prescott, Jones, and Milich (1967; 1969; 1970) had completed definitive studies of group day care, and their work had alerted those concerned with the lives of young children to the limits, restrictions, and possible dangers of the large day care center. It was our task to examine an alternative form of out-of-home care for children and to assess its potential in delivering developmental services.

POTENTIAL BENEFITS

We hypothesized that the small, personal, neighborhood program provided by family day care mothers might provide a setting that would meet the needs of many children and their families for a wide variety of reasons.

Family day care provides for children of a wide age range, from 4 weeks old to school age. A family with children of varying ages may find their child care needs met under one roof, in one setting, and the wide age range of children in family day care provides a rich learning experience.

Family day care has the potential for horizontal diffusion. The family day care mother may be a neighbor and often has a life-style similar to that of the parents. The family day care home thus has the unique opportunity to provide a developmental program for the children, which assures continuity in learning experience from one setting to another. It is also quite possible for parents to enrich their own home by replicating the child-rearing practices and developmental environment that they find in the family day care home. This is not usually the case in center-type programs that are viewed as "school" and therefore not duplicable by parents in their own homes. Life-style similarities are a plus in another way, too: like values between users and givers of services are more likely to be attained.

The opportunity for a child to feel himself more personally responsible and responded to in an intimate setting is more likely to be found in family day care, where a motherly woman is caring for relatively few children without pressure for the aloofness that the "teacher" role implies.

Family day care is more easily responsive to the convenience of day care users than group programs can ordinarily be. Schedules can be flexible and more easily tailored to work schedules of parents. The neighborhood location eliminates difficult transportation arrangements, and the day care mother can ease the working parents' fear of missing work because of children's illness. Upper respiratory ailments, common among young children, are usually acceptable in family day care homes but not in centers. Illness may go undetected in larger programs, but mothers are more likely to report the illness to family day care mothers so that measures such as rest and quiet may be insured. Family day care may help to reduce mothers' work absenteeism, while at the same time providing proper care for the children

Finally—and no small consideration it is for many day care users—the cost of family day care is usually less than that of group center care.

GETTING STARTED

The first problem facing anyone who wants to study family day care is how to discover the network of family day care services. Our search was particularly difficult because residents of the multiracial and economic area in which we established our Project center are suspicious of anyone who comes asking questions, having been endlessly surveyed but with no tangible results. That is doubly true in the *barrio,* where the isolation is more acute because of language barriers.

We could have started with the list of licensed family day care mothers provided by the Department of Public Social Services, but we knew that a large number of day care mothers were not licensed. We needed them in our study, too. Using the "gatekeeper" technique (Lewin, 1947), we identified local people who would likely be trusted by residents of the area in which we were to work. We introduced ourselves to the "gatekeepers" (in many cases merely re-establishing long-time relationships made through the good offices of Pacific Oaks), who in turn helped us identify, or introduced us to, the women providing child care in their homes. We also used some of the techniques described by the founders of the Portland Day Care Neighbor Service (Collins & Watson, 1969; Emlen, 1970), as well as door-to-door screening and publicity. In all, we talked to 69 women providing some form of child care in our immediate area.

Contracts were made with 22 family day care mothers thus identified to act as consultants to our program. The contract specified that the day care mothers would demonstrate their methods and techniques of child care to a Pacific Oaks student and would attend monthly Project center meetings with the staff.

The family day care mothers represented a broad variation in age, ethnic background, and socioeconomic status. Seven of the 22 women were in their 30s and had 19 children of their own, 16 years and younger, living at home. Five were in their 40s and 5 in their 50s. More than 77% were of the working or lower class. Twelve were black, 5 were white, and 5 were of Latin heritage or Mexican-American (4 spoke only Spanish, and 1 was bilingual). Twelve were licensed and 10 were unlicensed.

OUR PROGRAM

The program we set up with the 22 day care mothers sought answers to two prime questions: What is the nature of existing family day care programs? and, How would our Project be able to enrich these programs, while at the same time protecting the integrity and unique quality of each? We acted on the assumption clearly stated by Solnit (1968) that "the act of rendering a service, an essential variable in research, makes possible the continuity of observation and provides access to relevant data in child development which otherwise will be missed." We assumed that we must provide tangible, immediate, and credible service in order to establish and maintain trust. The services were based on enrichment of the lives of the family day care mothers and their programs for children, as well as the environments. There were eight major facets of our program and they are described below.

THE CENTER MEETINGS

The Project staff met each week with five or six consultant family day care mothers, so that each mother was included once a month. The women were paid a token $10 for each meeting they attended. The meetings were structured to help us learn and assess the ways in which family day care functioned from the point of view of the family day care mothers. We carefully avoided a position of being "experts" in the field of child care in a home situation, since, in fact, the family day care mothers were the "authorities" and we were the learners.

The center meetings were free floating and generally covered areas of concern, as well as some of the solutions to problems that were part of family day care. The taped discussions covered such subjects as how to encourage independence in children, methods of discipline, how to work with aggressive children, feeding and nutrition, weaning, toilet training, sex identification, how to work with parents, different value systems of parents and family day care mothers, emergency day care, fees charged, collection of fees, advantages of licensing, morals, and morale. The meetings provided a place for family day care mothers to discuss problems of mutual concern, as well as a social respite away from children, thus serving the dual purpose of meeting the family day care mothers' needs for socializing and problem solving and the staff's need for information.

FIELD DEMONSTRATION ASSISTANTS

Seven students (five women and two men) from Pacific Oaks College enrolled in a practicum and seminar related to the Project. Each field demonstration assistant related to the same three or four family day care mothers for the duration of the Project. A student went to each of his family day care homes once a month for 4 hours on Monday and Wednesday of the same week. On Monday morning the family day care mother demonstrated her methods of working with the children in her care. On Wednesday morning the student cared for the children in the home, while the family day care mother attended a center meeting. The field demonstration assistants kept logs of their work, which proved rich sources of information on how family day care works. We found that students are vital to this type of project but require a good deal of supervision and tender, loving attention to many of the unresolved problems this kind of program may aggravate within them. The staff must be aware of the fine line required to maintain a balance between the experiences of students and family day care mothers, so that neither loses in perspective, values, or integrity.

TOY LOAN

A toy loan of equipment and toys ordered primarily by the family day care mothers was established. This assisted the women by permitting them to test and try, for a month at a time, materials that they could not afford to purchase unless they were convinced of the products' worth. The family day care mothers reported that the toys were useful in providing new experiences for the children, and also served to stimulate the mothers into thinking about new ideas and concepts concerning the role of play for young children.

COOPERATIVE NURSERY SCHOOL

The Project purchased six 2-day scholarships in the Mothers' Club Cooperative Nursery School for children from the day care homes who might benefit from a peer-group relationship in a school setting. The family day care mother had to work 1 day a month in the Cooperative in order to qualify for the arrangement. The Mothers' Club provided care for the rest of the children while the family day care mother worked at the Cooperative.

COMMUNITY RESOURCES

The Project staff developed a resource manual cataloguing the many resources for the family day care mothers, the children, and their families. In addition, we acted as catalysts in helping the women to make contact with appropriate agencies in the community that could offer help when needed.

MONTHLY BULLETIN

A monthly bulletin focusing on local needs and issues was edited and translated into Spanish by family day care mothers.

CHILD DEVELOPMENT CLASS

A class entitled "How Children Learn and Grow" was requested by the family day care mothers. This course was a pilot for a certificate program that is presently being offered by the extension division of Pacific Oaks College for family day care mothers and others who care for children.

PLACEMENT SERVICE

In gathering information about the informal and formal day care networks in the immediate area, our field staff and students found a number of vacancies for children in group centers as well as in family day care homes. The center staff soon found itself acting as a referral service for parents seeking child care placements. We also found ourselves helping women who wanted to become family day care mothers in areas where there seemed to be no services available. We thus have helped to increase the alternatives for parents seeking child care arrangements.

In continuing our work, we find that the whole matter of referrals and matchmaking remains an area that must have more attention given to it. It is our belief that parents must make decisions that are real for them and should be given alternatives from which to choose. Following this principle, we give out the names of four family day care mothers who would be close to the home of the working parent, and we provide them with a checklist that helps to frame some of the questions we have found critical in establishing a contract between users and givers. We then suggest that the parents visit and talk with the women providing the service before they make a decision. This procedure is not always practical when the need for immediate placement is urgent, nor is it necessarily one that makes a good match, but we are presently investigating methods to improve the process. We continue to find this area of matchmaking most difficult.

After a year of working with this program, we have found that the potential of family day care is authentic and exciting. It is important to remember that what is being described is a natural network, where there is no control of program, content, salaries, or children's placement. This is the kind of network that probably exists in most neighborhoods—invisible, unheralded, and quietly doing its thing, most often very well. Some of the kinds of child development services offered can be only briefly sketched here but are detailed in a report of the Project (Sale & Torres, 1971).

SERVICES AND FEES

Services offered and fees charged in family day care demonstrate its flexibility. Most of the family day care mothers had developed a sliding scale, based on what the family could afford and the number and ages of the children involved. The weekly fees ranged from $7.00 to $22.50 per week per child. We believe that these low rates resulted from the fact that 19 of the 22 family day care mothers had husbands living at home and none was the sole support of her household; three received supplementary income from pensions or other family support. (Indeed, one of the requirements for licensing in Los Angeles County is that the family have sufficient income to meet its basic needs.) Having an interested male in the household added much to the enrichment of the children. After all, it really is nice to have "grandpa" come home from work on the night shift and invite Tom to make a snack with him or to have "Uncle John" invite Janie to watch while the car tire is changed.

Comparing the fees to proprietary day care centers, family day care charges were usually less and the services greater. Most private centers charge a minimum of $22.50 per week in Pasadena. Even where a sliding scale, based on the family's earnings, is used in public centers, the fee charged is still prohibitive for the working poor.

Most of the private and public day are centers in the area were open from 7:00 a.m. to 6:00 p.m. Some of the women in the Project provided care for children as early as 5:50 a.m. and as late as midnight to 1:00 a.m.; one child was cared for from 1:00 to 11:30 p.m. on a regular basis. Picture a child arriving at a day care center at 5:30 a.m. (Also picture the staff.) In family day care, the early-arriving child is generally brought in his pajamas and is put back to sleep and allowed to awaken when he is ready for breakfast with the family. If he is picked up late, he is put to bed after an evening meal and story time and later transported in his pajamas to complete his rest in his own bed at home.

Other services found in family day care relate to the well-being of the children and their families. For example, family day care mothers reported that they took children to the doctor, dentist, and barber. All of the women took great pride in the food that they prepared for the children (and the field demonstration assistants attested to the justification of the pride). Special diets were prepared when the requests were made and one woman described the semi-kosher meals she arranged, not on demand but out of respect for the family. All of the family day care mothers assumed responsibility for toilet training and weaning, and some would wash and iron clothes for children in their care. The majority of women took the approach described by the American Academy of Pediatrics (1971, p. 1) in dealing with illness of children. These family day care mothers believed that if the children were exposed to an illness as a "family" member, they could not be rejected from the family—rather, that a regimen of quiet, semi-isolated care, with the giving of prescribed medicine, rest, and diet, was the best policy to follow.

CHILDREN SERVED

Most of the children placed in our family day care homes were in the 1–3-year age range. Since there was no group center care for children under the age of 2½, this is a logical outcome. The 143 children involved ranged from 6 weeks to 11 years of age. Over 24% were 2 years or younger; 53% were 3–5 years old; over 22% were of elementary school age.

Almost 48% were from working-class families, 28% from homes of professional parents, 17% from lower-class or welfare homes, and over 6% from the middle class. More than half of the children in the study were black and less than 5% were of Mexican or Latin extraction. Almost half of the family day care homes had children of various racial background; all of the homes had children representing a variety of socioeconomic classes. This democratic mix was of great interest, since 72% of the children lived within a 1- or 2-mile radius of their family day care homes.

NOW AND THE FUTURE

One of our goals was to learn how a network such as family day care could be improved and supported. Not every one of the 22 homes in which we worked was an ideal place for children, in our view. In fact, there was one home —overcrowded and rigidly regimented—that we would never recommend. We believe this licensed home should no longer be permitted to operate. What made the difference between the homes we found to be excellent environments and those we found needed improvement? It became obvious to us that the key to quality had to do with the family day care mother herself. It also became clear that licensing had little to do with a guarantee of quality. The whole area of licensing in family day care should be further explored and some experimenting with alternatives such as registration, accreditation, or a voucher system would be worth pursuing.

With respect to quality, we are doing several things in our program in its second year that we hope will upgrade and give some needed status to family day care. We—meaning both the Pacific Oaks staff and the family day care mothers—have developed a core curriculum that will lead to a certificate for family day care mothers. More important, we are helping family day care mothers to create a self-help organization in which they may work together to improve family day care for the children, their families, and the day care mothers themselves. If doctors can set standards for doctors and enforce those standards, if lawyers can set standards for lawyers and enforce them, if teachers can set standards for teachers and enforce them, then why can't family day care mothers do the same?

We are aware that funding support of a project such as ours comes to an end, and that its worth may be measured by what happens after the staff, the center, and the money are gone. The fledgling self-help organization is beginning to struggle with this reality. A system of program-enrichment volunteers is now being developed that will provide some of the supports necessary for the sustenance of a hard-working group such as family day care mothers. In addition, the connection with Pacific Oaks is a real one—it serves the self-interest of both groups in maintaining an ongoing program of student field placements in family day care homes. All meetings of the day care mothers' organization are held at Pacific Oaks College as an ongoing reminder of the relationship. A regional conference on family day care was held at Pacific Oaks, with the organization members acting as hosts and participants.

The question remains open as to whether such an organization will last. Family day care mothers are women who have not been part of organizations in the past; they are not paper pushers or people who have responded to influences outside the home. We have found in the initial meetings of the organization, however, a common sense and flexible approach to working together. The structure for officers was developed by the women to meet their needs. Selection of toy loan and library chairwomen was the first order of business because of the desire for improving environments for the children in their care. It was also quickly decided that the organization should be open to any persons interested in family day care who wished to join, a proviso that helps eliminate the possibility of an elite group forming.

CONCLUSION: WITH AN APPEAL

This chapter has described the formation, introduction, and some of the ongoing program of the Community Family Day Care Project in the Pasadena community. But beyond the goal of mere description, we have a further desire—that there will be in the broader community, and among child care professionals, some appreciation of the child development services offered by the existing network of family day care. Most often these programs are labeled "custodial" or "babysitting," and little attention is paid to the natural and relevant learning environment provided by an aware family day care mother in a home setting.

Prescott is now finishing a comparative study of family day care, group center, and nursery school-home settings, and her preliminary results indicate high frequencies of cognitive and language input by family day care mothers in their unsophisticated programming. In observations of group day care settings, those found most appealing are the centers that try to replicate the warm climate found in a home. Let us be careful, when we "discover" the potential of family day care, that we do not bring the worst of center day care to the home by attempting to duplicate the school. The flexibility, informality, and lack of a fixed curriculum is part of what makes the family day care environment relevant and useful.

This is not to say that family day care is all of an excellent quality as it now functions. On the contrary, it needs much support, change, and improvement. But while ways that it may be supported and improved are being considered, the unique quality of the family and home setting must be preserved.

Let us not prescribe academic formulas and methods of teaching number concepts for a family day care mother who shows children how an apple may be sectioned into halves, quarters, and eighths. Let us not prescribe an academic formula for language development for a family day care mother who will answer questions about the picture of a deceased grandparent above the fireplace, about the dog who has just had six puppies, or about why a ring remains in the bathtub after a bath. Let us not prescribe psychosocial or cognitive input of a stereotyped nature that will deny the richness of the real world in which we live. In short, let us not prescribe play-dough where real dough is available.

REFERENCES

American Academy of Pediatrics: *Standards for day care centers for infants and children under three years of age.* Evanston: American Academy of Pediatrics, 1971.

Collins, A., & Watson, E. *The day care neighbor service: A handbook for the organization and operation of a new approach to family day care.* Portland: Tri-County Community Council, 1969.

Dubos, R. *Man adapting.* New Haven: Yale University Press, 1965.

Emlen, A. Neighborhood family day care as a child-rearing environment. Presented at the annual meeting of the National Association for the Education of Young Children, 1970.

Grotberg, E. (Ed.). *Day care: Resources for decision.* Washington: Office of Economic Opportunity, 1971.

Keyserling, M. *Windows on day care.* New York: National Council of Jewish Women, 1972.

Lewin, K. Frontiers in group dynamics. *Human Relationships,* 1947, *1,* 145.

Milich, C., Prescott, E., & Jones, E. *Group day care: A study in diversity.* Pasadena: Pacific Oaks College, 1969.

Prescott, E., & Jones, E. *Group day care as a child-rearing environment.* Pasadena: Pacific Oaks College, 1967.

Prescott, E., & Jones, E. *An institutional analysis of day care.* Pasadena: Pacific Oaks College, 1970.

Ruderman, F. *Child care and working mothers: A study of arrangements made for the daytime care of children.* New York: Child Welfare League of America, 1968.

Sale, J., & Torres, Y. *I'm not just a babysitter.* Pasadena: Pacific Oaks College, 1971.

Solnit, A. Acquisition and application of knowledge about children: A modern dilemma. Presented at the annual meeting of the American Orthopsychiatric Association, 1968.

Willner, M. Unsupervised family day care in New York City. In *The changing dimensions of day care.* New York: Child Welfare League of America, 1970.

Willner, M. Family day care: An escape from poverty. *Social Work,* 1971, *16,* 30–35.

Chapter Five

FAMILY DAY CARE: THE HUMANISTIC SIDE

Lorraine B. Wallach and Maria W. Piers

A recent item in Chicago papers concerned the death of six children, all under the age of 5, in a fire that swept through the family care home in which they spent their days and nights. Investigation revealed that the ramshackle frame house was a death trap that should have been torn down long ago and that the care the children were receiving did not meet minimum standards of decency.

A young child care student told her supervisor about a family care setting not far from the scene of the fire. She had observed a second-grader sitting at the kitchen table, engrossed in his homework, assisted by an 11-year-old boy, while the care mother looked after a little girl, perhaps 2, who was whiny and uncomfortable and seemed to be coming down with a cold. At the same time two preschool youngsters, a boy and a girl, were having a wonderful time in an area partitioned off in the kitchen, ordinarily used as a broom closet, but at the moment "a manned spacecraft." The atmosphere was not quiet, but it was serene.

Article first appeared in *Child Welfare* Vol. LII, No. 7, July 1973, and is reprinted here with permission.

The two incidents epitomize the worst and the best in family day care. Since private homes frequently defy inspection, family day care can be hazardous to the children's bodily and emotional well-being. On the other hand, it can be flexible and offer many options of space distribution and activities, thus meeting the needs of children of many age levels and of varying personalities. In principle, family care offers infant care as well as afterschool supervision—a sound place for children to be regardless of the working hours of their parents or the children's school schedule. It is evident that family day care exists, indeed, proliferates. Because of its blurred visibility, however, there is constant danger of poor services. Therefore we have to make doubly sure that the human needs in family home settings are well defined, well provided for, and adequately met.

THE REQUISITE COMMON DENOMINATORS

There is a considerable variety of homes that are in principle suitable for family day care. There are others that are not. Suitable homes should have the following common denominators:

Number of adults. There should be, at least from time to time, more than one adult available. Taking care of children for long hours each day can be physically and emotionally so exhausting that it is in the interest of the children that the family day care mother's burden be shared by another adult. Rested care givers are better care givers.

Maturity. The care giver should be of an age that permits her to assume legal responsibility for children other than her own, but it is equally important that she be sufficiently mature to be able to attend to the needs of others without feeling deprived or envious.

Sense of responsibility. It is essential that the care giver be reliable, consistent, and predictable, both in her physical presence and her emotional makeup. All people, of course, have good days and bad days. In the case of a care giver it is important that these swings not be excessive, and that her behavior not be withdrawn. Even a "nagging housewife" is preferable to one who "turns off."

Orderliness. The care giver must be organized so as to convey to the children a sense of time and space and a fairly predictable sequence of events. Meals should be on schedule, work and play time should be regular, and places should be set aside to be used for specific purposes. Yet the care giver should not be compulsively clean and orderly. It is admittedly difficult to determine the right admixture here, but preference should be given to care givers who place the needs of human beings above a spotless kitchen.

Affection and Discipline. The care giver has to be capable of kindness and affection, and show such feelings when the child has need of them. But she must also be able to discipline the child, not on the basis of her own moods, but when the child's behavior demands attention. In a family day care situation there has to be flexibility in defining right and wrong. Nonetheless, we might all agree that willful injury to persons or damage to property is wrong and that helpfulness is right.

Various standards. The care giver's personal standards about more trivial matters may, however, differ from those of the families she serves. Sometimes she will find herself annoyed with the kind of behavior a child's own family tolerates. If there is considerable discrepancy in standards, she should be able to spell this out and tell the child which kind of behavior "goes at the care home" and which "goes at your house."

Eagerness to learn. It is of great help if the care giver is herself eager to learn new things, almost regardless of the subject. Whether she enjoys baking, reading, gardening, or playing music, her enthusiasm is usually contagious and encourages the children's curiosity and initiative, and hence their learning.

Cooperation versus regimentation. A measure of conformity is, of course, a necessity in any household, but the demands of the care giver should not amount to regimentation. She should be capable of seeing each child as an individual and of perceiving the specific talents and aptitudes, virtues, and weaknesses of the children in her charge, rather than the similarities.

Biases. None of us can help preferring some children to others, but precautions should be taken not to select a highly biased care giver, whether the bias refers to skin color, sex, or developmental stage ("I think babies are cute, but big boys are a pain in the neck.") She must, under all circumstances, be objective enough to attend to all children in her care.

About the house. Both adults and children need a certain amount of privacy in the course of a whole day. Privacy for the care giver may simply be her bedroom with the door closed, so she can rest by herself, while another trusted adult or older teenager watches the children. Nooks and crannies or even an empty closet (without a lock on the door) often serve the younger child's need for privacy. Older ones require some well-lit area in which they can study. In addition, it is important to have a comfortable room, such as the kitchen or the living room with the TV set where all can congregate.

Daily Routine. Children who spend the better part of the day away from their own family need to feel as comfortable with the care family as with their own. One way to facilitate this is to let children participate as much as possible in the daily routines and in holiday events. Activities such as cooking, cleaning, marketing, errands, excursions, visiting, and parties should include the children. Another way to make the dual home situation a positive rather than a confusing experience is to let the children bring some favorite possession from their own homes. A cherished object gives persons of all ages a sense of continuity. A pipe or wristwatch constitutes a piece of home away from home for the adult. A blanket or trinket or toy does the same for a child.

Insuring lasting quality. It must be remembered that a home applying for a license tends to look its best at first and only gradually shows its flaws. This reflects human nature. Because of this, however, it is important that machinery be set up to insure ongoing quality in home care.

Local sources, social agencies, and schools of higher learning should be called upon in the interest of both the care family and the biological family for services and supervision. Such services may be offered in a number of ways, though home visits, group meetings, formal classes, and so forth. If home care is to be more than babysitting, care givers must be helped to use current information on child development and rearing. They should be instructed in recognizing early signs of emotional disturbance and learning problems, and be able to plan a course of action together with the biological parents and the supervisors.

Obviously, ongoing instruction, support, supervision, and collaboration cost money. So does all quality service. That all aspects of family care must be adequately financed becomes immediately clear if alternatives are considered. Which corners should be cut? What is it we might do without? Proper food for family day care children? Healthy, well-informed care givers? Space to play and work in? Medical services? None of these is expendable. All are vital for family day care children.

Children in two environments. Care givers must learn about the complexities of rearing children in two different homes simultaneously, and how to help the children adjust to a new environment. Some adults take it for granted that all children will adapt to any number of standards at the same time. Other adults are overly worried about exposing a youngster to divergent expectations. The truth is frequently somewhere in between. Differences in customs and manners are usually readily absorbed by the child, especially if the important adults spell them out. It is important, however, that the children's parents always be regarded as the final authority and the ultimate and lasting source of comfort. Their house must be recognized as the place where the child really belongs. Of equal importance is that both parents and care giver trust each other's handling of important issues, such as injuring others, taking what belongs to someone else, sharing, etc. Even if care givers and parents work out ways of coexistence, there may be feelings of uneasiness, rivalry, or jealousy. Such feelings, if they persist, may require intervention by a skilled, objective person. A social worker, a child care specialist, or a parent educator may be able to help the adults work out their differences and thus avoid moving a child from one home to another.

NEEDS OF CARE GIVERS

So far our concern has been with the optimal interaction among a child, the parents, and a care giver. A care giver is, however, a person whose needs, strengths, and limits must be taken into consideration. All too often it is assumed that long hours of unlimited togetherness with children constitute a natural state of affairs, and that a care giver is tireless. On the contrary, being with young children is exceedingly strenuous, and even the strongest and most dedicated care giver wears out. She must, therefore, be helped to arrange for regular time off from children, especially if her working day is longer than 8 hours. Such time off is no more than plain mental hygiene and crisis prevention. In addition, care givers who are self-employed should have access to someone they can consult on business matters such as taxes, social security, and insurance, to safeguard their own interests and the interests of the families they serve. The care giver should also be able to get help in business matters concerning herself and the families. Matters such as payments, transportation, times of pickup and delivery of children may seem trivial, and so they are if they have been settled in advance. If not, they can lead to friction.

Above all, the care giver must be helped to plan for those crises that inevitably arise with children and those caring for them. Plans should be made in advance to deal with illness of either the adults or the children included in the care arrangement. And even the most accident-proof household has its share of accidents. Toddlers invariably find a door to smash their fingers in; school-age children hurt themselves in sports; and persons of all ages slip on wet kitchen floors. A concrete plan of action, including access to community resources for emergency help, is therefore a necessity.

SETTING REALISTIC STANDARDS

Finding a home is a difficult task under the best of conditions. To forestall disappointment and maintain a level of hope, we should be aware that the perfect home for family day care simply does not exist—but then neither does the perfect own-family home. The human element in providing day care for children has long been underestimated, despite the findings of developmental research that it is the adults in charge of the children who make the difference between optimal development and the stunting of physical, emotional, and intellectual growth. The current wave of interest in child care provides an opportunity to set new patterns based on this research. Emphasis on humanistic considerations must be part of all plans for children, rich or poor, of all ages, in all settings, particularly in the new and promising, but still somewhat experimental, family day care programs.

Chapter Six

REACHING FAMILY DAY CARE HOMES

Bertha Addison

Thousands of young children receive day care in small groups in private homes. Many of these homes lack a staff trained even in the rudiments of child development, are unlicensed and unregulated, and lack adequate facilities and materials to provide more than just custodial care. The Far West Laboratory for Educational Research and Development has responded to the interest shown by many day care providers in improving their skills and keeping informed about the latest methods of child development.

Child care providers in day care homes suffer from isolation from the mainstream of direct educational services. As a consequence, there are few opportunities for a systematic provision of training opportunities. The Far West Lab provided me as a trainer to the Contra Costa family day care homes. The training program I initiated utilized the parent/child toy lending library as one of its components. The specially designed toys are one component of the Responsive Model Program of the Far West Lab.

The toy library was originally designed exclusively for parental use. Through using the toys, parents provide meaningful and useful educational experiences for their children. The toys facilitate the development of a healthy self-concept in children, they promote the children's intellectual development, each by teaching specific skills, concepts, and problem-solving abilities. By working with the toys and their children, parents stimulate the children's intellectual abilities and improve their interaction with them. In addition, the toy library enables parents to participate in the decision-making process that affects the education of their children.

The Parent/Child Educational Program is an 8-week course which meets weekly for 2 hour sessions with parents. The sessions include discussions of basic ideas about child growth and development and demonstrations of the use of educational toys and games to help children learn important skills and concepts. Each week the parent takes one of the eight training toys (see appendix), and instructions for its use at home, to play games with their children. The parent returns the toy the following week and takes another.

The toy lending library contains a variety of educational toys, games, puzzles, and other materials which participating parents may borrow for use at home. Typical classroom sessions include descriptions and explanations of the toys, films, or filmstrips dealing with an aspect of childhood development, and a discussion period.

From experiences with the Toy Lending Library Program, a competency unit for teacher assistants in preschool and day care programs was developed. Without training, day care staff usually provides only custodial care—serving meals, picking up after the children, and taking them to the bathroom.

The training procedure for the competency unit, outlined in the *Handbook for Teacher Assistants,* is similar to that used with parents, and it uses the same toys as well. Each toy provides a specific responsive learning experience. After mastering the use of the toys, the teacher assistants learn to generalize to other responsive experiences.

In the fall of 1971 the Far West Laboratory, in cooperation with Contra Costa College and Richmond Model Cities offered a training program in the use of toys and games for day care operators. The program served two purposes. First, day care operators receive training and college credits, in response to the Richmond Model Cities Programs desire for an educational program for children in day care homes. Of the 12 required units in the Early Childhood Department of Contra Costa College, the Training Unit on Toys and Games fulfills 3 of the credits. Second, the program provided another opportunity, in addition to parental home use, to test the toys for eventual use in a day care setting.

Since many of the day care operators had never had formal training, the Director of the Child Care Program for Model Cities requested a program that would be academically unthreatening and would include not only a basic introduction to child development, but also the groundwork for later courses that would be needed to complete the requirements.

The program for the day care operators consisted of 10 weekly 2-hour evening class meetings. In addition to the class meetings, participants in the program completed 6 weeks of individual study of the materials used in the course and suggestions for making and using other materials.

The program consisted of two basic parts. In the first, by using the toys with the children in their homes, each operator developed skills to provide learning activities for preschool children. Each week in the classroom the operators familiarized themselves with the skill or concept taught by a toy, then used the toy for the following week in his or her home.

In the second part, day care operators were assigned readings in child growth and development which were then discussed and analyzed at the next class meeting. The outline for the 10 weeks of class meetings follows.

Session 1. Orientation and introduction
Film: "Learning and Growing and Learning"
Reading Assignment: "How Young Children Learn"

Session 2. Discussion of reading assignment "How Young Children Learn"
Introduction of toy: sound cans, film strip, role play
Reading assignment: "Toys as Learning Tools"

Session 3 Discussion of reading assignment: "Toys as Learning Tools"
Introduction of toy: color lotto
Reading assignment: "Developing a Positive Self-Concept"

Session 4. Discussion of reading assignment: "Developing a Positive Self-Concept"
Introduction of toy: feely bag
Reading assignment: "Discipline Means to Teach"

Session 5. Discussion of reading assignment: "Discpline Means to Teach"
Film: "Discipline and Self-Control"
Introduction of toy: stacking toy
Reading assignment: "Language Development"

Session 6. Discussion of reading assignment: "Language Development"
Film: "Parents Are Teachers Too"
Introduction of toy: table blocks

Session 7. Reading assignment: "What is the Nursery School Curriculum?"
Discussion of reading assignment: "What is the Nursery School Curriculum?"
Film: "Talking Together"
Introduction of toy: numberite

Session 8. Reading assignment: "The Nursery School Teacher"
Discussion of reading assignment: "The Nursery School Teacher"
Introduction of toy: color cubes

Session 9. Reading assignment: "The Arts"
Discussion of reading assignment: "The Arts"
Film: "My Art Is Me"

Session 10. Introduction of toy: flannel board
Evaluation session
Film: "Head Start in Mississippi"

Before the start of the course, each of the day care operators was interviewed about his or her views on child development, day care, and his or her role as a home day care operator. The interview also raised questions about the program, about the facilities of each of the day care homes, and about the operators' expectations concerning the course.

The operators answered questions about the number and ages of the children in their homes, the daily schedule, and the kinds and uses of materials available to the children. They also commented on their attitudes toward what they could and should provide beyond custodial care.

A general picture of the home day care in Contra Costa County emerged from the interviews. Each home cared for between one to five children, aged from 6 months to 7 years. (The school-age children used the homes after school.) The age range limited the use of materials in the course, since the toys were designed primarily for 3-, 4-, and 5-year-old children. However the course suggested other, similar materials and toys for children of different ages.

The schedule in the day care homes generally followed what might be a typical schedule in the childrens' own homes. The operators either picked up the children or had the children brought to them, sometimes as early as 6:00 A.M. After breakfast at the day care home, the children played either indoors or outdoors, depending on the weather, while the operator attended to her own household work.

Most homes had only a limited selection of materials, puzzles, dolls, clay, bricks, cars, and other toys. One home had only a toy telephone which one of the mothers had supplied. The materials were provided by Model Cities.

The children in all of the homes played alone or among themselves; the operators made little or no conscious effort to involve themselves in the children's activities. Consequently, apart from occasionally helping school-age children with their written assignments, operators did nothing actively to encourage development.

Among the things the operators felt the children should learn while in their care and before they entered school were good manners, politeness, the alphabet, their name, address, and phone number, not to talk to strangers, and to get along with other children. From the course the operators hoped to learn how children think and how to handle them better.

The interviews led the interviewer to conclude that the operators saw themselves as babysitters rather than as persons charged with the responsibility for fostering the mental and social development of the children. The course therefore attempted to define and prepare the operators for assuming a more professional role. Before the course began none of the operators, all middle-aged women, had had any formal training in early childhood education, but all had a wealth of experience raising their own children.

One of the day care homes had a separate playroom for the children, and most of the others used the living room or dining room as the playroom during the day.

By the end of the 16 weeks of field tests, the operators were proficient in using the toys presented in the course. However only two of the women were able to generalize concepts from the toys and use materials other than those presented in the course or in individual sessions. Recognizing this, we suggested that a future program consist of two parts, the first duplicating the original course, the second concentrating on applying the lessons and techniques of the toys to other materials the operators might use in other activities with the children in their care.

On completing the course, the operators responded positively to the experience, appreciating especially the opportunity to talk with other operators about their common problems and experiences. They also felt that the course gave them new insights into dealing with children and helping them to grow intellectually and socially.

An important aspect of this program was that it encouraged day care providers for the first time to define areas of need and to suggest approaches to dealing with these needs. The successful experiment with the toy lending library strongly suggested that it should be incorporated into future educational programs for day care operators.

Development of a successful program for day care operators requires coordination of all the components of the program. One important element of a successful day care program not incorporated in the course was parental involvement. Future plans for day care should include involvement by parents.

The toy library has proven its usefulness, but all of the services in day care, including physical facilities, health services, educational programs, and parent-staff communication, are crucial in complementing the effectiveness of the toy library.

APPENDIX

SOUND CANS

This toy is comprised of two sets of small, covered metal film cans; a set consists of six cans, each of which contains a different object or substance, for example, water or a bead. Thus each can in a set sounds different when it is shaken. One set is for the adult, the other set for the child.

The purpose of the sound cans is to help children learn to listen carefully, to identify sounds that are the same and to distinguish those that are not the same.

COLOR LOTTO

The color lotto consists of a square wooden board divided into nine differently colored squares, and a loose set of nine small squares. The loose squares are the same size and color as the squares on the board. One set of squares is for the adult, the other for the child.

The toy helps children learn to identify differences in colors and to match colors that are the same.

FEELY BAG

The feely bag is a drawstring bag and two sets of masonite cutouts. Each set consists of a circle, a square, a triangle, and a rectangle.

It introduces the four basic shapes and helps the child learn to recognize the shapes by using only the sense of touch.

STACKING SQUARES

The toy is constructed of 16 wooden squares of four graduated sizes which fit on a wooden spindle. There is a blue, a yellow, a red, and a green square in each size. The center-holds of the squares are graduated with the size, and the spindle diameter is graduated likewise, so that the toy is self-correcting: If the squares are not stacked in order of size, all the squares will not fit.

The toy teaches the concept of size, discrimination, color identification, and extension and repetition of patterns.

WOODEN TABLE BLOCKS

This toy consists of a set of 10 wooden blocks. The largest is ten times as large as the smallest, and the others represent the units between one and ten.

It provides experience in discriminating various size relationships—e.g. tallest, shortest, equal to—and the concept of number units (1–10) and number relationships.

NUMBER PUZZLE

This toy is a ten-piece masonite puzzle, each piece of which represents a number from 1 to 10. On each piece are peg holds corresponding to the number the piece represents, and the appropriate numeral.

The number puzzle helps children learn to associate numerals with the quantities they represent and to count sequentially.

COLOR BLOCKS

This toy consists of small cubic blocks in several colors. Its purpose is to teach children relative positions and pattern extension.

FLANNEL BOARD

This toy is made up of a flannel board and 36 felt shapes. The shapes are circles, squares, and triangles. There are two sizes of each shape and in each size there are three colors—red, yellow, and blue. Thus there are 18 different combinations of size, color, and shape, and two shapes in each combination.

The toy helps teach the skills of classifying and problem solving according to the attributes of color, shape, and size.

Far West Laboratory for Educational Research & Development *A Guide to Securing & Installing the Parent/Child Toy-lending Library.* San Francisco, Ca. 1972 or US Government Printing Office, Wash. D.C., 20402 # 1780–0993. 60¢.

Chapter Seven

DEVELOPING QUALITY FOR FAMILY DAY CARE

Margaret Ann Brostrom

Mrs. G's daughter, Maria, is 3 years old. She has been attending a day care center for 6 months while her mother is at work. Maria's physician is concerned about the number of times he has seen Maria for colds, ear infections, and flu. He suggests to Mrs. G that Maria's health seems to indicate that she should be in a day care setting where her exposure to infection would be limited.

Mr. R is a single working father who cares for his three children: David, age 11, Paul, 5, and Susan, 3. This is a closely knit family and the children depend strongly on one another for emotional support. Mr. R would prefer to have the children kept together and cared for by one care giver whose home is close enough to the older children's school to allow them to walk or take the school bus to the day care home.

Mrs. D is a working parent with a 3-year-old boy, Bernie, who is physically and developmentally immature. He is small in stature and poorly coordinated physically. His emotional and mental growth is minimally retarded. Mrs. D feels that in a day care center Bernie would be overwhelmed by the large number of children and would have to share an adult's time with many other children. She feels that he needs both a great deal of individual help and attention, and a few other children to play with.

Mrs. W's daughter, Donna, is an extremely active child who needs frequent limits set on her behavior. Mrs. W's frustration in dealing with Donna's difficult behavior results in the fear that she may physically abuse her child. The authorities and her psychiatrist are trying to help Mrs. W find a place that will care for Donna for part of the day, to give each of them some time apart from one another.

Rafael is a Mexican-American boy whose parents speak only Spanish. His father works and his mother is in a job training program. Rafael will be going to kindergarten next year. His parents want Rafael to learn English and to learn how to play with other children cooperatively. They also want him to continue learning the values of his culture, especially those concerning the man's role in the Mexican-American community.

What do all five of these parents have in common? First, all of them are either working, in job training, or cannot otherwise care for their children for part of the day. Second, their income is average or less than average ($12,000 a year or less) and they cannot afford to pay a great deal for quality child care. Third, they all love their children deeply and want a safe, secure, stimulatingly creative and individualistic environment for their children while they must be apart.

The special needs of these children and their parents fit within the day care home model (Note 1). Care for children outside of their own home has long been provided by day care homes. Parents have sought home care through relatives, neighbors, or friends. Statistics show that by far the greatest number of children receiving day care get that care in someone else's home (Department of HEW, 1974). Most states, including California, have licensing laws that provide a system for licensing and monitoring homes in which an adult cares for other people's children (Note 2).

WHAT IS A DAY CARE HOME?

California defines two kinds of day care homes (Note 3). One is the family day care home, in which a private home is used to provide supervision and nonmedical care for less than 24 hours to 6 or fewer children not related to the day care provider. The second is the group day care home, which provides the same kind of care on the same basis to 10 or fewer children.

WHAT IS INVOLVED IN GETTING A LICENSE?

In California the local county health offices process applications for licensing. The applicant calls the day care licensing unit and talks with a licensing worker—often a social worker with some background in preschool or early childhood education. The type of license in which the applicant is interested is determined: a license for 5 children, which allows for children up to age 6; for 6, which allows for children 3–14 years old; or for 10, which also allows for children 3–14 years old. With each license the total number of children allowed includes the number who reside in that home full-time. For instance, an applicant with two children of his or her own under 16 years of age can be issued a license for only three more children, 0–6 years of age. Before a license is issued, the applicant's file must include (a) the results of an interview by the licensing worker with both the applicant and spouse. (Licensing workers prefer to license the traditional home of a married couple where the husband is working full-time at a day job and the wife is looking for a means of earning a supplemental income. They say that experience has shown that this plan is the most successful.) (b) A medical form including a negative TB test, signed by a physician and substantiating the good health of both the care giver and spouse. (c) Fingerprint clearances for both husband and wife. (d) Written responses from three personal references supplied by the applicants. (e) A clearance from the County Environmentalist (formerly the Health and Sanitation Officer) attesting to the fact that the house meets local building codes as well as health and safety standards.

When the applicant seeks a license for 10, four additional conditions must be met: (a) a health assistant 18 years or older must be in the home when more than six children are in attendance; (b) the home must be visited and approved by a fire marshall; (c) an outdoor drinking fountain, fire extinguisher, and fire alarm system must be installed; and (d) the location of the home must meet the zoning regulations of the local community (Note 4).

The process usually takes about 2 months to complete, with no cost to the licensee. Some county offices maintain a service that refers parents seeking day care licenses to day care home operators near their home or work. In San Mateo County the charge for full-time day care for an infant or toddler averages $30 a week, and $25 for a preschooler. School-age children are prorated according to the number of hours spent in the day care home each week (Note 5).

Though seemingly well planned this system unfortunately has many flaws. The most outstanding is that a great many care givers simply do not apply for a license. It has been said that if you want someone to do something, you have to make it worth their while. Nonlicensed care givers often do not think licensing is worth their while. There are a variety of reasons for their reticence to apply. Some are not aware that a license is required in California. Some feel it is just too much bother. Some resist the "meddling" of bureaucracy into their privacy, and perhaps some fear the possible power of the licensing agency. Setting standards for quality day care in these homes becomes impossible, and officials are reluctant to pursue the monumental task of closing unlicensed homes. Yet the number of cases of child abuse or neglect originating in unlicensed homes comprises an appalling percentage of Child Protective Service's case load (Streuer, 1974).

Who is to blame for this situation? It is extremely difficult to pinpoint one source. Day care licensing units are understaffed and find it difficult enough to license, evaluate, and monitor their existing case load, without the additional task of pursuing unlicensed homes. Parents often cannot afford the tremendous cost of quality day care—estimated at between $1200 and $3000 a year (Department of Public Health, 1973)—so must seek day care at a price within their means, but often at the risk of their children's physical and emotional needs. Finding and closing unlicensed homes is as elusive and frustrating a task for law-enforcement officials as finding the elusive "floating crap game." And what about those unlicensed caregivers who truly give quality day care? Do we want to risk losing these day care slots when the need for child care is already so great that it cannot be met adequately?

STANDARDS IN LICENSED HOMES

The philosophy of day care licensing units varies from county to county and is the cause of much confusion for both agency officials and day care licensees. Some counties feel that by licensing a great number of homes they better meet the need for child care and therefore reduce the number of unlicensed homes. The resulting problem is often that the staff is too small to evaluate and support the many licensed homes. Other counties prefer to license fewer homes and to stay within the number to which the available staff is able to give adequate support. The result of this approach is often a stronger support system for licensees, but greater numbers of unlicensed homes. Neither approach has been properly researched to test validity of the hypotheses on which they are based.

In 1975 new regulations and guidelines were implemented in California (Note 6). Several significant changes have occurred. The terms used to designate the two types of homes were changed to "small family home children" and "large family home children." Secondly, in large family homes, the former requirement of subtracting the number of children residing in the home from the licensable number was eliminated, and the maximum limit was increased to 12. The kind of experience that children in care receive has been expanded from simply establishing plans for personal care (including personal hygiene and napping), to protection, supervision, assistance, and guidance on an individual basis. The new regulations include requirements for activities that provide for socialization through group projects, pets, arts, crafts, and music. Leisure time skills are to be developed through recreation and play, and physical skills through games, sports, and exercise. The regulations specify the necessity of education to increase community awareness, language, and conceptual skills.

On paper, the addition of these activities to improve the quality of the experience for children by meeting their emotional, intellectual, social, and physical needs is exciting. But one wonders how this section will be implemented inasmuch as no training requirements are included in the regulations. The ability of the care giver to comply with the regulations seems to rest entirely on a subjective evaluation by the licensing worker of the local licensing unit. It seems, then, that priority at the local level must be given to the selection and employment of the licensing workers. Perhaps a citizen's advisory group could monitor local departments to assure the community of quality selection and unbiased supervision of care givers.

In a similar attempt to improve the quality and standards of all day care in California, a licensing task force was convened in the fall of 1974 by the Office of Educational Liaison of the Health and Welfare Agency, State of California. The task force members were divided into subgroups whose intent was to examine the present licensing practices and recommend revisions and/or new directions in philosophy, administration, enforcement, standards, supervision, and consultation. Some of the questions to which the task force addressed itself were, "What agency should be responsible for licensing?" "Should consultation be included in the supervisory process?" and "How do zoning requirements restrict licensing?" The final report of the task force was made public in 1975 and covers the licensing of nursery schools and day care centers, as well as family day care homes.

FAMILY DAY CARE HOME SYSTEMS

One of the vehicles used by several states, including California, to improve the quality of family day care is a system or network of family day care homes. Generally speaking, the family day care home system incorporates a more workable solution for adequate supervision and training of staff than the Department of Health is able to supply. The Day Care and Child Development Council of America described the advantages of a network.

> In the family day care system, homes can be supervised and assisted by a central administrative-coordinating agency. Mothers belonging to it may be trained in a group center linked to the system or in local community and four-year colleges. A system can provide educational and play materials, employee benefits and career ladder opportunities, administrative back-up and provisions for substitute homes for vacations and emergencies. Caregivers may be further assisted by child development specialists who can visit them and give helpful advice. Ultimately, the benefits of a family day care system may contribute to improved quality care for the children.

With the advent of AB99 legislation, the State Department of Education began to evaluate, albeit minimally, possible family day care home systems. The primary significance of the involvement of the Department of Education is the subsidizing of child care costs by government, which allows low-income families quality day care at a cost they can afford. Although the Department of Education has included Children's Centers under their supervision since World War II, passage of AB99 in 1972 allowed federal money to be channeled into proposals for innovative child care delivery systems. Ten of the proposals accepted included use of family day care homes (FDCH) (Note 7). Some of the systems use FDCH as sick care facilities in conjunction with a children's center. Others use the center as as training ground for FDCH providers. Another approach used FDCH exclusive of centers, as a network in and of itself. One of these networks or systems is described in detail here.

DETAILED DESCRIPTION OF AN FDCH SYSTEM

The Neighborhood Day Care Program (NDCP) of the Family Service Agency of San Mateo County now includes six licensed group family day care homes. Five homes are located in Redwood City and Menlo Park, in an unincorporated area which has been designated as a target area of low-income population by the Economic Opportunities Council. The sixth home is located in a similar area in San Mateo. All homes are within walking or busing distance of elementary schools, and most of the children enrolled live in the same neighborhood as the licensed day care home. Approximately 70 children ranging in age from 2.9 years to 9 years receive care 5 days a week, 52 weeks a year.

How does a system of this type get started? What are the steps involved in setting up such a program? What kinds of priorities are established to insure quality care for the children enrolled? Let's take these questions one at a time.

HOW DOES A SYSTEM GET STARTED?

The idea for this program was conceived out of a need in the community. The Family Service Agency (FSA) is a private, nonprofit agency which employs social workers who specialize in marriage, family, and child counseling. In 1971 the community-based Board of Directors of FSA recognized the need to provide counseling within the Spanish-speaking, low-income community. An Advocacy Program for Spanish-speaking families was implemented, and as a direct result of the needs of the people who sought help from the social worker and the community worker of the Advocacy Program, the Board began to direct their thoughts and efforts into establishing some kind of child care for working parents.

Two years of planning went into the writing of the final proposal, which was accepted for funding by the California Department of Education in September 1973. Seventy-five percent of the first year's budget was covered by the grant from the Child Development Unit of the California Department of Education. The remaining 25 percent came from a special grant from the United Bay Area Crusade.

WHAT ARE THE STEPS INVOLVED IN SETTING UP SUCH A PROGRAM?

First, an experienced nursery school director with an early childhood education credential was hired to organize and supervise the program.

Second, homes and day care providers were recruited with the help of the community worker of the Advocacy Program and the Licensing Unit of the County Department of Health.

Third, negotiations with the County Planning Commission resulted in a zoning ruling which allowed each home in unincorporated county areas to be licensed to provide child care for 10 children without the usual use permits. (Interestingly, restrictive zoning regulations by local *cities* has continued to be a deterrent to licensing homes in city residential areas.)

Fourth, each home was licensed by the County Department of Health according to the regulations referred to earlier in this Chapter.

Fifth, children of low-income families whose parents needed child care while they were working or in job training were solicited in an exhaustive, multimedia approach. This process turned out to be slower than was originally anticipated. We knew that the children were there in the community, but finding them took time—more time than we had thought. We used public service radio spot announcements on local stations, ads in the local newspaper, and flyers on community bulletin boards. We informed public agencies and community organizations who could make referrals, we scoured waiting lists from existing children's center programs, both public and private, and ultimately we relied on word of mouth.

We were hampered by two factors: First, we were virtually invisible to the community; there was not one big center to see and "inquire within." And second, since referrals most commonly come from parents already enrolled who tell their friends and neighbors, a new program has very few parents to pass the word along.

While the homes were being licensed and the children recruited, the entire staff—four day care mothers and four assistants—spent 30 hours in a pre-employment training program. With the help of public and private agencies, the staff were taught basic first-aid techniques and given child development information, ideas for activities, help in planning low-cost, nutritional meals, and a general orientation to the program. However, on October 29—2 months after the money was secured—the first two homes opened with seven children between them. All the homes were open and operating by December.

WHAT KIND OF PRIORITIES WERE ESTABLISHED?

First, care for the children had to be more than custodial (Note 8). This priority led to the requirement of staff training: pre-employment, on-going and on-site. Pre-employment training is described in the paragraph above. On-going training occurs at monthly staff meetings where speakers, workshops, and general problem-sharing discussions increase our knowledge about dealing with the individual needs of the children as well as with staff needs. Interestingly, these monthly meetings have had a secondary effect in that they help to relieve the feelings of isolation many home care givers experience. On-site training is conducted in the day care home by the director. The philosophy of the Program encourages the paraprofessional staff members to think of themselves as teachers rather than as babysitters.

Second, financial compensation to the staff had to be more than equal to present standards within the county. We know that employees in low-paying jobs often have a lesser image of themselves and their work. To upgrade the staff positions, the budget includes employee benefits such as paid holidays, vacation, and sick leave, payroll deductions, and enrollment in a health care plan. Salaries now range from $400 to $800 a month, based on the employee's position and the number of child care hours delivered. These figures represent at least a 25 percent increase over the average salary of similarly trained employees in private centers.

Third, we wanted to strengthen each family unit enrolled. Therefore parent services and parent involvement are an important part of the Program. Parents are encouraged to participate with their children in the day care home whenever possible. In addition, parents often share outgrown clothing and toys, food, and just plain conversation with one another as well as with the staff. As one father was overheard saying to another father who was having difficulty starting his car, "Oh, I don't mind helping you out a bit. You'll find that around here we all help one another. We're all one big family." A quarterly newsletter and parent meetings link one day care home with another and help to give the total picture of the program to parents. Free consultation with a professional in the counseling program of the Family Service Agency is available to any parent, child, or staff member.

Fourth, each child's uniqueness had to be recognized. The program includes day care providers who are white, black, and Hispanic, and the cultural values of each child are carefully protected and fostered. Each child receives educational training based on his or her developmental growth level and his or her needs. Good health habits, nutrition, and self-directed responsibility are encouraged.

Activities for the children range from a tooth brushing routine to games that teach mathematical concepts; from teaching a 2½-year-old to dress himself to helping a 9-year-old with her homework; from introducing English-speaking children to chiote (a Mexican vegetable similar to squash) to watching baby spiders "hatch" from their eggs.

Awareness of the importance of adequate quality day care is becoming increasingly more widespread. This awareness emerges from a variety of sources, one of which is this quote from a booklet entitled "Industry's Share in Day Care" (Note 9).

> Widespread quality services will bring rewards to everyone—businessmen and women, parents, teachers, grandparents, community leaders and, most important, to children themselves.... Parents, communities and industries must work together for the expansion and development of services and facilities which will be adequate from preschool through early adolescent years. Healthy, positive educational experiences for the children early in life, strengthen the future of our country, for today's children become tomorrow's citizens and leaders. (pp. 17–18)

Family day care home systems are one more link in the chain providing quality day care for children and alternatives for parents.

REFERENCES

Day Care and Child Development Council of America. *Family day care systems.* Washington: Day Care Council of America, 1970.

Department of Health, Education, and Welfare. *Day care for your children.* Publication No. OHD 74-47. Washington: Department of HEW, 1974.

San Mateo County Department of Public Health and Welfare. *Fourth annual report.* San Mateo County: Department of Public Health and Welfare, Social Services Division, 1973-1974

Streuer, E. What feminists want. *Day Care and Early Childhood Education Magazine* 1974, *1*, 17.

NOTES

1. Metropolitan Life Insurance Company. *Day care—what and why.* Publication No. T 12571 (2-72). Metropolitan Life Insurance Company, Health & Welfare Division, 1 Madison Avenue, New York, NY 10010.
2. Keyserling, Mary *Windows on day care: A report on the findings of members of the national council of Jewish women on day care needs and services in their communities.* National Council of Jewish Women, 1 West 47th Street, New York, NY 10036.
3. California State Department of Health. Health and Safety Code, Section 1522.
4. *Licensed family day care.* County of San Mateo Department of Public Health and Welfare, Children's Day Care Services, 225 37th Avenue, San Mateo, California.

5. Recommended changes by the Day Care Parents Association, San Mateo County, California.
6. Proposed regulation changes, Health and Safety Code, California State Department of Health.
7. California State Department of Education. *Directory—California child development programs, 1974–75.*
8. Although based on the needs of our community, these priorities are substantially shared by people throughout the country, as indicated in *Day care: statement of principles.* Department of Health, Education, and Welfare. Publication No. (OCD) 73–2, 1973.
9. Metropolitan Life Insurance Company. *Industry's share in day care.* Publication No. T 12086. Metropolitan Life Insurance Company, 1 Madison Avenue, New York, NY 10010.

ADDITIONAL NOTES

1. *Proprietary Day Care,* a very informative booklet published by the Bank of America (Vol. 11, No. 8, 1973), discusses the problems of finding facilities, insurance, sample budgets, daily programs, meal service, and other pertinent information on running this type of small business.
2. *Guides for Day Care Licensing* (Department of Health, Education, and Welfare Publication No. 73–1053) presents the federal recommendations for a day care licensing and regulatory model to be used by state personnel. It is a persuasive resource when dealing with city and county interpretations of zoning restrictions and licensing regulations.
3. *The Politics of Day Care, Vol. 1* and *Day Care as a Child-Rearing Environment, Vol. 2,* by E. Prescott and E. Jones, are two valuable aids in determining day care staff training, program objectives, and physical settings for day care homes. National Association for the Education

of Young Children, 1834 Connecticut Avenue, N. W., Washington, D.C. 20009.
4. *Pacifica Survey Report* is an excellent example of a survey of need. Pacifica Parent Advocates for Children, Pacifica Park and Recreation Department, 170 Santa Maria Avenue, Pacifica, California 94044.
5. *Child Day Care Services in the San Francisco Bay Area* is another good example of such a survey. Bay Area Social Planning Council, 364 14th Street, Oakland, California 94612.

Chapter Eight

LICENSING CHILD CARE

Edna H. Hughes

The intent of this article is to provide a brief review of the changing and developing role and function of child day care facility licensing in the day care system. Specifically, it speaks to concepts and principles, now identifiable, which enable licensing to be correctly defined, sharply focused to its regulatory purpose, and consequently better equipped to set and guarantee a baseline of quality.

It draws some distinctions between what licensing is and what it is often misunderstood to be; reviews changes in the conception of licensing beginning two decades ago; enumerates some even more recent developments in its administration; and identifies some problems still to be solved if licensing is to fulfill its present promise of becoming a fully professional, effective, and efficient state service in behalf of children.

The reader, whether student, day care provider, parent, or concerned citizen with a voice and vote for policy, needs to keep in mind that the conceptualization of licensing presented here is a mere sketch; that few state licensing administrations, even when familiar with it, have fully integrated it into practice; and that national agencies and professional schools are only beginning to familiarize themselves with it. Nevertheless, the reader should be aware that many of the changing perceptions and practices in states are due to this conceptualization.

THE DAY CARE SYSTEM AND LICENSING

Major components in the day care system for the present and immediate future can be identified as:

• A variety of day care settings—in the child's own home and elsewhere in family homes, group homes, and centers.

• A variety of auspices—proprietary, philanthropic, and governmental.

• A mix of funding sources—parents, federal and state governments, church, industry, and community-organized voluntary giving.

• State regulation—licensing of private facilities, both profit and nonprofit, fiscal regulation in purchase of care, approval procedures for publicly-operated facilities—for baseline, mandatory standards.

• The beginning of accreditation and credentialing under public and private auspices, to recognize achievement of quality care above that mandated by state and federal statutes.

• Community understanding, interpretation, and support through the media, educational institutions, and citizen organizations.

Licensing must be seen as only one of the several kinds of state regulation in day care, just as all state regulation itself is only one of the six major components identified above.

Does licensing then have strategic importance? The answer is yes, and it comes from three facts: (a) licensing is now operational in every state; (b) most day care facilities are private and proprietary, including family day care homes which perhaps outnumber other kinds by at least 10 to 1; and (c) more children are presently safeguarded by licensing than by all other forms of regulation together.

Does licensing also have significance? The answer again is yes, when its proper function of providing a baseline of quality, below which no private child day care will be permitted to operate, is understood. At that time and in those states, child care advocates have a solid foundation upon which to build child care of the excellence children deserve as the trustees of posterity.

LICENSING IS STATE ACCEPTANCE OF RESPONSIBILITY

When children are regularly under the care and supervision of persons other than their parents for a considerable portion of the day or night, they may be presumed to need a measure of the state's concern and protection. Licensing is the means by which state government carries out its part in a three-way sharing of responsibility for children in private day care situations.

In making child care arrangements, parents retain all their natural guardianship rights and divest themselves of none of their obligations. What they do is assign or delegate the duties and tasks involved in the daily care and supervision of their children.

Day care providers, in assuming the care and supervision of children for whom they have no legally transferred rights or obligations, do so on the basis of their stated policies, on the terms of their agreement with parents, and within the framework of common law and statutory provisions applicable to caring for the children of others.

The responsibility of licensing is to insure the level and kind of care which all children must have in relation to their age, stage of development, and any special problems or handicaps. Its constraints are always upon the operator and the setting, and never upon the day care child or his parents.

With regard to the day care "day," three-way sharing means that parents are ultimately responsible, providers are immediately responsible, and the state is responsible overall for a quality of care that is in the public interest. All three parties may be said to have moral and ethical responsibilities, i.e., societal and psychological "contracts" as well as those specific obligations that are governmentally imposed and legally enforceable.

WHAT LICENSING IS

Police power, "the way of the state with its subjects," is a broad and general power deriving from the people, delegated by them through their elected representatives, and administered by whichever department of the executive branch the legislature designates.

It is intended to prohibit what is harmful or dangerous and to safeguard the citizenry—their lives, health, peace, and comfort. It serves such ends as public safety, public health, public morals, and public welfare. Police power encompasses regulation over the mails, taxation, interstate commerce, and the welfare of children, other dependent persons, and even adults in such areas as food and drug, and fire and building safety. Its safeguarding is always at a basic or minimal level. It is implicit that only those constraints necessary to the public interest are to be imposed on private persons.

Licensing is an exercise of the police power. By definition it can apply only to individuals or associations of individuals in their private undertaking. It cannot apply, historically or by definition, to the agents (personnel) of government or to the undertakings of government—federal, state, or local. Other kinds of regulation and standard setting—not the subject of this statement—do apply to persons in and activities carried out by government.

Specific to private day care facilities, licensing's function is to safeguard children from harm in the three broad areas of their health, safety, and well-being. It does this through setting and enforcing basic, minimum standards upon the providers. When promulgated as rules or regulations, these standards have the force and effect of law—"statute plus rule and regulation equals law."

The would-be day care operator, just like the would-be automobile operator, must apply for the license, establish his eligibility for it, and, once he has it, continue to maintain his operations at the required standards level. To operate without a license is to be in violation of the law and liable to its sanctions, such as an injunction to stop operations.

WHAT LICENSING IS NOT

Other forms of federal, state, and local regulation are frequently confused with licensing. Some of these forms apply to private day care facilities, so that they overlap with licensing.

Fiscal regulation is the setting and requiring of certain standards as a condition of receiving money.

The Federal government may require any facility which receives its dollars to meet its requirements. Examples are Head Start funding standards and the Federal Interagency Day Care Requirements.

State and local governments may also set requirements which facilities must meet to receive tax funds, either on a case-by-case, purchase of care basis or on the basis of an agreement to use a certain number of day care placements (slots).

The private day care facility must therefore be (a) licensed in order to operate legally, and (b) approved in addition on the basis of fiscal standards to receive federal, state, or local tax dollars in payment for child care.

Here there is an overlap of licensing with one or more sets of fiscal regulations.

Ordinances and regulations for fire and building safety, sanitation, and zoning are requirements which state constitutions and statutes authorize local governments to set and enforce. State statutes and state personnel usually regulate to insure safety in rural areas where local government may choose not to regulate. These regulations apply to private day care settings on the same basis as they apply to other private buildings, such as residences, boarding houses, restaurants, and so on.

Most state licensing administrations require evidence that facilities meet these regulations before they issue their own licenses. Many assist licensing applicants by referring them to these authorities and coordinating the entire process of securing these permits with the licensing process in order to save the applicant time and expense.

It should be remembered that requirements in these areas are not licensing requirements, that they apply to facilities under statutes other than the licensing statute, and that they would apply anyway, even if there were no state licensing of day care facilities.

Approvals and other forms of regulation are applicable to facilities owned, operated, or leased by state or local governmental agencies. These agencies receive their authority to establish, set standards, approve, use, and supervise child care facilities by act of their law-making bodies, state or local.

State or local operation of day care facilities is usually authorized in connection with the provision of a service to a particular target group, such as the recipients of public assistance grants and services, where the provision of day care is essential to training mothers for employment.

There is no overlap here with licensing, but a common misconception is that public facilities should be licensed, rather than approved, monitored, investigated and reported, and included within the state's administrative supervision over local operations.

STAGE OF DEVELOPMENT OF A THEORETICAL LITERATURE

No conceptual writing on licensing as police power and a process in the field of administrative law appeared in the social work and child development literature until the late 1950s. Yet state authority to license began as early as 1885. The few articles in professional journals and the few monographs appearing earlier perceived licensing as a mix of regulation and professional help via the caseworker-client model, or as state supervision somewhat vaguely based on the *parens patriae* doctrine.

The years following 1955 have produced a small literature, but one likely to stand the test of time. It is oriented to the theory that licensing is an exercise of police power by an administrative agency of state government. This literature is in the form of journal articles, monographs, conference proceedings, a chapter in a child welfare services textbook, etc. Much is in draft or in unpublished papers, as is characteristic of a developing professional specialization.

This theoretical underpinning has been the work largely of one educator, through research, adaptation from the general literature on administrative law, and testing through classroom teaching and consultation with state licensing personnel. His writing, published and unpublished, constitutes the substantial beginnings of a theoretical-conceptual literature. A few other educators are now writing within this conceptual framework. Some of them are beginning to use the concepts in fresh ways, having grasped their basic import.

Almost no writing based on practice or experience has yet appeared. There are no reports on the effectiveness of methods and techniques, workload assignments and expectations, community attitudes and how to use or modify them, research into the effect of this or that requirement, or an analytical assessment of this or that statute. An exception is a number of useful reports on the process of formulating standards requirements.

Understanding and accepting this emerging concept of licensing means modifying, if not renouncing, some of the philosophy and some of the techniques acquired by licensing from its proximity to and confusion with social services, early childhood growth and development, and other direct helping and supporting disciplines. It means almost a complete turnaround in ways of thinking and acting.

The new conceptualization seems to be sound, firm, and catching on, although not yet fully developed.

EMERGING SUPPORT FROM NATIONAL AGENCIES

Day care licensing, beginning chiefly with the 1962 amendments to the Social Security Act, has benefited from four kinds of support from the constituent agencies of the U.S. Department of Health, Education, and Welfare. These four types of support are partial funding of the licensing service and small outright grants to states to improve licensing, plus some special studies and audits; a state-of-the-field survey reaching into every state; consultation in regulatory administration focused on licensing; and the development and distribution of information, guides, and conceptual formulations.

Federal dollars have helped to extend the state licensing service and to improve its administration. The survey by the Office of Child Development, in addition to producing reports and guides, is the first effort under any sponsorship to call national attention to licensing, and in so doing to bring together wide representation of agencies, child care advocates, licensing officials, and day care providers and consumers. The Children's Bureau initiation of consultation in regulatory administration and the underwriting of some professional literature, have contributed to the conceptualization of licensing; calling its attention to national voluntary agencies and professional schools; and a change in the perceptions and practices of many state licensing agencies.

National voluntary agencies are beginning to recognize the role and function of licensing, by providing continuing rather than occasional panels or institutes at their regional and national meetings; by a willingness and sometimes a reaching out to publish an article; and in a few instances by an effort in support of licensing as good social policy.

PROFESSIONAL SCHOOLS AND REGULATORY EDUCATION

Perhaps no professional school, whether oriented to social work, health, or early childhood growth and development, is currently offering as much as one quarter or one semester of content in regulatory administration. On the other hand, two social work and one child growth and development oriented schools are providing annually 3 to 5 days of day care licensing content under the aegis of continuing education. Another six or eight schools are considering adding either regulatory content to their regular curriculum, or a short offering under their continuing education programs.

Here and there, leaders in this field are just beginning to recognize the serious gap in education with respect to regulatory administration, especially licensing and even more especially day care licensing. And they are beginning to recognize that there is a conceptual framework and a fragmentary literature, only partially developed yet sufficient to support a concentration in regulation comparable to other concentrations presently offered.

CLASS ADVOCACY THROUGH LICENSING

Licensing is a form of class advocacy for children. Advocacy of licensing by national agencies, governmental or nongovernmental, and by professional schools, can take one of two forms: (a) the role of broker to assist their constituent agency members to be licensed, if appropriate; to support licensing as a necessary component in the day care system; and to offer constructive criticism; and (b) to contribute to knowledge and skill through articles, guides, and the inclusion of regulatory content in their education and training programs.

The recognition that advocacy of a high quality licensing service is or can be advocacy of a baseline of quality care for out-of-home children has not yet come to national agencies, professional schools, or organized children's services advocates. Hope lies in the fact that a few persons in strategic positions do recognize that licensing must be perceived as class advocacy and good social policy, and that action will follow.

CHANGING PERCEPTIONS AND PRACTICES

Three developments previously identified are influencing change in the administration of the licensing service, if indeed change could take place without them. These developments are: (a) the conceptualization of licensing as a process within administrative law, an exercise of police power, freeing it of its overlay of some inappropriate social service philosophy and techniques; (b) the beginnings of a theoretical literature and classroom teaching under continuing education auspices; and (c) federal support through partial, formula funding of this state service, a survey, special grants, guides, and consultation on licensing as regulatory administration.

Two additional developments have coincided with and

are reinforcing the first three, both in perception and in practice.

Administrative Procedures Acts. As more and more states have passed administrative procedures acts, licensing administrations are hearing their messages and observing their directives. This means that more states are holding better attended public hearings on proposed rules and regulations before their promulgation. As a result, there is more public awareness of due process and constitutional safeguarding, more involvement of parents, providers, and concerned citizens, and better opportunity for public education and decision making on matters affecting the needs and rights of children, and the needs and rights of persons whose livelihoods depend on day care operations. These acts also mean that fair hearings mechanisms are being set up which allow applicants and licensees to contest the fairness or legality of licensing requirements and decisions.

Public Records Acts. Although only a few records acts have been passed recently, their implications are being felt even in states where none exists. They are putting teeth into the regulatory axion that licensing records are public records whose content must be restricted to their regulatory use and kept free of inappropriate personal information and subjective judgments.

Reaction to Past Neglect. Exposure of extreme neglect and abuse of children in certain residential facilities in a few states has served to bring about reactions advantageous to the licensing service in some of these states and in others heeding the warning. These reactions included a shocked awareness at top administrative levels that indefinitely tolerating some substandard facilities in the false hope that casework and teaching will change them must be replaced with administrative actions to deny licenses, plus actions by attorneys general and the courts to close illegal operations.

There has also been growing awareness of the need for subtle and not so subtle pressures, ranging from acceptance of poor facilities "because they're no worse than where the children come from" to political pressure to override denials of licenses. Finally, there have been some increases here and there in funds for enough staff to deliver the licensing service more effectively, including legal counsel as well as licensing staff.

All these developments are moving licensing administration toward more awareness of its legal base and those legal remedies which it must understand and begin to use where they are needed. A tightening of the delivery process has been encouraged, as has the use of a wider range of advice on statute writing and standards formulation, both from legal sources and from the other five members of the day care system.

At the same time, licensing staff, whose historical and professional commitment has always been to children, have some anxiety lest child care licensing become overly legalistic, cold, and remote.

Improvements visible and helpful to day care licensing staff, applicants, and licensees may be grouped under administration standards and opening up the licensing system itself. The reader is cautioned, however, that all these improvements have not taken place in every state, and that the writer is including as improvements those that are in process as well as those that have been completed.

Administration. Better and more frequently updated information is necessary in such forms as staff manuals, flyers, question-and-answer leaflets, and instruction booklets to assist would-be day care providers with the application and study process. Records and forms should be simpler and better organized, if not always fewer.

A number of meaningful services only tangentially related to licensing should be provided—in particular, consultation to licensing applicants on day care management, budgeting, and programs; and newsletters, informational reprints, and original teaching aids on program, food, creative materials, play, and so on.

Standards or Rules and Regulations. Most state licensing staff once perceived their job chiefly as assisting facilities to upgrade their program and its setting, first up to licensing requirements and then above and beyond them. It consisted of minimal attention to enforcement and maximum emphasis on consultation and teaching, focused to high if not ideal standards. Now most staff accept their job chiefly as one of requiring all facilities to meet and maintain basic standards, and most of their consultation and teaching is focused on assisting applicants to understand what each required standards item means to children and how they can meet requirements.

Now there is almost nationwide agreement that licensing standards should set a basic, enforceable level of care below which the state will not permit the care of children to fall, and then to see to it that all facilities do comply. This change is evidenced by the facts that standards publications have all but ceased to include recommended practices, and that "rules and regulations" are beginning to replace "minimum standards." Procedures related to enforcement, action on complaints, and fair hearings are appearing more and more in the publications, and in simple, everyday, nonprofessional language.

The substantive standards themselves are becoming more objective, less subjective, more realistic, more measurable, and more capable of uniform and consistent enforcement.

Opening Up the Licensing System. In the past, most state licensing staffs concentrated almost completely on safeguards and benefits for the child in care. But they have now broadened their thinking to a concern for parents, who must have a place, even if not ideal, in which to leave their children. This concern also extends to the providers, who should not have to meet requirements so high and costly that they would be forced out of business or into illegal operations.

The licensing agency's old practice of setting up a small, elite standards advisory committee, made up chiefly of educators and community-financed day care agency representatives, is being replaced by larger committees cutting across a broader constituency, including providers, concerned citizens, and parents of children in care. In some states the standards are circulated in draft form to all licensees for suggestions and reactions before they go to public hearings.

Both day care licensing statutes and the rules and regulations that amplify them are being revised at frequencies geared to meeting changing needs, and with good representation from the entire day care system.

FUTURE-ORIENTED NEEDS IN BEHALF OF LICENSING

Perhaps no state would consider that it has a model day care licensing statute, the perfect set of standards, and certainly not a staff large enough and equipped with the kind or amount of training in regulatory administration needed to deliver the licensing service. Most have statutory exemptions of some kinds of daytime care facilities whose children need the protections of licensing. Most states are able to reach no more than a tenth of the estimated number of their family day care homes. Very few states can make regular supervisory visits on a quarterly basis, and only a few can make visits semiannually, even to group day care facilities.

Nevertheless, this old state service has undergone a quiet revolution in the past 10 years, with changes for the better in its goals and in the delivery of its services. If licensing is to fulfill the beginnings of constructive change sketched above, the following four needs must be met.

- State and federal governments must recognize that licensing is class advocacy for children, worthy of policies sympathetic to its adequate funding and a place of stature and status in their arrangement of functions and services.

- Professional schools at all levels must recognize and incorporate into their curricula, both in on-going and shortterm programs, the content of regulatory administration focused to the uses of licensors, licensees, and child care advocates.

- Community leaders must accept responsibility for community education and support of day care licensing as one of the components necessary to the day care system.

- Licensing officials and personnel must develop sufficient identification with this emerging professional specialization to demand its fair share of funds and educational preparation, and the opportunity to do its job.

Licensing can serve the public interest, benefiting children, their parents, providers, and the entire community when it has the necessary support to realize its two major goals—preventing common hazards and foreseeable dangers, and insuring a nurturing environment. These two goals, when achieved, provide that baseline of quality which is licensing's correctly defined function.

For further information contact The Association for Regulatory Administration, Tulane School of Social Work, 3217 Westover Rd., Topeka Kansas 66604.

Chapter Nine

REGISTRATION OF FAMILY DAY CARE HOMES IN MASSACHUSETTS

Linda McCauley

In October 1974 the Massachusetts Office for Children changed its method of regulating family day care homes by replacing traditional licensing practices with a program of regulation called *Registration*. There are several models of registration that could have been implemented (Morgan, 1974). Massachusetts chose a model which is actually a form of licensure: the legislature prohibits the service, the Office for Children is delegated the responsibility to lift that prohibition when minimum requirements are met, and positive and negative sanctions are applied and enforced. Certain licensing methods which have become traditional practices, however, such as requiring proof of compliance with requirements through on-site inspections before a license is issued, have been changed a great deal.

In making the change from licensure to registration of family day care homes, we have essentially taken the position that the methods are not of themselves sacred, and that if they are ineffective or inappropriate for a particular service, they can be changed. To understand the reasons for making such a change, it is necessary to look at the nature of family day care and the regulatory processes applied to the service.

What is family day care? In the Massachusetts licensing statute (Note 1), it is defined as the provision of day care services to six or fewer children, unrelated to the provider, in a private residence. Children served may range from infancy to 7 years of age. Although the legislation does not regulate facilities caring for children over age 7, a family day care home often provides a natural setting for children needing out-of-school care as well. At its best, family day care provides a warm and stimulating family life experience in a safe setting, for children who are away from their parents for part of the day. It is not a "mini" day care center. By definition, it may be provided without major changes in the living quarters and manner of living. A flexible service, family day care often begins quickly, as the need arises. The hours of care are subject only to the willingness of the provider, and they may accommodate what would be an otherwise unwieldy schedule of a parent, or be adjusted easily when an unforeseen situation arises. Finally, family day care, like group day care, is a service which contributes significantly to a child's growth and development by complementing the care given by a child's parents.

How to regulate such a service without requiring it to become something other than what it is, is a matter for some thought. Regulation is appropriate for services when (a) their nature is such that the average person (a person without some orientation to, or knowledge of, the discipline characterizing the service) does not have the expertise to assess the competency of the provider of the service, or (b) when a person is not in a position to have enough information about the daily operation of the service, or the right to enter and inspect the facility where a service is provided. When either of these conditions exists, the state has traditionally assumed a protective role toward those people being served by regulating the service.

The first condition does not relate to family day care, but the second does, as a result of rapid social and economic changes in this country. Parents are no longer in the position to know personally the people who will care for their children while they work. Stable neighborhoods are becoming rarer; the nuclear family is the norm; more women need and wish to work outside the home. Parents are forced, and indeed may prefer, to look outside their circle of neighbors, friends, and relatives to find day care for their children.

There is, in addition, an increasing awareness of the importance of the early years in human development, and an increasing concern for children's rights. In some ways regulation can act as an indicator of the importance of a service, in this case, to raise the status of the family day care provider. In a country that verbalizes reverence for its children, child care workers and others in nurturant roles have a surprisingly low status. At the very least, regulation implies that one is important enough to have the state interested in what one is doing!

The kind of regulation chosen for family day care should acknowledge its emphasis on family living and the small size of the facility where the child care takes place. Family day care must not be forced into the traditional licensing mold for group care, such as day care centers and institutions, thereby denying the very qualities which make it family day care. Registration, as an alternate method of regulation, is an attempt to regulate family day care in a new, creative, and more suitable way than that provided by traditional licensing methods.

It became increasingly clear during the several years that family day care licensing was operational in Massachusetts that the application of traditional licensing methods to family day care was not practically or philosophically sound. A review of other state's methods of regulating the service yielded little helpful information, because nearly every state has encountered the same types of problems as Massachusetts. In general, states have chosen (a) virtually to ignore the licensing of family day care, (b) to define family day care in such a way that licensure is required only when a certain arbitrary number of children (three, four, or five) are being cared for, (c) to make minimal staff commitments to the licensure of family day care, (d) to make some staff commitments while maintaining traditional licensing methods, and (e) to license only those homes from which care is purchased with federal or state funds.

The practical problems involved in licensing family day care homes, which became apparent very quickly, precluded any success in the efforts of a small licensing staff. The volume of family day care homes alone would necessitate larger staffs than Massachusetts could ever hope to have. It is discriminatory to license only a small percentage of the family day care homes in existence, when the licensing statute applies to all homes providing the service. The public correctly perceives licensing as a guarantee of a certain level of quality of care. When family day care licensing staff, limited in number because of budget constraints, were not able to visit homes regularly for supervisory purposes, an expectation was set up that could not be met.

In addition to the practical problems, however, the methods used to license family day care homes seemed excessively cumbersome given the size and nature of the service. The licensing process often took months to complete, despite the fact that the applicant was able to prepare to offer the service in a short period of time. Staff experience in Massachusetts tended to confirm two things: (a) that the vast majority of homes met, without extensive modifications, those minimum requirements that could be measured before the service began, and (b) that on-site inspection before the initiation of the service yielded little information about the quality of care which would be provided. Supervision of the home when it was actually operating, which might have yielded useful information, was impossible because staff were busy keeping up with initial licensing studies. The large number of homes and the high rate of turnover in family day care resulted in the misuse of staff time and the abuse of provider's right to offer the service.

REGISTRATION CONCEPTUALIZED

Registration of family day care, as it has been conceptualized in Massachusetts, is a process of initial self-evaluation according to minimum requirements, supported by technical assistance (or consultation toward registration), and safeguarded through a number of other program components.

PROCESS OF INITIAL SELF-EVALUATION

The self-evaluation component is based on the assumption that the applicant, given correct information and clear directions, is able in most cases to make a sound decision about whether he or she meets the minimum requirements set by the state for the operation of a family day care home.

Self-evaluation occurs primarily through the mechanics of registration, which are intentionally as simple as possible. A person interested in operating a family day care home calls or comes into one of seven regional offices. After talking with a staff person, the applicant receives a copy of the family day care regulations and a self-evaluation form designed to reflect regulatory compliance. The applicant is then requested to name two persons who can attest to her ability to care for children, preferably persons for whose children she has cared. The applicant is also given an instruction sheet to guide her through the process, and a brief written statement of why family day care is regulated by the state and what it means to become registered. Upon completion of the registration forms, the applicant is asked to certify that, to the best of her knowledge, she meets family day care requirements.

The Office for Children then issues a Certificate of Registration, which grants permission to operate a family day care home, and which enables the provider to advertise the service.

TECHNICAL ASSISTANCE (CONSULTATION TOWARD REGISTRATION)

The goal of registration is to substitute a variety of contacts with family day care providers, some of which are regulatory, for the previous one or two on-site inspections before an operating license is issued. Technical assistance (or consultation toward registration) is one of the ways that the applicant is given the assistance and information necessary to complete the registration process quickly and successfully.

The first telephone contact is important in establishing the helping and listening attitude under which continuing contacts will occur. If possible, interested persons are encouraged to come into the office to pick up registration materials and to talk with a staff member at that time. A clear and simple explanation of the procedures the applicant will need to follow and of the forms she will receive is a must. In addition, family day care staff teach the regulations to the applicant and review selected requirements. This is done both to familiarize the applicant with the content of the regulations, and to allow the staff person to highlight those requirements which he or she knows from experience are most likely to be misunderstood. Reviewing some regulations may also relieve some of the applicant's anxiety about becoming registered, because it shows her that the meeting of requirements is probably an attainable goal.

Family day care staff try to keep in touch with as many applicants and providers as possible. People whose applications (self-evaluation forms) have not been returned are routinely called to see if the person is having difficulty completing the process. Finally, calls are made to providers within a few weeks of registering to find out whether they are running into any problems.

SAFEGUARDING PROGRAM QUALITY

The safeguarding component of the registration program consists of processes that occur over a period of time, and includes both regulatory and nonregulatory safeguards.

One regulatory form of quality control is the spot-checking of family day care homes. A spot-check is an on-site inspection of a family day care home, announced or unannounced, to measure compliance with the family day care regulations. The Office has the authority to visit and inspect any family day care home, and the responsibility to inspect whenever questions have been raised about a person's ability to comply with regulations.

Top priority for spot-checking goes to complaints and questionable applications. Other priorities are homes that are registered for the maximum number of children and homes that have been in operation for a full year. Although these are the priorities, as many inspections as possible will be made during the first year of program operation. The data collected by spot-checking will be used to decide on a reasonable amount of supervision, to provide more information about what the priorities for spot-checking ought to be, and to aid in the assessment of the feasibility of the program.

The establishment of an effective mechanism for responding to and following up on complaints is a second regulatory safeguard. There is no doubt that less than adequate child care can occur in any setting. We all know a few "horror stories." To this end, it became a priority to establish such a mechanism, and to publicize the fact that the Office for Children wants to hear complaints, and will use its legal authority to follow up and resolve such complaints when it is appropriate. The Office receives complaints about unregistered family day care homes, about situations in which too many children are being cared for in one home, and about inadequate child care, as well as the usual number of complaints resulting from personality conflicts. Some are easily resolved; others are not, and may require holding a hearing on the case, with the eventual possibility of going to court.

Family day care staff are also involved in a number of nonregulatory functions designed to increase the visibility of family day care services, to help parents find and make knowledgeable choices about child care and to support family day care providers.

No regulatory program, however sound, can be developed without public awareness of the service and the law regulating it. As a result, much staff time has been spent educating the communities in which they work. Approaches to public education vary, as does each region of the state itself, but they include the following kinds of activities.

1. Education of new applicants for family day care certificates about the regulatory process. In turn, they spread information, since word-of-mouth contacts occur often within this population.
2. Education of the other units within the Office for Children (Note 2), such as local Councils for Children, and Help for Children staff, who are well acquainted with the activities in their areas.
3. Contacts with newspapers to ask that they cooperate with our efforts by not accepting child care advertisements from unregistered providers, or least that they inform the advertiser of the law.
4. Interviews with newspapers which result in articles about family day care and the Office for Children's role in regulating the service.
5. Information-sharing meetings with Public Health Departments, Welfare Service Offices, social service agencies,

community action programs, day care centers, resource centers, schools, hospitals, and any other agencies, groups, or individual in the community who might be interested in this information.
6. Speaking on radio talk shows and public service announcements.
7. Development of a simple, explanatory brochure, which briefly outlines the law and the registration process, and answers a few of the most commonly asked questions about family day care.
8. Development of a brochure which outlines some of the things parents may wish to consider in choosing a family day care home.

In practice, family day care staff also find themselves giving technical assistance different from the consultation toward registration described above. Providers have many questions about things such as billing the Welfare Department for child care services, zoning and building safety issues, parent-provider relationships, liability insurance, the going rate for family day care services, and how best to make their service known in the community. These questions are obviously not regulatory concerns, but are nevertheless areas which can subtly affect program quality. Responding to these concerns is an appropriate role for staff, whose experience with state government and a variety of family day care providers often allows them to assume a supportive role toward the family day care provider. It is necessary, however, for staff to constantly clarify, both to themselves and the providers, the difference between this kind of technical assistance, which is an information-sharing, supportive, and nonmandatory relationship, and the regulatory function which is their primary job role.

One vehicle for providing some supportive services to providers which has shown promise is the holding of provider meetings at the local level. Beyond offering a forum to talk about those issues and questions that are consistently raised in family day care, the meetings offer providers a chance to get to know other people in the community who do the same kind of work. The meetings give a feeling of group solidarity and are often useful as consciousness-raising sessions. More experienced providers can often "bring along" newer providers by sharing ways of caring for children and of dealing with common problems which the provider may encounter. More importantly, the meetings are a place where the self-esteem of the provider can grow, where she can begin to take her place in the child care community, and where the group can begin to gather power to make the changes they see as necessary. The role of the family day care staff person is to set up the meetings, to provide the initial incentives for attending, to be as responsive as possible to the needs the providers indicate, and eventually to take a back seat as the group becomes more autonomous.

Provider meetings are not yet widespread in Massachusetts. Staff time is simply not available for this kind of development, and the inherent conflict between the regulatory and supportive roles creates further difficulties. Ideally, supportive and organizational functions that are intended to raise the quality of a service like family day care, would be offered by some group or agency which is not attached to the regulatory function of the state.

PROGRAM ADMINISTRATION

On a regional basis the job of implementing the registration program is functionally divided between two persons: the registrar and the regional family day care coordinator.

THE REGISTRAR

The registrar's job role might be described as "clerical-PLUS." This position did not exist before the change from licensure to registration. The job description is still evolving, but it encompasses at least the following responsibilities.

1. Responsible for insuring that the mechanics of registration run smoothly, quickly, and efficiently. This is no small task. It includes mailing and following up applications for registration, taking references, updating control cards, notifying providers of renewal, screening completed applications for compliance with requirements, issuing Certificates of Registration, and preparing and mailing quarterly listings of family day care homes. This part of the job also includes large amounts of telephone work, because the registrars are the initial teachers of regulations and must explain the registration process, call the laggers, give out referrals of registered family day care homes, answer all routine family day care questions, and provide office coverage.
2. Responsible for recording statistical data which will be used to assess program workability.
3. Responsible for being conversant with the law, regulations, and all issues and questions relating to family day care.
4. Responsible for participating in and helping to define on-going training.
5. Responsible for special assigned projects which will contribute to program development, depending on the skills and interest of the registrar and the time available for such projects.

THE REGIONAL FAMILY DAY CARE COORDINATOR

The role of the original family day care licensors changed a good deal when the Office for Children began to implement a program of registration. The regional family day care coordinator now has the following job responsibilities.

1. Responsible for responding to and following up on complaints.
2. Responsible for spot-checking family day care homes.
3. Responsible for the program of public education in the region.
4. Responsible for developing support services.
5. Responsible for participating in and helping to define on-going training.
6. Responsible for much of the training of registrars.
7. Responsible, in addition to the above, for the regulation of Massachusetts' 25 family day care systems.

All family day care staff participate heavily in program planning and development. Their field experience, and their knowledge of what works and what does not work, shape the direction and the priorities of the program.

An agency administering a program of registration for family day care homes must concern itself with several tasks, the first of which is to define to the public exactly what a change from licensure to registration means with regard to the state's authority and responsibility in regulating family day care services. Much of this can be accomplished by well-trained staff, by careful wording of public education materials, and by requiring providers to give parents written information about registration, the regulations and the complaint process. But the agency itself must deliver a message to the public indicating its expectation that communities will share in the responsibility of assessing child care facilities and will report inadequate child care to the regulatory unit.

The development of requirements is an important task in any regulatory program. The requirements must establish a minimum acceptable level of quality below which no facility can legally be operated, and must be written in such a way as to be enforceable. In fact the credibility of any licensing function rests heavily upon the content of the regulations. In a program of registration, the requirements must meet an additional criterion: they must be written in such a way that family day care providers can read them. Regulatory language may be a difficult hurdle for a provider, and no one, to my knowledge, has ever described regulations as being seductive reading material. Nonetheless, the provider will not only need to evaluate her service according to them, but must also be able to understand from them exactly what she must do to bring her service into compliance and to keep it that way.

Finally, the agency must be prepared to support the change from licensure to registration. I would go so far as to say that the administrators of the agency must be convinced that registration is potentially a more appropriate method of regulation for family day care, not just a possible solution to practical problems. After all, no change is ever made without criticism.

PRELIMINARY OBSERVATIONS ABOUT REGISTRATION

Most of the program assessment will begin as the Office moves into its second year of registration. Statistical data will not be forthcoming for a while yet. However the Office did have certain expectations about the results of a change from licensure to registration, and certain perceptible changes can be reported at this time.

Observation: Intake has increased and the number of family day care providers who are now regulated has tripled, when the high rate of turnover is not taken into account. *Apparent Reason:* Public education and the ability to follow-up on complaints.

Observation: The premise that the vast majority of providers are and will remain substantially in compliance with family day care regulations appears to be valid at this time. Spot-checking has yielded little in the way of noncompliance, and most noncompliance is in a few areas that seem to be unclear to providers. This premise began to be retested when the Office promulgated new family day care requirements early in 1976. The new regulations require more of the provider, but are also clearer and more specific. *Apparent Reason:* Basic honesty and desire to perform competently; the ability to meet requirements; or low requirements.

Observation: Administrative delays are largely curtailed. *Apparent Reason:* Addition of the registrar job function; simplification of the regulatory process.

These preliminary observations must be very general at this time; more specific information will be compiled by June 1976. Meanwhile it is probably true that no one can appreciate the possibilities of a program of registration quite like the licensors who were involved in the endless futility and certain failure of licensing family day care. The Office certainly anticipates many modifications and refinements in the program. There are philosophical, political, and practical problems to be solved, but unlike the situation with traditional licensure of family day care, those solutions are not unattainable goals.

Chapter Ten

SUGGESTIONS FOR DESIGNING A CHILDREN'S CENTER

Excerpted and Edited by James Rivaldo from *Patterns for Designing a Children's Center* by Fred Osmon

Too often the design of buildings does not serve the needs of the people who occupy them or the activities they conduct within them. In too many cases the client hands the architect a list of room requirements, the architect devises a single plan including these rooms, the client approves the plan without being able to relate blueprints to the functions to take place within the building, and the building is built.

This chapter is excerpted and paraphrased with the author's permission from the book, *Patterns for Designing Children's Centers,* by Fred Osmon, published by the Educational Facilities Laboratories. The book can be considered as part of a continuing dialogue between early childhood educators and architects who take the time to articulate their ideas on educational needs and required physical solutions. It is a summary of this dialogue as gleaned from the literature, from visits to many centers, and from conversations with preschool educators across the United States. Many general guidelines, adaptable to many varying situations, have emerged from this extensive research.

As an architect Mr. Osmon has tried to avoid the disputes among early childhood educators regarding the "right" curriculum for a preschool program. This was possible because there are now only three distinct group programs in early childhood education—free activity choice, slow pace, and highly structured. This limited number allows each pattern to suggest a different physical solution for each program type whenever a different solution is appropriate. The free activity choice program dominates this discussion since it is oriented more toward the use of the physical environment as a teaching tool, whereas the highly structured approach is oriented toward words and books as the primary educational mode and treats the physical environment only as supportive or neutral.

Because the physical environment plays such a crucial role in determining the program of a children's center, the design team should include not only the architects, but also the center's staff, working in close cooperation from the beginning, whether the project consists of minor alterations to a storefront or of building an entirely new facility from scratch. In addition to familiarizing themselves with the literature on the subject, the design team should try visiting a number of different centers in its community to learn from their mistakes as well as their successes.

THE ORGANIZATION OF A CHILDREN'S CENTER

The organization of a children's center is determined by three major factors: the approach to early childhood education that will guide the program, the general knowledge of how best to organize young children in groups, and the economics of operating a self-sufficient center. For the purposes of our discussion, we have gleaned from various educational experts three distinct approaches to the structure of the daily program:

Free Choice: This program approach emphasizes cognitive, social, and emotional development and allows a free choice of materials and activities by the children. The structure resides in the materials and the teacher's individual contact with each child, but she does not teach.

Slow Pace: This program approach emphasizes the same triad as the free choice program, but it places heavier emphasis on cognitive development. The daily curriculum is centered on activities planned by the teacher, but generally includes some free play, especially in an all-day program.

Highly Structured: The third program approach is centered primarily on cognitive or symbol development within a highly structured daily program. The primary motivation is to prepare the child for the standard elementary school program.

These three programs differ in the degree to which they structure the child's activities, and this difference has a direct parallel in the physical environment. The different types of activities in which children involve themselves have different optimal space requirements. Some activities require plenty of room for many active children, others require a quiet corner for a single child or a small group of children. The center should therefore be subdivided into activity centers with access routes between them. In general, children require a sense of security from their environment, but also the opportunity for exploration and expansive activity.

A MULTIREALM ENVIRONMENT FOR CHILD AND ADULT

The physical environment of the center can contribute substantially to the development or impedance of the child's sense of adequacy and independence. If the clothes, lockers, drinking fountains, furniture, tables, storage units, clocks, windows, etc., are convenient for a child's use, he can attend to his own physical needs and embark on a variety of play activities. A functional world within the child' level of manual dexterity and muscle capability affirms his sense of competence and encourages him to explore from that secure base.

Not everything, however, should be made to adapt to the child. He must learn that he needs to adapt to this environment as well, and that adults can help him to do certain things beyond his reach. The adult staff should also feel comfortable in the center environment, so that they can function in maximum comfort and efficiency. Sinks, doorknobs, windows, etc., should be built at two levels —one for adults and one for children—if the budget allows.

As children develop their sense of independence and competence, and begin to test their motor coordination, reaction time, and judgment, safety becomes a prime consideration. Shatter-proof glass, rounded corners on furniture, shock-proof electrical outlets, slip-proof rugs and floors, controlled hot water temperature, and storing potentially dangerous items beyond the children's reach can prevent injury.

In an environment in which formal teaching by an adult is minimized, the question of adult dominance becomes important. The structure of the center affects the degree of the adults' physical presence. For example, a small room or a room with a low ceiling is overwhelmed by the presence of an adult, to a degree that adults often cannot appreciate. Our studies suggest that a ceiling height from 10 feet to 12 feet achieves the balance between intimacy and expansiveness needed by small children. In addition, to minimize adult dominance even further, the circulation paths and activity centers of the staff should be on the periphery and not in the middle of the children's activity centers.

RELATIONSHIP OF THE CENTER TO THE SURROUNDING COMMUNITY

The center in most cases represents the child's first venture into the community outside his family home. The center, in its relationship to the surrounding community, can therefore play a role in determining whether the children feel either isolated or a part of the activity going on outside the center. Ideally, the center should have a cheerful, inviting entrance, windows to allow the children to see passersby and to allow passersby to see the children, and an outdoor play area self-contained for security, but not walled off like a prison. Parents should have an area to congregate without interfering with the childrens' activities, but this area should not be structured to make the parents merely observers of the children, rather than co-participants of the Center.

Vandalism always presents problems and the individual location of the center will determine the security measures necessary. Often the lack of challenging barriers, such as chain link fences, deters vandalism.

THE PLAY ENVIRONMENT

A free activity choice program succeeds most readily in an open environment with easy access to the different activity centers. A common problem in centers with these programs is overlap and conflict among children engaged in different activities. Also, young children need a certain degree of structure and familiar landmarks to stimulate use and to minimize the need for rules governing their interaction with different spaces and other children.

The center can use many devices to provide minimal separations and delineations of activity centers without sacrificing openness. Different floor surfaces, either rugs or linoleum, can either insulate against noise or contain certain activities. Similarly, different colors on the floor can provide a more subtle delineation of space. Movable or low shelves and storage modules—less imposing barriers than walls—can direct traffic in certain areas of the center. Lighting can be utilized to create an environment distinct from adjacent darker areas. Earphones and telephones can isolate an activity within space without disruption to adjacent spaces. Acoustic materials can create different sound levels and differing moods in adjacent areas.

The major difference between slow-paced and highly-structured programs and the free activity choice program is the degree of guidance the teacher offers in selecting activities for the children and, to a certain extent, in enforcing longer attention spans on these activites. Consequently the flow of traffic in these centers is more structured and restricted, with more permanent barriers and subdivisions of space. Smaller, quieter activity centers, sometimes resembling the traditional classroom, accentuate the physical presence, and hence the authority of the teacher.

Ideally, the total square footage of the play area will be the space needed for each activity plus circulation, utilities, and structural elements, but modified by any multiuse criteria. The square footage needed for a particular activity varies significantly with the materials used in that activity and program emphasis given to it, and so the footage should be developed by the design team. Although many educators suggest between 30 and 50 square feet as a minimum guideline per child per center, I suggest 60 square feet a minimum for an all-day center program, especially if it includes provisions for napping during the course of the day.

PLACES TO PAUSE FOR A WHILE

When involved in natural play, children take a break from time to time and go "off duty." These breaks reduce excitement and help a child to stay on an even keel at a time when his mechanisms for emotional stability have not yet developed completely. Children usually seek out smaller, isolated, or enclosed spaces where they can pass some time either alone or in the company of one or two other children. These enclosures can be produced by the children with blocks, cardboard boxes, or furniture, or they can be provided in the form of furniture-like elements placed throughout the group play environment.

As an alternative to enclosed spaces, the center might provide watching places, either near a window or in a raised location in a loft or tree from which children can quietly observe the activity of others inside or outside the center.

Children will be attracted to elements within the environment that have a quality of delight and constant change. These places tend to be objects that become "events." Children will pause at these places and watch or participate depending on the demands of the event.

A teacher can place these points of interest throughout the group play environment in the form of mirrors, shells that contain the sound of the sea, a fish tank or a pet cage, and the architect can build these events into the center's structural fabric. Windows in the roof from which children can watch the clouds and rain or gutters that spray falling rain into gravel pits in the yard rather than into silent pipes in the ground emphasize the drama of changing weather. In general, children are attracted to small details, irregularities and surprises, and a simple but thoughtful improvisation can provide enormous interest and delight.

PRESENTING AND STORING PLAY MATERIALS

The type of program in the children's center, whether free activity or highly structured, determines to a certain extent the degree of accessibility by children to the materials used in the center, and hence determines the proportion of open and closed storage facilities. To make play materials accessible to children, the storage shelving should have the following dimensions: Maximum shelf height, age 2.0 to 3.0 years—2'11"; age 3.0 to 4.0 years—3'1"; and age 4.0 to 5.0 years—3'3". A program that mixes children of different ages will need a single in-between height of 3'0" for shelving and a height of 22" for a storage unit that will also act as a stand-up work surface.

The presentation of materials to encourage use has a number of parameters. First, the items should be displayed so that they can be clearly distinguished from adjacent items. This is helpful to all children, but especially valuable to disadvantaged children. Dr. Jerome Kagan, a noted child expert, has said that ". . . what is often termed 'enrichment' . . . a hodge-podge of things to see, touch and hear in an overstuffed classrooom. . . is largely useless to many children. Instead, people who plan such programs should provide single, distinctive stimuli to be presented in a context of quiet. Culturally disadvantaged children are not deprived of stimulation, they are deprived of distinctive 'stimulation'." This distinctness can be accomplished by separating the items with space, with shelf separators or by contrasting qualities. Another way to suggest use is to provide work space adjacent to the stored item.

To insure that the stored items are always convenient and distinctly presented to the children, they must be returned to their original condition after each use. Sometimes the children can help the teacher, but in most cases a child under 6 is not orderly and should not be forced to pick up after himself. He has enough things to learn without the additional stress of learning orderliness, which comes more naturally at a later age.

Provisions for closed storage enable the teacher to introduce new materials gradually or to store potentially dangerous things away from the children.

THE FLOOR AS FURNITURE

To children the floor is more than just a walking surface; it is also the primary playing surface. The layout and materials used in the center's flooring deserve careful attention by the design team.

Several criteria should be considered in planning the flooring surface. The floor should be free from drafts and warm to the touch, since children enjoy sitting and playing on it. It should be easily maintained to prevent or minimize slipping hazards and to minimize germ retention. The floor should be resilient to minimize accidents from falls and also to minimize its production of sound. It should be designed with a minimum of changes in level along major circulation paths to eliminate places to stumble. The floor should be considered for its potential as work/play surface to minimize the clutter of furniture and to maximize the number of play/work postures.

Since the flooring surface alone does not determine the warmth of the floor or the prevelence of drafts, the planning team should consider such matters as subfloor construction and insulation, including the possibility of a radiantly-heated floor slab. Although effective such slabs have been found in many cases to be too fatiguing to the occupants. The planners should also consider air-lock doors, perimeter heating systems, and other means of eliminating drafts.

Both resilient flooring and carpeting offer advantages and disadvantages. Resilient flooring, whether vinyl asbestos tile or seamless flooring applied as a liquid, is easily cleaned and kept dry and is a good surface over which to slide furniture and storage units. Carpeting offers greater sound insulation and is a more comfortable surface on which to sit and play. However cleaning up spills poses more problems than on a resilient surface.

It follows, therefore, that the type of flooring should

be chosen to fulfill the needs of a particular indoor activity; resilient flooring should be used in wet, messy, heavily used areas, and carpeting should be used in passive or noisy but not play areas.

If children use the floor as a play/work surface, they in fact make it a substitute for tables and chairs. Some educators and designers have begun to manipulate the floor to create a new kind of built-in furniture. Many centers have introduced sunken or raised areas, covered with the same carpeting as the general floor, to facilitate different playing postures. This innovation reduces the constriction and clutter of tables and chairs. However the raised and lowered areas should not be so extensive that they eliminate the flat, open area required for the group multiuse area, nor should they interfere with safe paths of circulation about the center.

A CHILD'S PERSONAL POSSESSIONS

The center should provide storage areas for children's coats, rubbers, and outer garments, preferably near both the entrance to the center and the exit to the outdoor play area, but outside a circulation path with which the inevitable clutter might interfere. Children also should have a place to keep their personal possessions, including mats or blankets if the center includes a sleeping period in its program.

CHILDREN'S TOILET AREA

Toilet training is a source of stress for many young children. Therefore the center should do everything possible to make toileting easy and pleasurable. To accomplish this, the toilet should be a sociable, friendly place that is free from scoldings and where an air of enjoyment as well as duty exists.

To aid in creating a cheerful toilet environment the architect will need to minimize the coldness usually produced by "easy-to-maintain" surfaces. Sunlight, view windows to outdoor play areas, ledges for potted plants and flowers, bright colors, and wood surfaces help to relieve this coldness.

The size of the toilet fixtures can also aid the teacher and child in toilet training. Although some argue that having adult-sized fixtures minimizes the differences between the home and the center, the weight of opinion lies with maximum convenience to the child.

The recommended height for water closets for children aged 3 to 5 is 11 inches. Although this height corresponds to the typical junior fixtures available from most plumbing manufactures, it still may be too high to accomodate children aged 2 to 3. Portable potties, steps, platforms, or fixtures sunken into the floor a few inches may solve the problems encountered by younger children.

Many centers recommend the use of urinals, usually troughs set 12 inches above the floor, to minimize wet toilet seats and floors. Rather than an enclosed room, some centers prefer low barriers around toilet fixtures to provide a measure of privacy, but also to allow teacher supervision. The average recommendation for the number of water closets is one per 10 children, with one 4-foot-long urinal trough per 30 children.

Some often-overlooked details include a clean-out to allow retrieval of flushed toys blocking the drain line; sound insulation for flushing, especially if the napping area is nearby; placement of toilet paper, hand towels, and mirrors at child height; and a seamless floor (liquid plastic, ceramic tile, or sheet vinyl) to minimize retention of water and germs. Raw concrete is not a good material because urine will find its way into hairline cracks and produce odors.

CHILDREN'S SINKS

The sinks in a children's center typically serve three purposes.

The first is child hand washing, usually after using the toilet or before eating. Teachers generally prefer that hand-washing facilities be located outside, but convenient to, the toilet area to deemphasize the association between the toilet and hand washing and to avoid the development of neurotic traits associated with the function of elimination. Also, the hand-washing sink can then be used for other purposes as well.

Second, various activities in the group play environment require a multipurpose sink for play as well as cleanup. These sinks should have adjacent work spaces that drain into them, and temperature controls accessible only to the teacher or no hot water at all. Multipurpose sinks are generally larger, deeper, and accessible to more children at one time than are the hand-washing sinks.

Third, in the course of play, especially outside, children often get excessively dirty, or they may have a bowel relapse, or they may sustain an injury requiring washing. Therefore many centers find that it is useful to have a special child-washing sink, either one specially designed for that purpose, or a standard service sink at teacher height. A drinking fountain, perhaps attached to a sink, helps to encourage a child's self-sufficiency.

FOOD PREPARATION

Centers that prepare complete hot lunches and breakfasts for the children usually have a professional cook. Their kitchen requirements are therefore fairly standard. If the center program involves the teacher in the preparation of either meals or snacks, or if it involves the children as well, the design team must consider certain special requirements.

Generally, the kitchen area should grant an open view of the center for the teacher engaged in preparing the food. The elaborateness of the food prepared will determine the size and complexity of refrigerators and heating elements. A serving counter 22 inches high and near the kitchen allows the children to pick up their food themselves and to carry it to a table. If the children participate in preparing the food, many centers use portable appliances set on the child-height counters.

WATER PLAY

Most educators and psychologists attest to the value of water play in a preschool environment. Few other activities offer as much potential for flexibility, sensation, experimentation, and exploration. However water play also creates many problems for the teacher, and often so many restrictions have to be placed on water play that the value of the experience is severely limited. To prevent this the center should have a water play environment designed to minimize water cleanup and slipping, to help keep children dry, to provide a generous supply of props and water surfaces, and to provide protection to the water play area from children engaged in other activities.

The requirement for protection implies that the water play area should be out of the main traffic flow. A permanent water table creates its own area and is available for long periods of uninterrupted play. A water tub on wheels (one- or two-child size), standing 22 inches from the floor, would allow the teacher to place the tub either in a quiet corner for passive, protected play, or in an action area for more vigorous play.

When water does splash on to the floor, the flooring

material should collect it in some way and still retain a slip-proof surface. An ideal solution is a wooden drain board set flush with the floor and containing a drain underneath. A rubber mat with a deep pile also works well and is less expensive. The water play area should not have floor seams into which water can seep and cause damage.

Some teachers prefer to limit water play to the outdoor yard on warm days. Outdoor facilities can take many forms, including a fountain or sprinkler, a wading pool, or boat-sailing pool. In any case the water should not be deeper than 9 inches, and walking surfaces should not become slippery when wet. An empty pool can become a hazard when not in use. Therefore any permanent structure should be designed for other play activities, such as a trike run, a seating area, or a climbing element.

Rain water can also be utilized for water play and has wonderful "found" quality children enjoy. The rain can be allowed to puddle or form rivulets, or it can be given expression in spurting rain spouts and gurgling catch basins, or by tapping on a tin roof.

CONSTRUCTION ACTIVITIES

Because of their almost universal popularity among children and the educational-psychological value assumed by teachers, construction activities are a common ingredient of most preschool programs. Whether using standard blocks, commercially manufactured building toys, or "junk" such as boxes, cartons, sawhorses, and planks, children find one of their greatest opportunities for expansive self-expression in building things. Blocks are excellent therapy for inhibited, timid, or disorganized children or children who find no comfort in people. Blocks can also foster cooperation among a group of children.

Several different environments should be provided for the use of the construction materials by individual children or by groups, and these areas should be sufficiently separated. The outdoor yard offers the opportunity for larger-scale projects.

Setting off the construction areas in raised or sunken areas of the floor helps to contain the activities. Carpeting in construction areas helps to reduce the noise generated by tumbling blocks and to minimize the stifling effects of teachers telling children to be quiet. The carpeting should have a dense, low pile to provide a stable building surface.

THE ART ACTIVITIES AREA

Whether paints, clay, glue, or fingerpaints are used most often in the art area, cleanup constitutes one of the most important considerations. Surfaces should be of linoleum, formica, oilcloth, or ceramic tile. Vinyl coating or enamel paint should protect the walls, and the floor should be surfaced with a resilient material.

Stand-up work tables should be 22 inches from the floor and sit-down/stand-up tables should be 17 inches for 2- to 3½-year-olds, or 19½ inches for 3½- to 5-year-olds. Besides adequate space and working suraces, the art area will need shelving, water and cleanup facilities, drying facilities, and display surfaces. Ideally the art area should be served by its own sink or at least by a sink peripheral to the area. This sink should have adequate work-top space to either side for cleanup and mixing.

Continuous expanses of wall, indoors or outdoors, can be used as a drawing or painting surface. The surface can be covered with blackboard or linoleum and used for chalk drawings, or it can be covered with paper for crayons or paints. Portions of an indoor wall can be covered with felt for use with stick-on felt letters, animals, cars, and so on. A free-standing panel of glass can be used on either or both sides as a fingerpainting surface.

PROPS FOR DRAMATIC PLAY

Dramatic play is a natural activity of children, especially during the preschool years. This activity serves the child's psychological growth by allowing him to act out and assimilate important emotional events; it serves his social growth by offering an intimate and personal means of communication; and it serves his intellectual growth by providing a means of organizing impressions at a time when the manipulation of abstract symbols is developing.

Although educators agree on the importance of dramatic play, they disagree on its role in a preschool program. Some centers encourage it, while others stress more formal instruction and reality-oriented tasks and leave dramatic play to the home. This discussion of dramatic play applies to those centers that encourage it in their daily program.

The center typically facilitates dramatic play by providing an area and props suggesting play themes. Several questions have recently been raised that suggest a fresh approach to the kinds of props provided for dramatic play. Children from lower socioeconomic classes tend to play roles centering on the home, whereas more affluent children play games involving a wider spectrum of topics, including train rides and airplane trips, construction activities, and so on. This has led many centers in disadvantaged areas to take their children on trips into the larger community, and it has led others to suggest that the housekeeping corner, which is so attractive to disadvantaged children, should be allowed as an introduction activity and then gradually be eliminated while the children are encouraged into different activities.

It follows that the children's center might be supporting the status quo of society by providing a housekeeping corner and its usual props, since the disadvantaged child and the middle-class child will play out only those roles they have experienced in their home environment. Traditional sex roles are also reinforced. We are not arguing against the value of play themes centering on the home, but we are suggesting that the housekeeping corner supports this limited range of experiences *too strongly*. To widen the child's range of experience, he should be introduced to the larger community outside of his immediate home environment. Field trips into the community and visits to the center by people from the community can help to broaden the horizons of the children.

Therefore the center should provide props for acting out the new experiences encountered by the children. A child can use familiar objects found in the housekeeping corner symbolically as well as literally, but other kinds of objects can provide additional stimulation. A middle ground must be found between a direct representation of an object and an object that is so abstract that it presents no stimulus to the child. This author believes that a group of objects can be chosen whose level of functional generality suggests a variety of man-made objects and functional tasks. Each object should be distinct from the others and should present only a few qualities very clearly.

Items suggested for this corner include gears, bottles, boxes, plumber's helpers, wheels, mugs, flower pots, balances, cans with no labels, sheets of material, ropes, baskets, hoses, sponges, spheres, cones, springs, brooms, pillows, mirrors, cardboard tubes, and navy surplus signal flags. These objects should be located in one place, preferably adjacent to a play area in which the children can act out a number of different roles— either an open area or an area shaped with large cardboard boxes, masonite, or plywood suggesting houses or walls with windows.

SAND PLAY

Sand play is one of the most popular activities among small children. The center can provide for it in a number of ways, on either indoor or outdoor sand tables. The problem associated with sand play is conflict among children in overlapping play areas. Sand in raised tables minimizes this problem, but areas in which children immerse their whole bodies generate more problems. There are several solutions, including an irregular-shaped pit which defines play areas within the pit to roughly 3-foot-radius circles, by introducing work tables into the middle of the pit, or by making several small pits in the yard.

Water drainage through the pit is important, and where soil drainage is good, the sand pit (usually with between 18 and 24 inches of sand) can have a brick underlayer with a gravel subbase below that. Where ground deepage is poor, a dry well should be dug or a drain line installed. An economical solution for placing a sand play area on an existing asphalt surface is to build *up* the sand pit without cutting asphalt. "Weep" holes will allow water to drain through the bounding element. The sand play area should provide some sun shelter, perhaps a tree, and should be covered, if possible, when it rains. Water should be available near the sand box to moisten sand for building projects, but it should have to be hand-carried in buckets to control the amount available to the sand pit. The children likewise should be able to wash sand from their bodies outside.

MUSIC

Music activities generally include quiet listening, phonograph or piano playing with child voice or bodily accompaniment, instrument playing, marching to music, and group singing.

Quiet listening, often with earphones, allows a child to take a break from other children and should be available in one or more quiet spots in the center.

Spontaneous dancing should be encouraged as a

means of releasing excess energy, whether joy or aggression. This can be stimulated by a phonograph available during free play, or it can be organized as a group activity with the teacher at a piano. In either case, a large, open area is needed.

NAPS

The inclusion of rest periods in the daily program varies among children's centers and varies with the length of the daily program. One or more of the following possibilities should be considered for the new center: a nap period for children who arrive very early; a midmorning rest period in which sleeping is not required, and in which children either stretch out on cots, put their heads down on a table, or quietly sit and listen to music; an afternoon nap period of 1 to 2 hours for an all-day program; a midafternoon rest period for a half-day program.

The different types and durations of nap periods suggest different sleeping accommodations. Many argue for a separate sleeping area which allows all or some of the children maximum quiet and gives the teaching staff an opportunity to rearrange the play area while the children nap. Space constraints in many centers do not allow a separate area for use only during nap time. In either case, noise and light abatement is necessary. Built-in cots permit easy cleaning and eliminate the bother of setting up and taking down to evolve their own napping schedules. This staggering of rest periods saves space and equipment.

THE SICK CHILD

Every children's center must provide for the child who becomes ill or who appears to be getting a possibly communicable illness. In many cases the mother is unable to pick up the child until the end of the work day. Therefore the center should provide an area away from the activities of the children, but not so isolated that the ill child feels unnecessarily lonely or unhappy. More than just a bedroom, the area might include provisions for quiet activities and play and should be as cheerful as possible.

Studies suggest one isolation bed per 25 children, or 50 square feet per 30 children. A center with 100 or more children warrants a separate infirmary under the direction of trained health personnel.

STAFF AND PARENT LOUNGE

Working with children can become an unendurable strain unless the teachers are relieved at reasonable intervals. They need more than just a trip to the toilet for that; a teachers' room should have a couch to stretch out on, and most importantly, it should afford privacy.

The teachers' toilet should be accessible from the general circulation path, but not the teachers' lounge. This insures greater privacy to both lounge and toilet, makes the toilet more accessible to the play area, and also allows parents and visitors to use the toilet, for economy. Teachers should also have a storage place for their personal belongings, preferably near the group play area so that their coats are easily available for outdoor play supervision.

Since interaction with parents is one of the most important aspects of a child care program, the center should provide a comfortable lounge or meeting room which encourages parents to visit and to chat among themselves and with the staff. The parents' lounge should afford a view of the play area, but it should be separate enough so that it does not interfere with the activities of the children. A public phone and a toilet, as well as a hot plate and sink, should be nearby. The teachers' and parents' lounges may be combined, but most teachers prefer them separate.

OUTDOOR PLAY

Outdoor play is an important component in almost every child care program. Outdoor play allows exuberant children to exercise the large muscles and to release excess energy. The square footage recommendations for outdoor play areas average 150 square feet per child.

Outdoor play areas are generally divided into active and passive play areas, distinguished by the degree of movement and noise. This distinction relates as well to large-muscle activities and manipulative activities. Active play requires approximately three times as much space as passive play.

The action area affords the opportunity to exercise large muscles. In addition to a variety of activities, the action area should challenge the child to develop gradually increasing his or her muscular skill and coordination. Ideally, the action area should challenge the most skillful child, but it should also offer the opportunity of successful achievement to the least skillful.

Play areas are usually arranged in nodes, or groupings of play equipment, which are separated for safety but also permit an easy flow of circulation among them. Above all, children seem to enjoy large, open areas in which they can run and tumble.

The passive play area facilitates activities which in most cases are extensions on a larger scale of indoor activities. These include painting, sand play, and construction. The passive play areas should be separated from the active area in which fast movement can disrupt the passive play activities.

The ideal ground surface of the outdoor play area would be soft enough for falls and tumbles but firm enough for good traction. Grass is good, but it does not hold up under sustained wear. Most centers use a combination of soft sand around play equipment, asphalt for circulation routes on which tricycles cruise, and occasionally outdoor carpeting. Drainage is an important consideration; the fastest drying areas should be nearest the door to the play yard.

Since the children may be quite active when moving between indoors and outdoors, the safety of path of flow must be considered. Any abrupt changes in level can produce accidents from tripping, and any changes in floor texture could produce an accident as a wet or sandy shoe moves abruptly from a rough surface (concrete) to a smooth surface (vinyl tile). Therefore the indoor-outdoor path must be level or ramped, the door threshold flush with adjoining surfaces, and the entry point provided with a transition place that allows a child to get traction when speeding up (going outside) or slowing down (coming inside). The door should be operable by a child, preferable with a window at child height.

This chapter presents only in the broadest outline of some of the more important considerations the children's center planning team should bear in mind. To reap the greatest potential from children's center programs, we must provide facilities that operate at maximum efficiency and provide greater developmental stimulation for the children.

DEVELOPING A FACILITY FOR CHILD CARE: A SHORT CHECK LIST

1. Bring your design team together at a very early point in the planning process. Many of the decisions that arise early do appear to have architectural consequences, but in fact do have implications that can limit future planning or increase the budget.

2. If the day care staff, parents, and the design team are looking for new ways to approach the problem at hand, then a preplanning stage should be initiated prior to schematic architectural design work. This phase

Figure 10.1 A center consisting of one room or building and some support area (offices, storage, toilets, etc.) for 15 to 30 children and 2 to 4 teachers.

Figure 10.3 A center consisting of several small buildings connected by a covered walkway or closed corridor. There are 15 to 30 children per "hut," either in separate age groupings or mixed age groupings. The main support facility is in a separate building, but there is some support in each hut.

1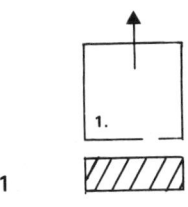

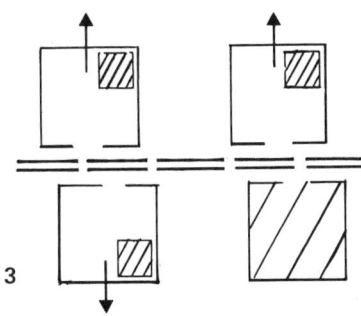
3

Figure 10.2 A center consisting of several distinct rooms all under one roof. Each room has space for 15 to 30 children, usually separated by age grouping. Support space is adjacent.

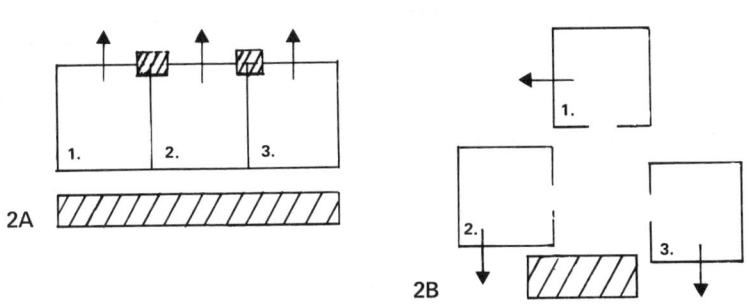
2A

2B

Figure 10.4 A center consisting of separate rooms that can be opened onto a central space. This layout allows mixing of children from different rooms for parts of the day.

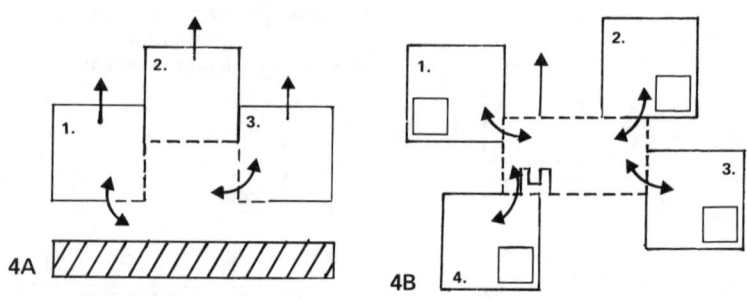

Figure 10.5 A center consisting of totally open classrooms arranged to provide a suggestion of home room space by the placement of support cores (toilets, sinks, storage, etc.). Home room groupings are in effect for part of day, and total flow throughout the space takes place at other times. Each home room has 15 to 30 children.

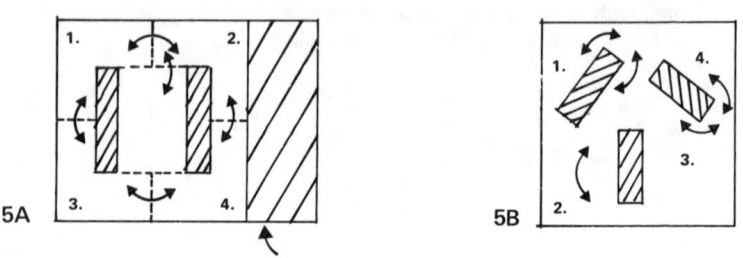

should include a perusal of the available literature and visits to other facilities in the local area. (See 3 and 4 below.)

3. The following books comprise a good introduction to the field of children center design. These books include a discussion of new on-site-built buildings, remodeled buildings, and factory-built modular buildings, and the relationship of financing to these three building types.

> *Patterns for Designing Childrens Centers.* New York: Educational Facilities Laboratories, 1971.
> *Schools for Early Childhood.* New York: Educational Facilities Laboratories, 1970.
> *Found Spaces and Equipment for Childrens Centers.* New York: Educational Facilities Laboratories, 1972.
> *Guide to Alternatives for Financing School Buildings.* New York: Educational Facilities Laboratories, 1971.
> *Schools, More Space/Less Money.* New York: Educational Facilities Laboratories, 1971.
> *Eveline Lowe Primary School.* Department of Education and Science, Great Britain. Building Bulletin 36, Her Majesty's Stationary Office, 1967.

All of the books, except *Eveline Lowe Primary School,* can be purchased from Educational Facilities Laboratories, 477 Madison Avenue, New York, New York 10022.

4. These books either discuss or show photos of outstanding facilities throughout the country. The examples are scattered geographically, so there should be a few that you can visit in your area. Other information on centers to visit would be available from the demonstration preschool at a local college or university, the local 4C office (Office of Health, Education, and Welfare) or the state office that handles preschool programs.

5. If the remodeling of an existing building is seriously contemplated, the local building inspector should be brought to the site for an inspection and report before any lease is signed. Interpretation of building codes regarding the housing of small children in an existing building is a highly subjective matter, and many buildings prove to be economically unfeasible when the necessary requirements are considered.

6. As a means to draw out the staff and parents on all program issues having an effect on the physical environment, I would strongly recommend Fred Osmon's book, *Patterns for Designing Children's Centers.* It covers the majority of issues in a way that encourages each group to develop a facility appropriate to its *own* particular requirements, but it does include a wide variety of solutions developed by others.

Chapter Eleven

CREATING INTERIOR SPACES FOR CHILD CARE

**Valerie Anixter
Alyson Kuhn**

Relatively few people in the field of day care have the exciting opportunity to design their own children's centers; most find themselves in the position of creating centers out of existing facilities, such as vacated public schools and church social halls. So rather than analyzing the particulars of a utopian children's center, this chapter will discuss how best to utilize available resources to create an interior that will nurture the total development—social, intellectual, personal, sensorial, and physical—of the children it will serve. Children are very sensitively attuned to their environment. Therefore designers of children's centers must pay special attention to creating a positive, cheerful, nonsterile, noninstitutional environment. A home-like atmosphere is desirable, because the center is the children's home for most of their waking hours. Austere, segregated bathrooms, staff-only institutional kitchens, and "regulation" furniture do not contribute to a warm, livable center.

Art work in this chapter by Sharon Skolnick and Alyson Kuhn.

THE ENTRANCE

The entrance(s) should be inviting and welcoming to the children, especially since many of them suffer some anxiety when their parents or other familiar figures leave them in an unknown situation. A massive, forbidding door into a dark entryway or a stark staircase is hardly reassuring. Decorate your door imaginatively. If you are actually choosing your own door, a partial or all-glass one has several points in its favor. Arriving children can see their peers within enjoying themselves, and, once inside, the children can see out and thus feel less shut in. In addition, the door serves as a source of a natural light, which also contributes to the children's feeling less confined. Transparent decals and plastic stained glass ornaments are attractive glass door decorations. If you must use a standard, heavy wooden door, paint it in brightly colored panels, free-form designs, or a castle facade. Perhaps the children would enjoy printing their names or drawing a favorite toy or pet on the door. If you cannot do anything permanent, one possibility is a fabric banner (again, designed and executed by the children) which could be hung up daily. If stairs led to the entrance, brightly painted bannisters are a necessity if the steps are not child-sized. The children might pot and care for plants along the staircase, or imprint or paint their hand and footprints and arrows on the pavement. The objective is to encourage the children to identify personally with the center, to enable them to feel it is "their place."

Practically speaking, keep the door mechanisms oiled to prevent irritating squeaks and sticking which make it difficult for the children to open and close the door unassisted. Similarly, if doorknobs or push-bars are at adult level, do provide footstools for the children. A hard-to-open door presents a frustrating barrier to children and contributes to feelings of confinement. The door's inner side is an excellent place for a bulletin board with announcements for parents.

WALLS

The biggest limitation on the versatility of wall space is a restricted imagination. If you are able to paint the walls, possible designs are the local skyline; an urban or rural scene, including various modes of transport; a detailed street map of your neighborhood; a map of Wonderland or the Land of Make Believe; nursery rhyme characters; or a fort or playhouse backdrop.

If you cannot do anything so radical but can repaint conventionally, be sure to choose a cheerful color, not a neutral and uninspiring one. The walls will unquestionably become battle-scarred. A darker color on the lower walls will disguise the dirt, while a lighter hue higher up will lighten and seemingly enlarge your space. As always, your primary consideration should be to satisfy the children's needs and tastes. It is absurd to have magnificently decorated walls which must be protected from the children, to restrict their behavior in order to preserve *your* decor.

Fabrics are also useful as wall coverings. Grass-cloth-look vinyl and burlap are durable, and an "upholstered wall" may break the monotony and give a special feel to one part of the room. Indian bedspreads are inexpensive; tie-dyed and batiked sheets have the added asset of being fun for the children to make. Such wall hangings lessen the institutional feel your walls may have. Fabrics can also be tacked to the ceiling to form canopies.

Walls have great potential as storage and display areas. Bulletin and cork boards, nailed or bolted onto the wall, or even built in as panels or suspended by ropes, are an effective means of mounting artworks. Tacks are difficult to use on plaster and wood and destructive as well, and tape tends to remove paint and to lose its stickiness. Cork and bulletin boards, however, are perfect for tacks and push-pins.

Pegboards can provide exposed and organized storage space for scissors, kitchen utensils, musical instruments, and dress-up clothes. Let the children decide where they want to keep things and place pegs accordingly. A storage arrangement that is logical to the children will help them to remember where materials belong; you can encourage them to put toys away by making it easy for them to do so. Small shelves that require precise stacking patterns and small drawers that get overloaded and stuck are discouraging and inefficient. Open shelves or cabinets on the wall save valuable floor space. A clothesline tacked onto the wall is handy for pinning up paintings or wet chalk drawings to dry, but make sure to spread some protective floor covering to catch drips. Actually, the children can keep all of their papers together on clips with their names, out of the way and safe from crinkling, but still visible, so that everyone can enjoy and comment on this daily changing art gallery.

WINDOWS

Windows are valuable assets, having the same merits as glass doors. They provide a link with the outside world, allow nature to overflow into the playroom, and are a source of natural light. Sometimes it is easy to forget that children are people. We do not condemn adults for rushing to the window to see accidents, fights, and parades, yet we often reprimand children for being concerned with happenings on the street. Everyday acts and typical passersby are worthy of scrutiny by children. Similarly, we admire living rooms and executive offices whose picture windows with good views allow us to enjoy the sunshine and the breeze and to watch the clouds and the rain. Is there any rationale for denying children such distractions?

Drapes or curtains have several advantages over shutters, shades, and blinds. The former are opened and drawn either manually, on metal or plastic curtain rings and rods, or with a simple pulley. Both are sturdy mechanisms, easy for children to use and understand, and relatively inexpensive to replace. Shutters, shades, and blinds on the other hand, are more fragile and complicated.

Of course, if your school is on a busy city street, you will probably look for a window covering that most effectively cuts off traffic noises; perhaps it will not be particularly desirable to use your windows as a source of ventilation, or perhaps they will not admit a significant amount of natural light. Conversely, if the sun pours in through the windows, making parts of the room uncomfortably warm, you will need a window covering that reflects rather than absorbs the heat, but does admit breezes. Similarly, in a room to be used for films, a covering which outside light cannot penetrate is desirable. This might also apply to a room in which children take their naps. Windows often opened for ventilation may need screens if bees, flies, or mosquitoes are a big problem in your area. If drafts are a problem, you will want heavy insulating curtains to warm up the room.

In choosing your windows, you may wish to consider the type that enables you to clean both sides from the inside. Disadvantages to these windows are that only half of each window opens and that their design prevents screening.

Sunny window sills are good spots for potted plants. Sills and frames are also excellent places for prisms, reflecting and transparent objects, tissue paper, cellophane, aluminum foil art projects, and plastic stained glass decorations. Once again you may have a window particularly well-suited for a clothesline on which to hang paintings to dry. Shelves may be extended from the sills to provide drying space for three-dimensional art projects. Large wooden storage chests with cushioned tops placed below windows do double duty as window seats which make lovely reading corners, or just quiet corners or sunny nap spots. Caged animals or those in terrariums would probably benefit from a spot near the sun and fresh air. If you inherit drab walls, investigate the possibility of painting all window frames and sills different colors.

Place yourself physically in the children's position and consider the windows' possible uses and drawbacks literally from their point of view.

CEILINGS

Ceilings also have some practical and decor-enriching uses. A light-colored ceiling heightens the room and reflects light well. If you are energetic, some ceiling painting possibilities are the solar system, sun and clouds, airplanes, helicopters, rockets, satellites, balloons, flying carpets, birds, and other sky travelers.

If you can leave adequately sized screw eyes or hooks in the ceiling, it will be a simple matter to hang and take down mobiles and potted plants with a crooked pole. If you can suspend a long dowel (broomstick) by means of a rope at each end, the children can use it as a support for sheet-tents, with no fear of collapse. Hula hoops can be suspended vertically from one point to form an indoor ball hoop, or laterally, by attaching ropes to four points on the hoop, to make a dress-up clothes rack, or a frame for a sheet to make a dressing room or a one- or two-person circular tent.

FLOORS

I consider floors to be perhaps the most important physical aspect of the entire center. Children walk, run, jump, sit, lie, somersault, and fall on the floors. Glue and juice and paint are spilled on them; crayons and cookies are ground into them; furniture is pushed across them. As always, the best way to approach the problem is by considering child behavior and then choosing floor coverings that conform to it. Since the floors serve many purposes, versatility is the key word.

Cement floors are very cold on feet and other body parts, even through tennis shoes and long pants, and walking on such a surface all day long is extremely fatiguing to the legs. Cement is also one of the most painful surfaces for children's inevitable stumbles and falls, and disastrous from an acoustical standpoint. Linoleum or wood floors are an improvement, being somewhat softer and warmer surfaces. They are also good surfaces for jacks, ball bouncing, toy trucks, wheel toys, and dancing.

Rugs are of course the most comfortable covering on which to lie and fall, and they also help to absorb noise. Unfortunately, they also absorb dirt and spills and are more difficult to clean than linoleum. Area rugs are good for quiet activities, particularly story telling, and they are practical because there is relatively little wear on them in such situations. If your entire room is carpeted, acquire big rubber or plastic sheets to place under craft tables and easels, perhaps even under eating areas. Have assorted sizes of protective sheets and rugs so that you can adapt your floor space precisely to your needs, as determined by the number of children involved in a given activity.

Cushions are an alternative to rugs. Each child could have his own pillow, perhaps decorated by his mother according to his specifications. Cushions large enough to accommodate several children comfortably effectively create activity islands for story telling or make-believe games. Quilts, blankets, foam rubber, and mattresses are other possible temporary floor coverings for gymnastics and roughhousing.

Chalk lines are a good way of temporarily designating activity areas. I worked in one school where the teacher drew a chalk circle for each child to sit in during story time and thus effectively eliminated shoving and shifting of positions.

In another school the wood floor was painted bright glossy yellow, which beautifully brightened an otherwise dark room.

CLEAN-UP

You can eliminate a great deal of the wear and tear on the floors by sensitizing the children, not by attempting to restrict their actions or sophisticate their behavior by imposing your values, but by helping them discover the advantages of cleaning up slippery messes, of avoiding spills, and of picking up obstacles. When the children complain about sitting on a gritty floor or finding a sticky spot on a blanket, raise the question of how the dirt got there and how it could have been avoided. If adults silently clean up after children, the children cannot be expected to comprehend what is involved and to exercise prudence.

To help involve the children in cleaning, do not keep all your cleaning supplies in a locked closet. Strong chemicals must be kept out of children's reach, but if you show the children how to use a broom and dust pan and sponge, how to make warm soapy water, and where to find paper towels and rags, you will increase their self-sufficiency and decrease your domestic duties. The children should not be made to feel like visitors in what is actually their home, nor should they be treated as guests. I strongly oppose allowing children to leave the dirty work for the custodial or teaching staff. If you let the children feel that the center is their center, they will treat the surroundings with greater pride and respect. (Adolescents who carve their names and thoughts into high school bathroom doors and desk tops and books do not vandalize their own homes.)

I am presently working in a preschool located in facilities used in the evenings for meetings and slide presentations. Consequently, all the preschool equipment must be put away daily, a procedure that occupies four teachers for close to a half-hour. I maintain that the children should be taught to stack their own little noncollapsing chairs, to stack the large cardboard blocks in the storage room, to rearrange books, puzzles, and wooden blocks in their folding cabinets, to wipe up their own spilt juice, and to put all the dolls back in the baby buggy. The teachers are even expected to amass forgotten shoes, socks, and sweaters from the playground. I honestly feel that the children would enjoy doing many of the tasks which teachers unthinkingly execute, such as putting paper cups on the juice tray. My experience has demonstrated the saying that children who are given responsibility become responsible. They also develop a sense of empathy with the teachers, rather than placing superhuman demands on them and regarding them as arbitrary authorities.

The lists and designs are included to give the reader specific suggestions for materials and equipment.

SUGGESTED EQUIPMENT AND AREAS

Framework tepee
Food and fun table
Hideout
Domes
Crawl
Storage
Nets
Drums
Bins
Phonograph in sick or rest area

Adhesive vinyl in designs
Carpet
Colors
Strips to define wall areas
Water Containers

Nature objects
Art objects
Science experiments
Bilingual labels with the object pictured hung around the room
Reading materials (child level)
Couches
Laundry baskets for containers
Umbrellas inverted and hung for visual effect, or see-through umbrellas raised by a rope and used for containers
Steps, platform, slides
Cloth wall hanging with pouch pockets
Boxes for play, seats, containers

All the above should be mobile. The room then has unlimited possibilities and changes can be made every few months.

Figure 11.1 Suspended Book Shelves: Hemp canvas with masonite or aluminum, or ½-inch plywood shelves and brass grommets and wood screws.

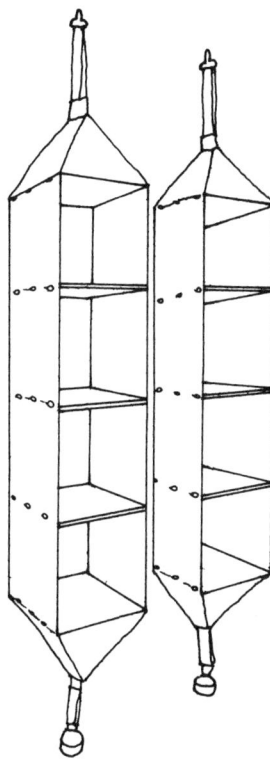

Figure 11.2 Hexagon Table Supports: You can vary sizes and materials.

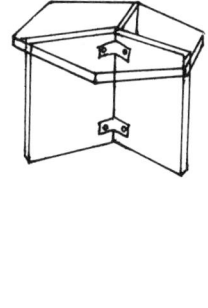

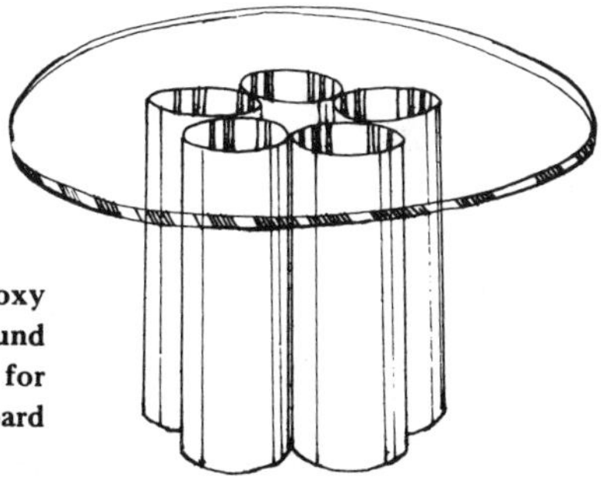

Figure 11.3 Fiber Tube: Epoxy together and paint 36-inch round tops. Fiber Drum (barrel): for a one-unit base or cardboard box.

Figure 11.4 Folding Hanging Cradle or Swing

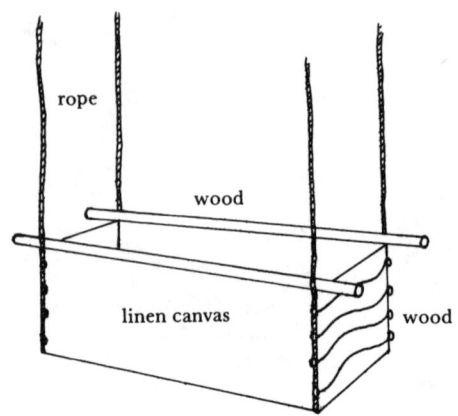

Figure 11.5 Collapsible Table and Drawer

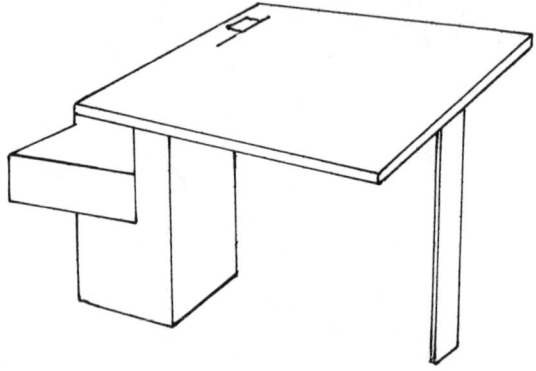

Figure 11.6 Cardboard Laced Room Dividers or Play Areas: Punch 3/8-inch diameter holes and space the holes at 1/2-inch intervals. Locate corners first and work toward the center.

Lacing pieces of cardboard with holes punched or drilled around the edges is easy and the child may help. Marine nylon rope is expensive but rope or hemp is cheap. The latter can be dyed different colors. Vinyl-covered clothesline is best because there is no fraying.

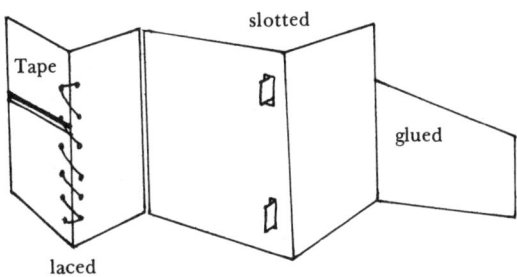

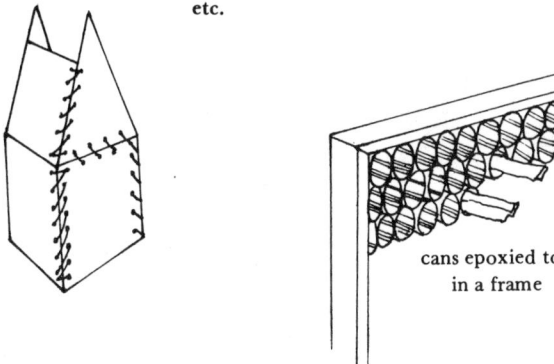

Figure 11.7 Tin Can Storage Units. Staggered or in-line, this unit will store rolled-up posters, etc.

Figure 11.8 Look-In Fantasy Box: Paint costumes on the inside walls of a wood or cardboard box. Cut look-in holes at different levels.

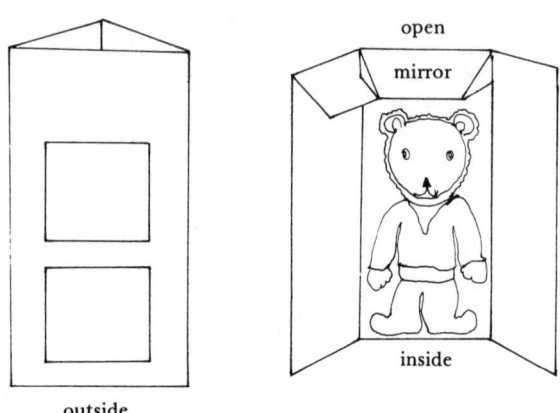

Figure 11.9 Heat Unit for Art Work: Insert for heating unit in a table used to melt crayons or wax. The plug can be in the wall or floor.

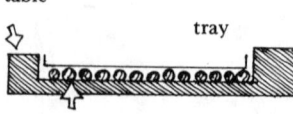

Figure 11.10 Table With Compartments for Art Supplies: Children may stand around the table and work together.

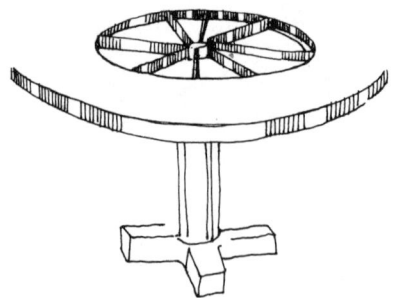

Figure 11.11 Cardboard Carpentry, Slotted or Glued

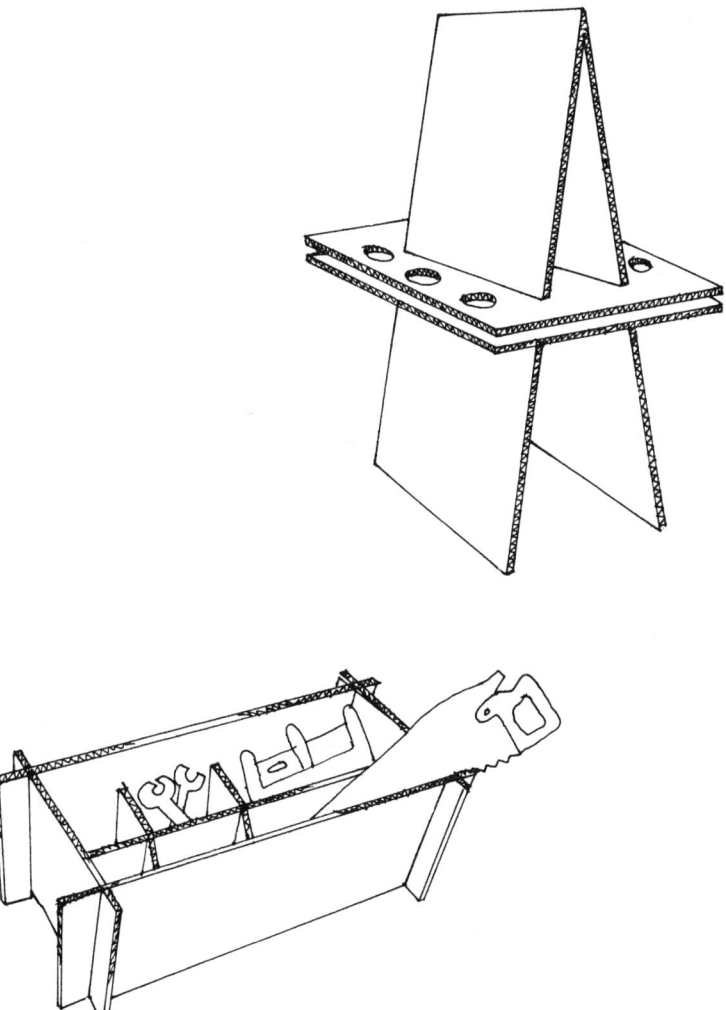

Figure 11.12 Simple Work Table

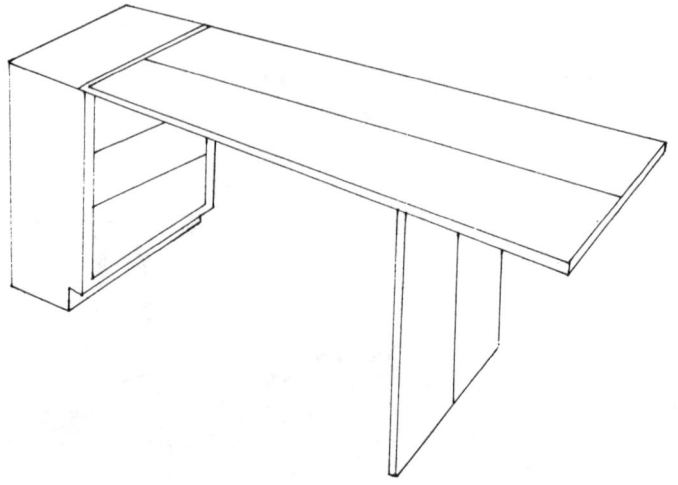

Figure 11.13 Square Tin Oil Storage Drum Wall Hanging Unit

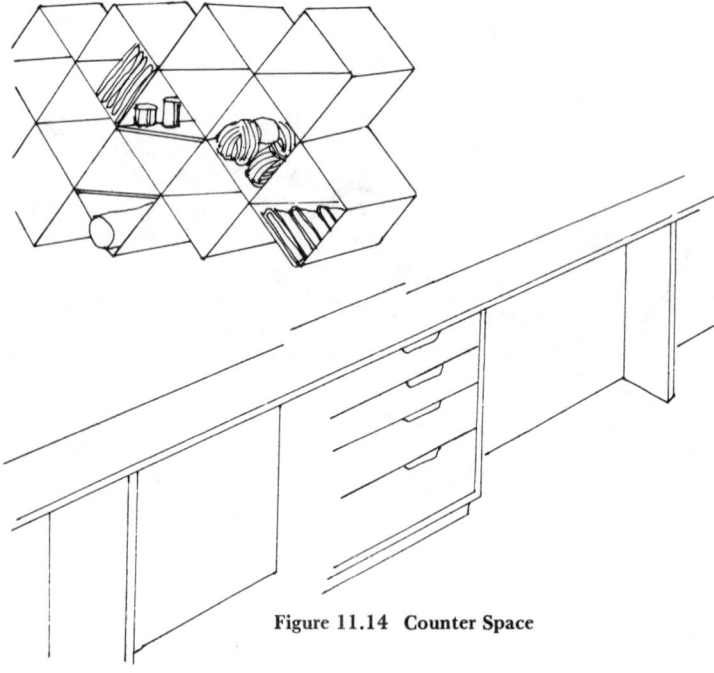

Figure 11.14 Counter Space

Figure 11.15 Playdesk and Three Toy Boxes on Castors: Three-quarter-inch plywood or chipboard painted bright colors. This unit can be covered with polyurethane foam cushions or fabric for seating and or storage.

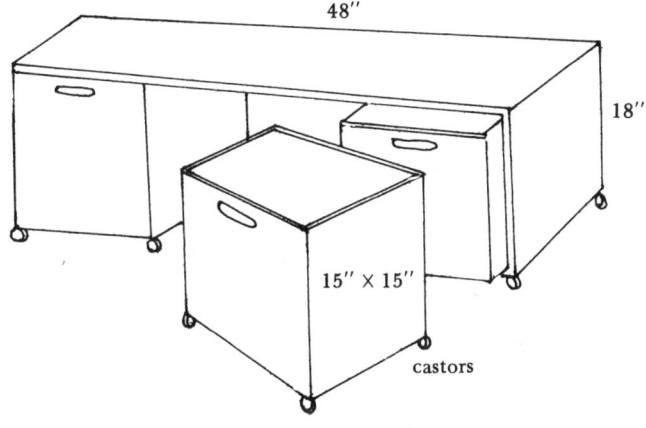

Figure 11.16 Blackboard/Easel and Crawl-in Playhouse

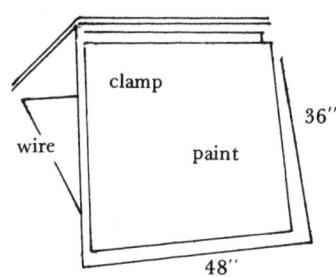

Figure 11.17 Stools or Tables With Wood Base and Formica Top: When one is turned, they fit together.

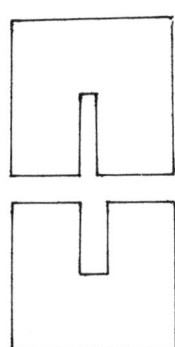

Figure 11.18 Appliance Boxes or Fiber Barrels: These boxes are available free! Paint designs, pictures, letters, numbers, and symbols, and cut windows and doors with a mat knife. The children can then build their own structures and spaces with privacy.

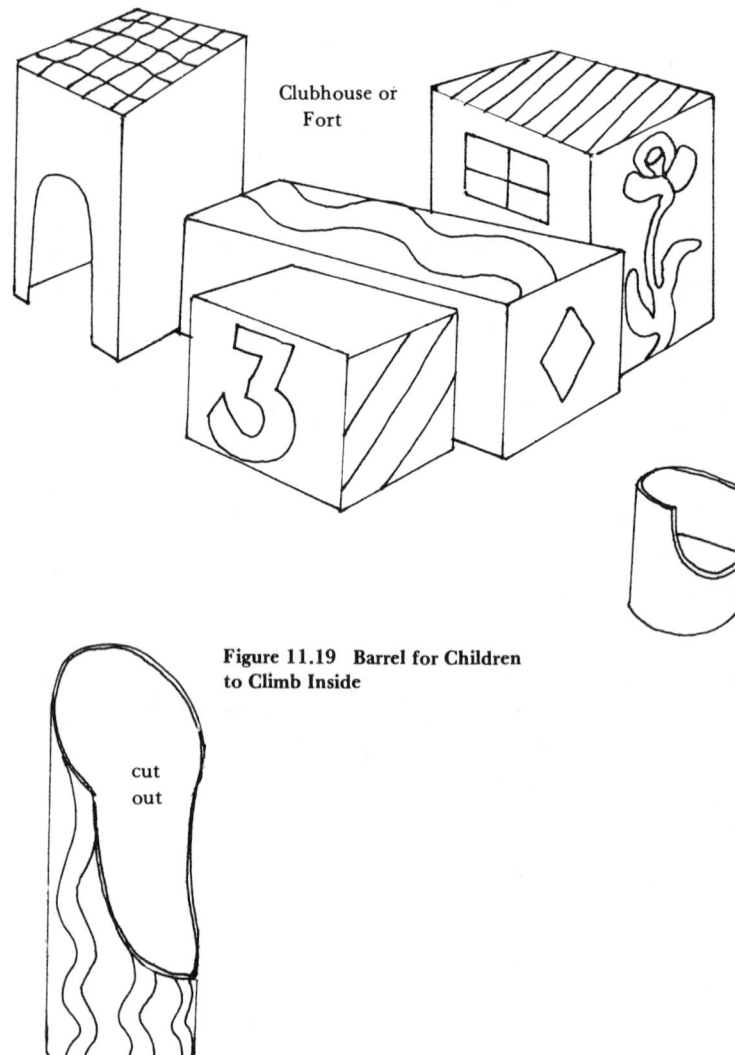

Figure 11.19 Barrel for Children to Climb Inside

Figure 11.20 Corrugated cardboard boxes will support up to 400 pounds. They are self-fastening but may also be glued, taped, or slotted. They can be used for bases or containers on the floor because they are a child's height.

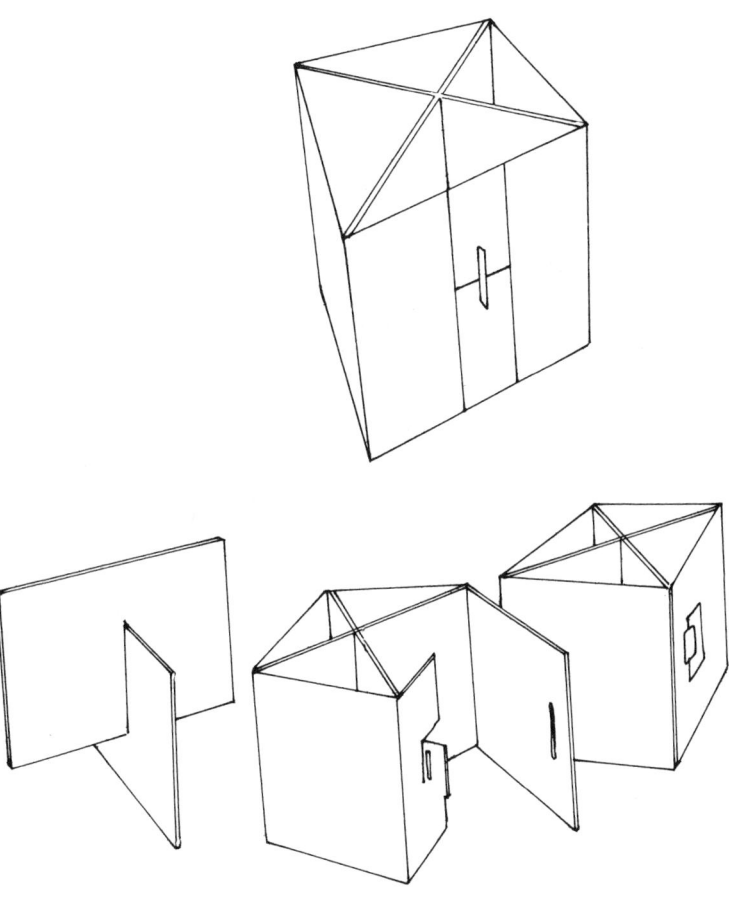

Figure 11.21 Play Equipment Design

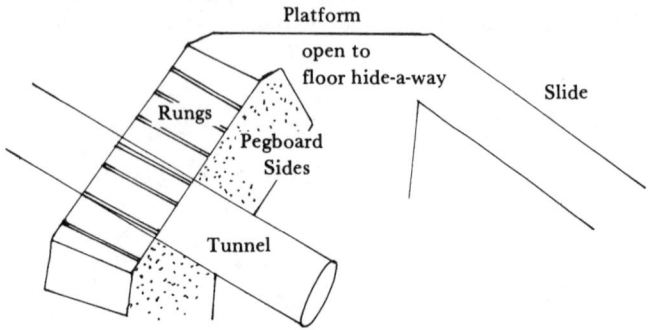

Figure 11.22 Barrels Full of Cornstarch on Flat Surface

Figure 11.23 Umbrella Catch-All

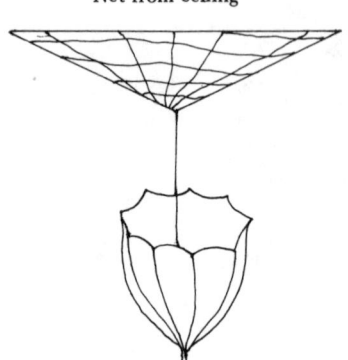

Figure 11.24 Clothes and Utility Closet: This drawing shows how to turn the dead end of a room into a clothes and utility closet with 4 × 8 foot plywood, ¾-inch fiber chipboards, 2 × 8 foot uprights, and 1½- or 2-inch steel pipe clothes rods. The entire unit can be hidden by a floor-to-ceiling curtain on a track in front.

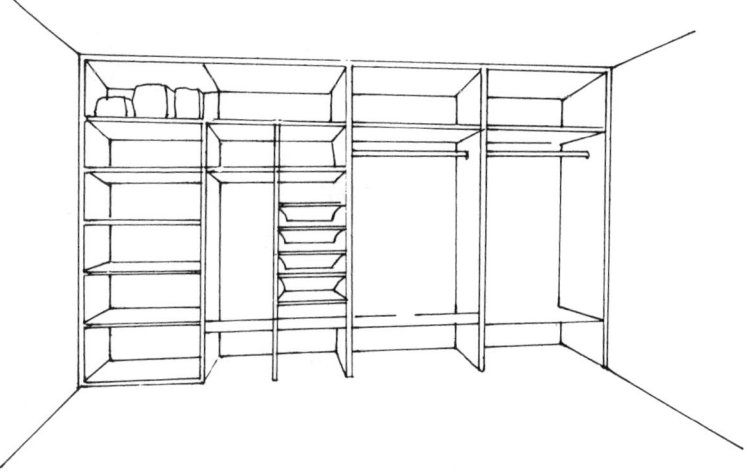

Figure 11.25 Japanese Paper Lanterns for Lighting: There is no wire. The lanterns are taped together and are hung from hooks and eyes. Christmas tree lights with white frosted bulbs are used inside and plugged into the floor outlet. The string of lights is placed inside an electric or gas dryer hose in white, 6-foot lengths.

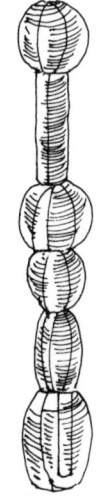

Chapter Twelve

DESIGNING STIMULATING ENVIRONMENTS FOR CHILDREN

Gloria Marshak Weissberg

Each season we live in a new and unique moment of the universe, a moment that never was before and will never be again. And what do we teach our children in school? We teach them that two and two make four, and that Paris is the capital of France. When will we also teach them what they are: You are a marvel. You are unique. In all the world there is no other child exactly like you. In the millions of years that have passed, there never has been another child exactly like you. And look at your body—what a wonder it is! Your legs, your arms, your cunning fingers, the way you move. You may become a Shakespeare, a Michelangelo, a Beethoven. You have the capacity for anything. Yes, you are a marvel.

Pablo Casals

Each day care facility has its unique flavor related to the community's location, values, and objectives. Therefore the first step in planning is to speak at length to the director, the teachers, the paraprofessionals, and the parents, as well as to the children. Observe the community in its streets and if possible in its home. While in fact each day care environment is a unique organism that grows out of the needs of its members, there are common objectives and creative concepts that apply to all such centers. Integrating general design concepts into the uniqueness of the community ideals is no easy matter. It requires a fresh approach in each project. A learning environment integrates floors, walls, doors, windows, ceilings, lighting, color, learning materials, and furnishings into an actual vital learning experience through which children adventure. Organize this space in an inconspicuous structure related to the daily requirement of children and adult helpers, keeping in mind that a day care center is not a classroom.

With an optimum budget the learning place can be an acre and a half of things like book gardens and vegetable gardens, fireplaces and sunken forums, inside drawbridges and outside scribble walls, tunnels and ladders and ramps, light places and dark places, quiet places and loud ones, hard and soft. It's a place with textures to feel and music to hear, things scattered around to eat, experiments to be made, and matchings and testings. It's a weather station and a dry creek bed, a wood shop and water places and sand places, and places made of color and others made of shapes. And places to be alone.

However, don't be dismayed if you are working within a limited budget, because creative integration of the environment can also be achieved on a mini-budget.

To design the optimum environment for teaching the very young, translate the following concepts into a learning place:

1. Use the environment to develop children's motor skills and their understanding of the ways they can affect different places in the center as they go about their different activities. Begin here by thinking vertically; create levels, ramps, circular spaces, big and small. Create spaces suited to the activity area and size of children.

2. Use the environment to liberate ideas about the creation and formation of objects surrounding the child,

ultimately to generate questions. Have areas where children can build environments of things and then take them apart without being told that this activity is destructive. Reinforced cartons of various sizes painted colors would serve well. Or a truck-load of junk can provide the materials with which to start.

3. Incorporate in the environment concepts such as up, down, under, over, near, far, etc.—prerequisites to learning reading and writing and understanding numbers. Window shades attached to ceilings can contain this information and can be rolled away when not in use. Styrofoam circles, squares, and triangles can be hung from the ceiling not only as decorations, but also to teach shape concepts. Arrows pointing in different directions on the walls, ceiling, and floor can teach directions of up, down, left and right. Use your imagination.

4. Create an environment through which children grow aware of their own feelings about physical space, people space, nature space, and respect for space. Talk about feelings children may have in various places of the environment. Encourage respect for their feelings, and encourage the child to seek out special places when they feel special ways.

5. Create an environment that facilitates learning through the senses of seeing, smelling, touching, hearing, and tasting. These are primary ways of learning for the very young, and careful creative thought is required. The cooking/eating area, where possible, should be in the center of the room. It can be partially sunken or counters may be regulated at different heights. Kids should have access to this area at all times (as they are at home). They may wander in or out, observe the preparation of their food, assist in preparation, pick up a snack or cook.

On pegboard panels, outline objects commonly used by children; scissors, brushes, yardsticks, right angles, etc. This will assist them in seeing and recognizing shapes as well as in putting objects back where they belong. Use large floor-to-ceiling mirrors on walls so they appreciate the way they look throughout the day. Create a special area covered with zillions of textures on all surfaces, vertical and horizontal. This area can be a tunnel which older children help to construct. The materials can be picked up in remnant shops and junk yards.

6. Use color to affect learning. Orange, red, green, and purple are colors that motivate children. Recent research indicates that skillful use of colors in a child's environment may help to increase his or her IQ. Don't be afraid to use more than one color in an area. Doors can be one color, baseboards a second color, walls different colors, floors a neutral color, and so on. Quiet colors such as blues and brown should be used in reading and listening places. Colored light bulbs can immediately change any area. Colors can be used as guidelines and in instruction. They can be used large scale with mobile forms suspended from ceilings, in supergraphics as toys and games, and on mobile partitions or on walls. Color alone can transform a dull space into a vital surrounding.

7. Create spaces that are commonly flexible by using multipurpose furnishings; cubes of varying sizes can be used in place of tables and chairs. They can be stacked and moved; they can be used to create environments built by children; they can be used to develop ideas of order and utility; they can be sat in and on. Sleeping mats can double for gym mats if pads are constructed of 2-inch rubber foam covered by colorful vinyls.

A physical environment for a young child may be facilitating or frustrating. An environment in which a young child can embark independently on a variety of play activities fosters a sense of adequacy.

In this area children work independently (Figure 12-1). Metal letter trays are organized with materials for different activities such as coloring and pasting or cutting and pasting. These trays are accessible to children when hung

Figure 12.1

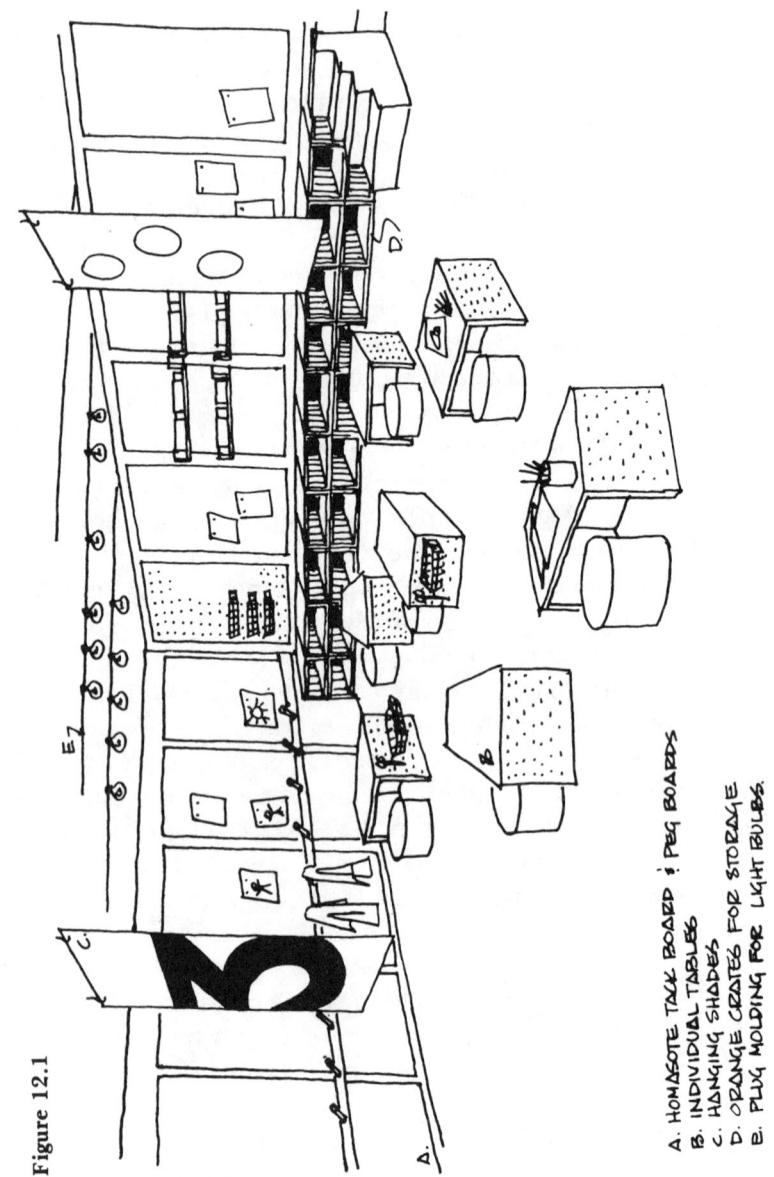

A. HOMASOTE TACK BOARD ; PEG BOARDS
B. INDIVIDUAL TABLES
C. HANGING SHADES
D. ORANGE CRATES FOR STORAGE
E. PLUG MOLDING FOR LIGHT BULBS.

from pegboards. A child may take the baskets and hang them from the side of his or her desk, which can also be made of pegboard. The tables, if placed on their front sides and put together, can be used for private places for children to sit. The circular stools can be stacked and played with in the environment center.

Above the storage units, which can be made of orange crates and either left natural and varnished or painted bright colors, you can fasten panels of pegboard and homasote (a compressed paper that serves as a tack board and is available at lumber yards in 4 x 8 sheets). These panels can be painted alternate colors.

More homasote panels can be used to hang children's work or learning information. Dowels placed on a 3 x 3 board provide a hanging place for aprons and smocks. Two of many window shades containing the three concepts can be pulled down. Window shades are easy to install and you can either paint directly on the surface with acrylic paint or apply cutout designs from contact paper. The learning concepts placed on these shades are easily changed by pulling up the shade. They also serve as dividers. Remember, all objects and materials utilized in the design must recognize children's dimensions.

PAINTING, CLAY, AND PLANT CENTER

If your center has windows, be sure to use that area for a garden (Figure 12-2). A large planter box built of plywood and painted a vibrant color can be filled with mulch. Children can put their own individual plants within the larger container. Also, plants can be removed and placed outdoors in spring and summer so that children can see enormous growth and gain pride in their own efforts. Seasonal botanical information can be posted on the adjoining walls in forms cut out of foam core. These cutouts can be made by the children or the teacher. The forms hung from

Figure 12.2

A. FOME CORE MOBILES ¦ SPACE DIVIDERS
B. GARDEN CENTER.
C. ARTS ¦ CRAFTS/CLAY STORAGE TABLES.

the ceiling can also be made of foam core. This simple material can be used for all sorts of learning. The forms can be hung from fishing tackle attached to a cup hook which is simply put into the ceiling.

The clay work tables are easily constructed from water pipes and cut-out plywood. Drawing wall boards are built by making two V-shaped hangers into which you place a roll of newspaper print. A board placed at the lower level allows children to tear off their work after they are completed. The area is lined with homasote and pegboard for storage as well as for hanging up individual work. Again, the panels can be painted different colors to make a cheerful environment.

THE COOKING FACILITY—THE CENTER OF THE DAY CARE ENVIRONMENT

If you can start with the cooking facility in the center of the day care environment you will have many advantages (Figure 12-3). The people who prepare the food can assist in providing warmth and companionship to the children as well as in teaching them the vital activities a child would otherwise learn at home. This time-consuming meal preparation does not remove paraprofessionals from the charge of children. There is no doubt that the kitchen is the center for young children. This open area eventually allows children to help in the kitchen where he may learn to measure, cook, count, familiarize himself with textures and sizes of objects and a realization of his personal needs.

Twenty-four-inch counters can serve as additions to arts and crafts centers; if they are contiguous to these centers, the initial cost of plumbing will be reduced. In addition, these counters can be used for eating surfaces with different height stools. Children can assist in serving and removing food. Therefore, the aide's time is freed to be

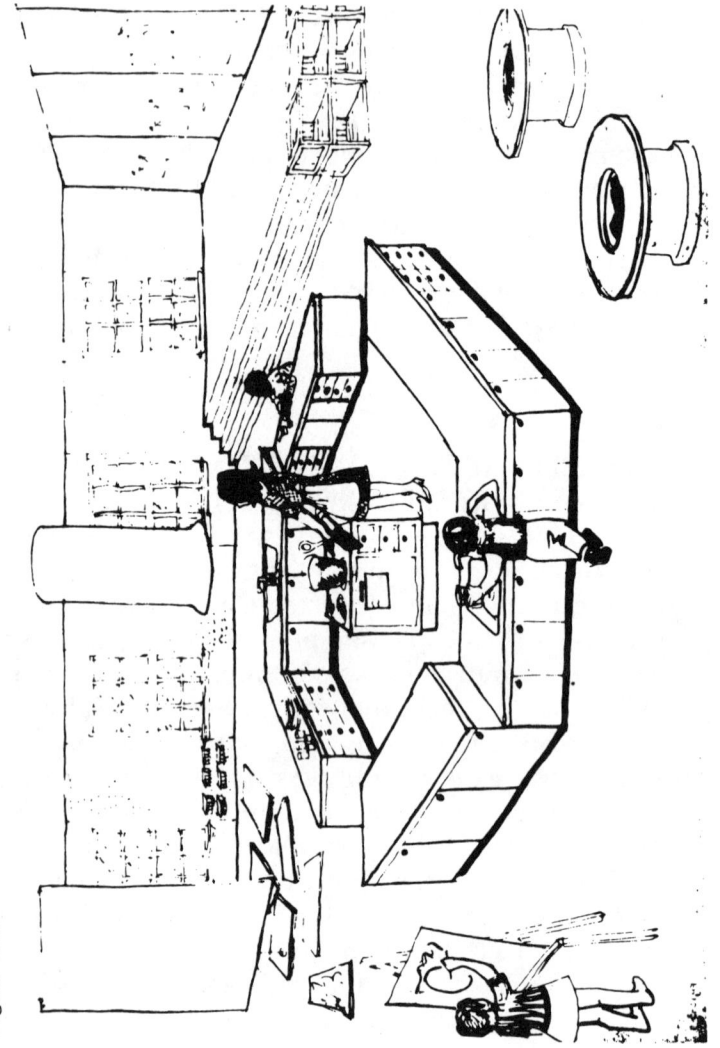

Figure 12.3

with the child rather than to serve the child, while the child learns independence.

If you're building a completely new kitchen and you have a small budget, visit your local wholesale kitchen supply house and ask for seconds or slightly damaged units. You can always paint the entire kitchen. In fact, color-coded drawers and storage units can help children to learn to put things in their proper places.

A MULTIPURPOSE PLATFORM AREA

Levels can be created with platforms into which storage compartments are built (Figure 12-4). The levels can be carpeted, and 2-inch foam (Omalon) placed under the carpet provides a secondary sleeping area. If you have a small budget, paint the platforms in bright deck paint. This can be an area where children and teacher sit during story time. Or children may come here and read, look at picture books, or listen to music. The homasote panels can contain pictures of storybook characters. Or if the children wish to put on a play, they can create backdrop scenery and tack the pictures on to the panels. In addition, window shades can be used again for learning, scenery, stage curtain, or storybook characters. When you are faced with a small space, always try to fit more than one activity into one center by clever use of different floor levels and by varying ceiling colors or textures within the center.

THE BATHROOM ENVIRONMENT

Think of the bathroom as a place children can learn good hygiene, then make it possible for them to do so (Figure 12-5). When possible, vanities should be designed for children's height. If you're faced with an old bathroom, build a sturdy platform and cover it with indoor-outdoor

Figure 12.4

READING/STAGE AREA WITH STORAGE SPACE BELOW

Figure 12.5

carpeting, or paint it with deck enamel. If you are starting from scratch, use tile or vinyl flooring. If the existing vinyl floor is dull, first thoroughly wash off all dirt and old wax and let the floor dry. Then paint it with Benjamin Moore Impervo enamel paint. After the floor dries, brush or roll on two coats of a clear plastic sealer.

Think about painting the entire wall behind the vanities a coordinated color on which you can paste bathroom articles. The articles, such as soap, toothpaste, and combs, can be designed first on contact paper, then attached to the brightly painted wall. Place mirrors cut in the shape of children's heads over the vanity, or put a full-size mirror cut in the shape of the child on another wall.

Hygiene cubbies placed on simple shelving may be used for each child's personal supplies. These hygiene cubbies, made of milk containers cut at a diagonal can be painted and labeled by each child with the help of the teacher. Label all articles to acquaint children with the name of the object and its spelling. Labeling with presstype lettering, available at all art supplies stores, facilitates this job. A simple supergraphic to cover walls that require painting enhances what otherwise would be a dull space. Remember, children spend time in this place.

Of course this is just a start. If you want your children to be creative, surround them with creative ideas within this unified environment. When you look at your space try to think of walls, ceilings, floors, and doors as vertical and horizontal forms on which you hang other vertical, horizontal, circular, or triangular forms to give dimension to the space. These forms have a dynamic quality, especially when painted colors that integrate the space.

If possible, light separate areas with different light systems, making some areas bright, others quiet. Colored bulbs give unique quality to an area and dimmers provide a soft, restful atmosphere when children are resting.

Most of the furniture can be made by the community. Tables can be made of plywood in different shapes or as described in this chapter. Clay tables, multipurpose stools, and storage units can be made of fruit crates. Costly manufactured furnishings will wipe out your budget. Incorporate the community's personality into the design of the center. For example, if children are from Spanish-speaking homes, label things in both English and Spanish. Utilize colors favored by the children in your community. Purple, a color white people shy away from, is enjoyed by all children. If children in your community require active movements, allocate space where they can feel free to move their bodies. Hang punching bags from the ceiling and chinning bars between doors.

In a carefully planned learning environment, each of the many aspects work together in a synergistic effect. Each detail has its own reason for being and acts in conjunction with other details; thus a total harmony of action is created. The whole of the environment is greater than any of its individually defined parts.

Figure 12.6

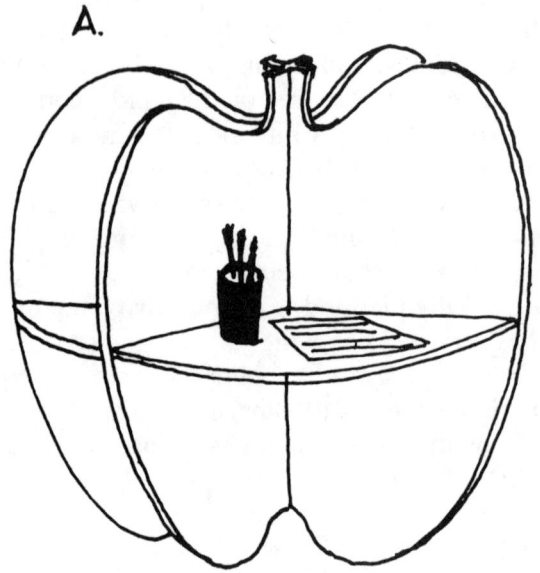

APPLE DESK

A. THIS DESK AREA OR PLAYFORM CAN BE CONSTRUCTED OF PLYWOOD, HOMASOTE BOARD OR FOME-CORE, DEPENDING ON THE STABILITY AND/OR DURABILITY REQUIRED.

TWO 4'×4' PIECES ARE REQUIRED — CUT OUT AS YOU WOULD A FOLDING STAND-UP CHRISTMAS TREE MADE OF CONSTRUCTION PAPER:

Figure 12.7

B. THIS LIGHT TRACK (PLUG STRIP) IS AVAILABLE FROM MOST ELECTRICAL COMANIES. IT CAN BE INSTALLED IN CEILING OR WALL AND USED AS A VISUAL AID TO HELP CHILDREN IDENTIFY GROUPS OR NUMBERS. FOR EXAMPLE, THREE LIGHT BULBS CAN BE PLUGGED IN NEXT TO A GRAPHIC NUMBER THREE TO HELP WITH ASSOCIATION.

C. COMFORTABLE SLEEPING PADS CAN BE MADE FROM SIX YARDS OF COLORFUL CANVAS FABRIC FILLED WITH EITHER A 1 INCH THICK FOAM RUBBER PAD OR COTTON KAPOK.

Figure 12.8

D. ART & CRAFTS / CLAY STORAGE TABLE

D. CLAY STORAGE TABLES CAN BE MADE FROM SECTIONS OF SEWER OR SIMILAR PIPING, BY PUTTING A CIRCULAR PIECE OF PLYWOOD WITH A HOLE CUT IN IT OVER THE TOP. THE WOOD SHOULD BE SANDED VERY SMOOTH, AND COVERED WITH SHELLAC OR BRIGHT LACQUER COLORS TO AVOID SPLINTERS. AT THE END OF THE DAY, THE STORAGE HOLE CAN BE COVERED OVER WITH A HEAVY PLASTIC TO KEEP THE CLAY FROM DRYING OUT.

Figure 12.9

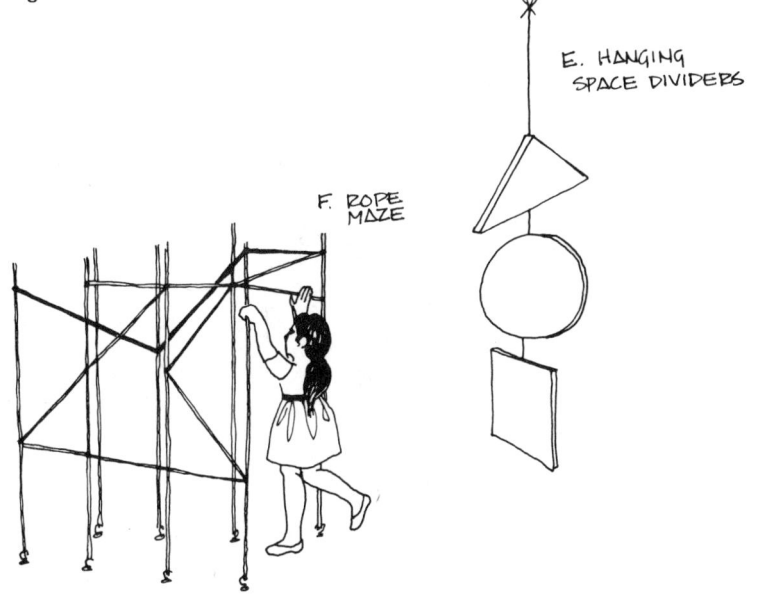

E. ONE OF THE GREATEST MATERIALS IN THE WORLD FOR HANGING ROOM DIVIDERS IS FOME-CORE, AVAILABLE AT ARCHITECTURAL SUPPY STORES OR AT ART STORES. IT IS EASILY CUT WITH A SHARP KNIFE, IS EXTREMELY LIGHT AND IS PAINTED EASILY.

F. THE ROPE MAZE IS OFFERED HERE AS AN AID TO SPACE CONCEPT. BY ATTACHING CUP HOOKS TO FLOOR AND CEILING AND STRINGING THE ROPES IN DIFFERENT SHAPES AND SIZES, YOU CAN CONSTRUCT A "TRANSPARENT" BUILDING INTO WHICH CHILDREN CAN CRAWL AND PERHAPS ATTACH THE ROPES THEMSELVES TO CREATE DIFFERENT KINDS OF SPACES.

Figure 12.10

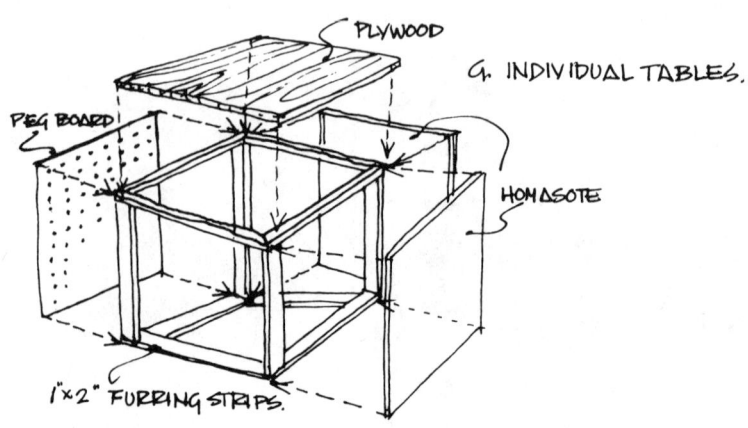

G. INDIVIDUAL TABLES.

G. INDIVIDUAL TABLES CAN BE MADE FROM 12-18" PIECES OF 1"x2" FURRING STRIP, 1 18"x18" PIECE OF PEG BOARD, 2 · 18"x18" PIECES OF HOMASOTE BOARD (TACK SURFACE), AND 1 18"x18" PIECE OF 1/2" PLYWOOD, HAMMERED TOGETHER WITH LONG, THIN FINISHING NAILS OR TACKS. AS WITH ALL WOOD, IT SHOULD BE SANDED AND LACQUERED OR PAINTED TO PREVENT SPLINTERS.
MIRROR SURFACES (18"x18") CAN ALSO BE ATTACHED BY TAPING THE EDGES AND USING CONTACT CEMENT TO ATTACH IT TO THE FRAME.

Figure 12.11

H. HANGING SHADES MAKE WONDERFUL ROOM DIVIDERS. THEY ARE ATTACHED EASILY TO THE CEILING WITH SCREW EYES OR CUP HOOKS AND CAN BE PAINTED WITH ANY DESIGN. THEY CAN ALSO BE USED AS BACKDROPS FOR PLAY PRODUCTION.

Figure 12.12

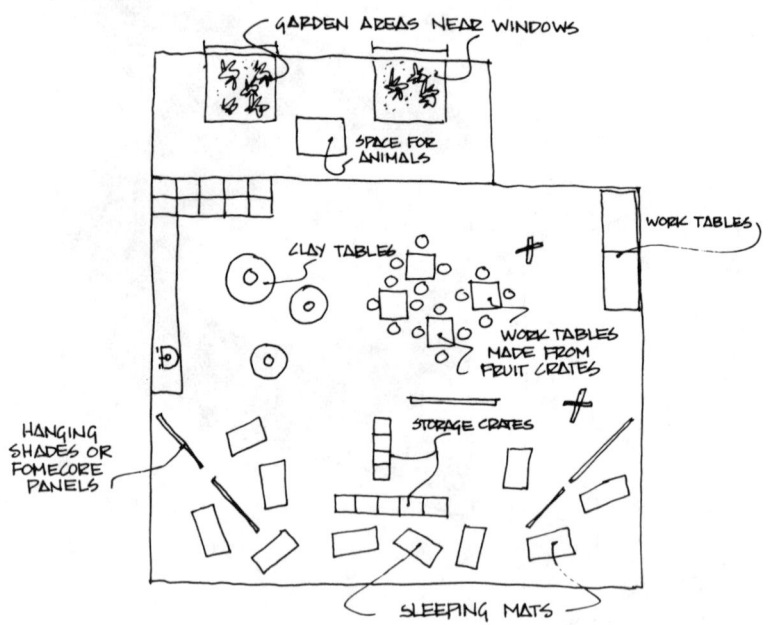

Figure 12.13

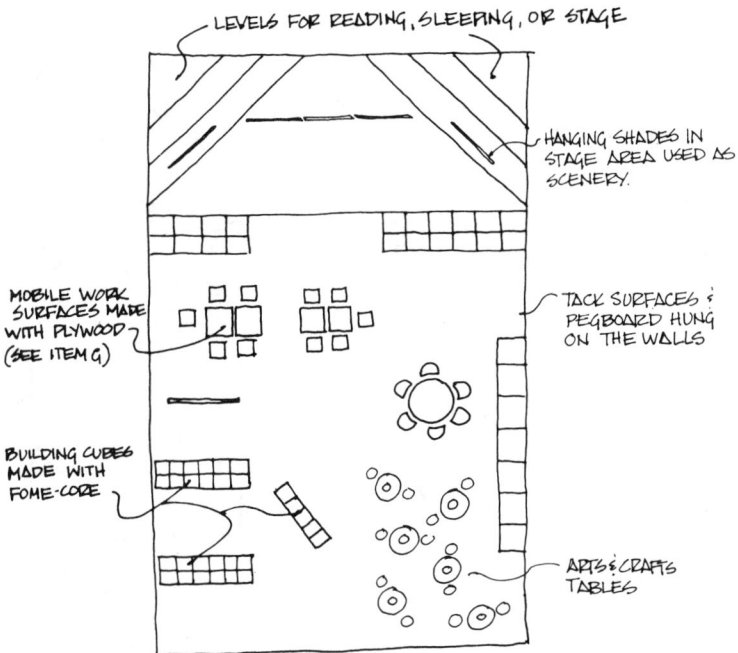

Figure 12.14

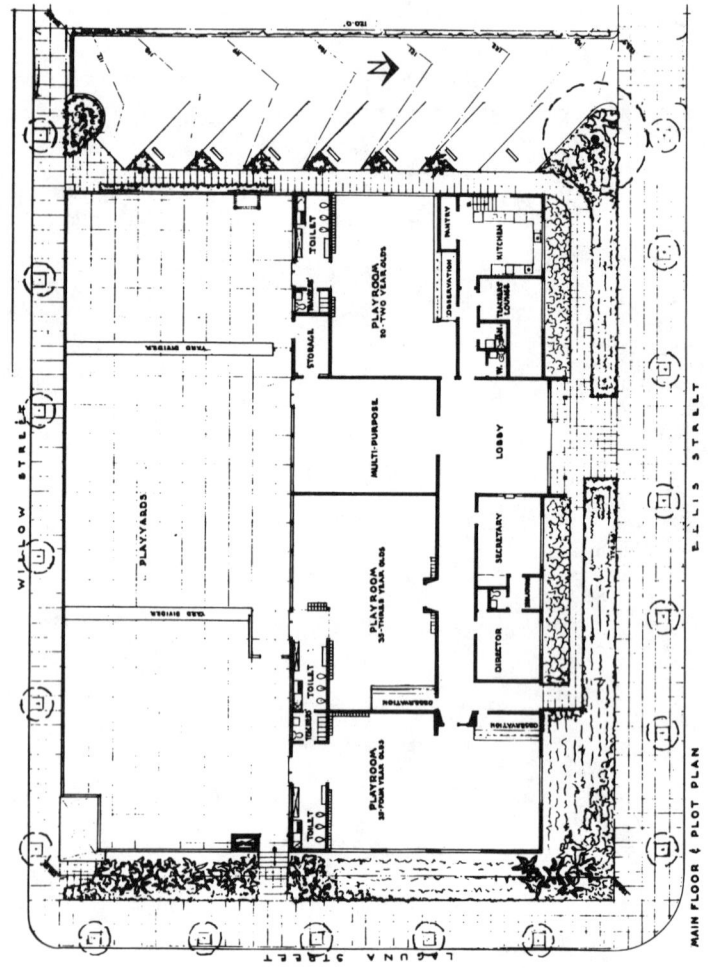

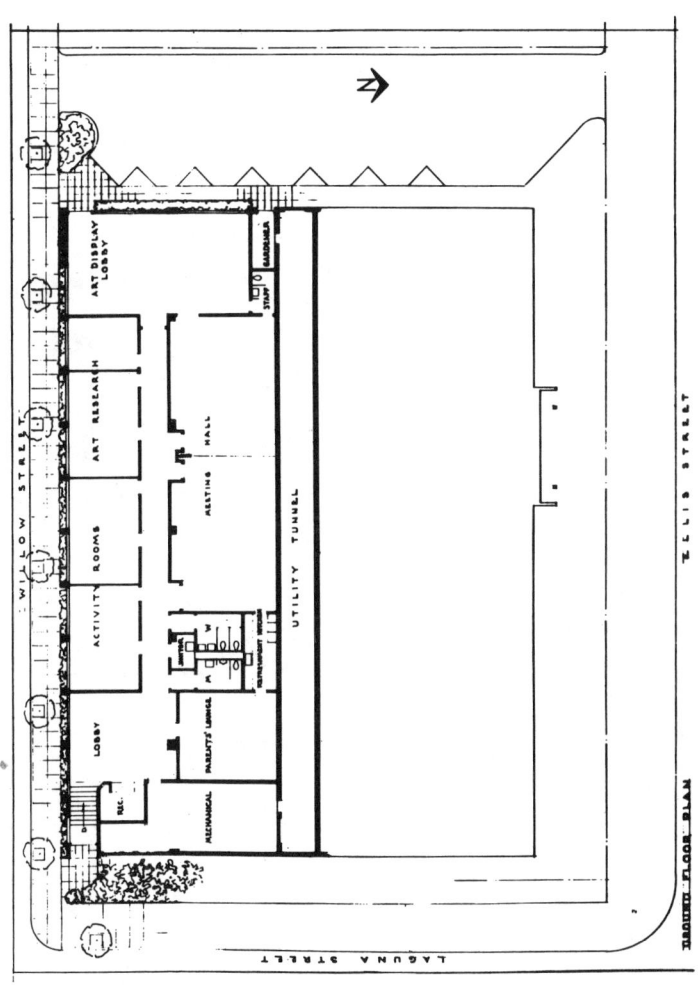

Figure 12.15

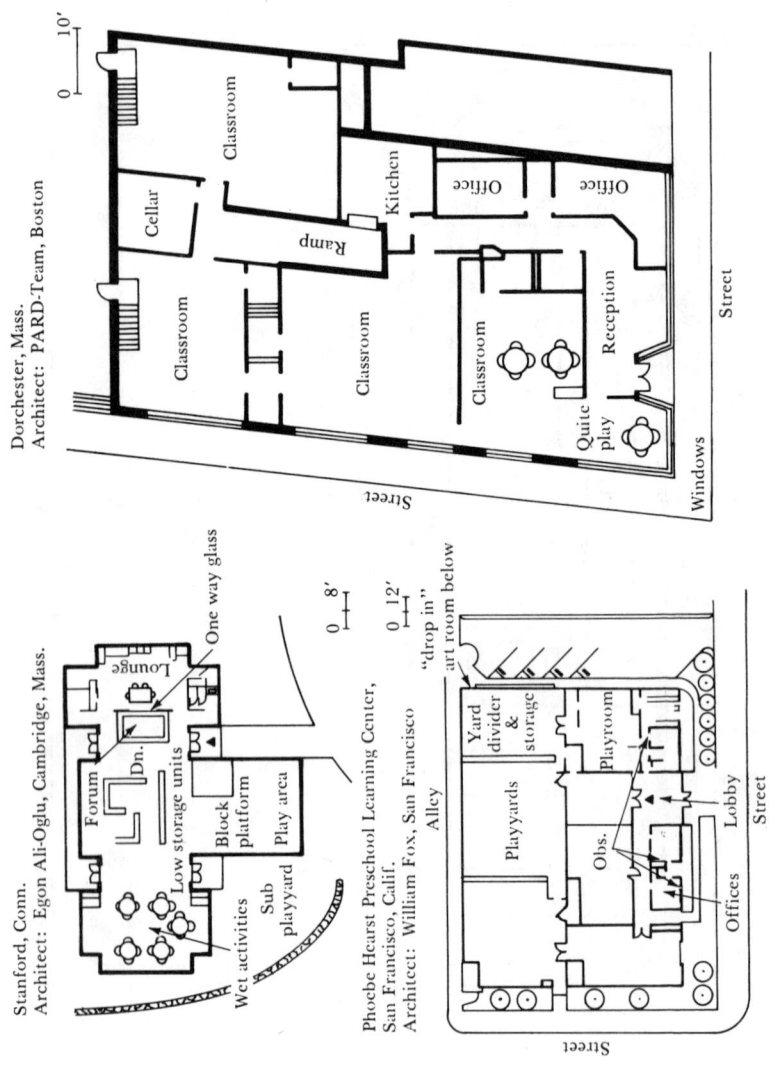

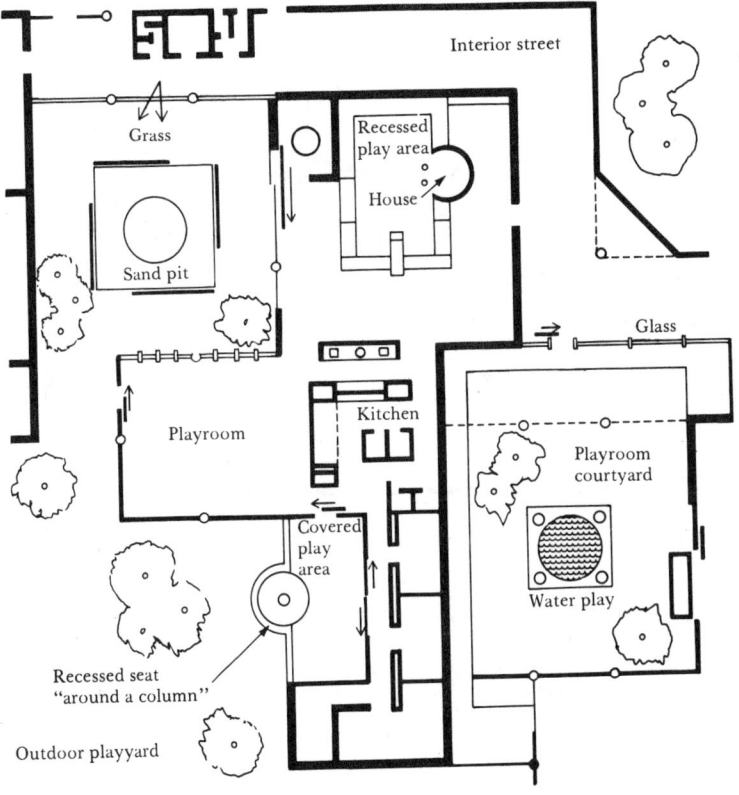

Figure 12.16

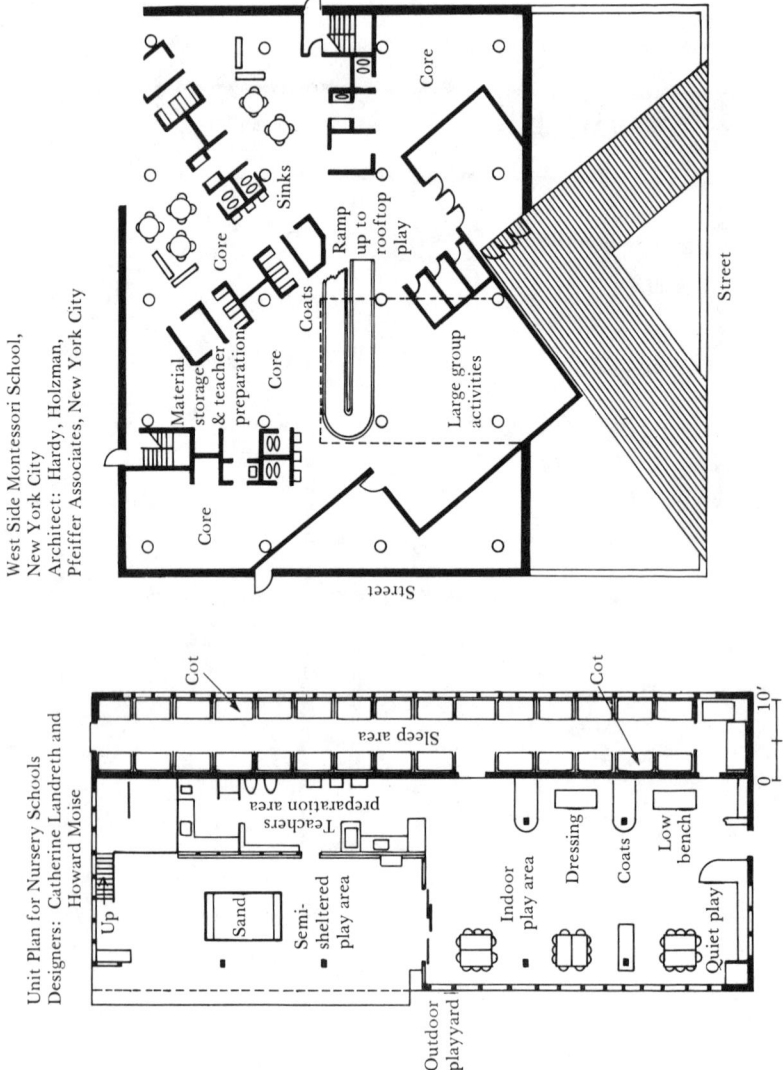

BIBLIOGRAPHY

Aaron, D., & Winawer, B. *Child's play.* New York: Harper & Row, 1965.

Alexander, C. *The city as a mechanism for sustaining human contact.* Berkeley: University of California Center for Planning and Development, 1966.

Alexander, C., Hirshen, S., Ishikawa, S., Coffin, C., Angel, S. *Houses generated by patients.* Berkeley: University of California Center for Environmental Structure, 1969.

Alexander, C., Ishikawa, S., Silverstein, M. A pattern language which generates multi-service centers. Berkeley: University of California Center for Environmental Structure, 1968.

Alexander, C., & Poyner, B. 26 entrance relations for a suburban home. In *The atoms of environmental structure.* London: Ministry of Public Buildings and Works, 1966.

Allen, L. A. *Planning for play.* Boston: MIT Press, 1958.

Benet, J. Bussing in Berkeley proves to be neither calamity or cure-all. *City,* 1970, June/July.

Bereiter, C., & Engelman, S. *Teaching disadvantaged children in preschool.* Englewood Cliffs, New Jersey: Prentice-Hall, Inc., 1966.

Berkeley Unified School District. *The early learning center: A new school.* Berkeley, California: Berkeley Unified School District, 1970.

Brown, D. S., & Venturi, R. A significance for A&P parking lots, or learning from Las Vegas. *Architectural Forum,* 1968, March.

Carew, T. Interview with Topper Carew. *Harvard Educational Review,* 1969, *39.*

Cockrell, D. A study of the play of children of pre-school age by an unobserved observer. *General Psychology,* 1935, December.

Coles, R. Those places they call schools. *Harvard Educational Review,* 1969, *39,* 4, 46–57.

Cooper, C. *The adventure playground: Creative play in an urban setting and a potential focus for community involvement.* Working Paper No. 118. Berkeley: University of California Center for Planning and Development Research, 1970.

D'Amico, V. *Experiments in creative art teaching.* New York: Museum of Modern Art, 1960.

Dattner, R. *Design for play.* New York: Van Nostrand-Reinhold Books, 1969.

Day Care and Child Development Council of America. *Proceedings of the 4-C pilot workshop, July 29–30, 1970.* Washington: Day Care and Child Development Council, 1971.

Department of Education and Science. *Eveline Lowe primary school.* Building Bulletin 36. London: Her Majesty's Stationery Office, 1967.

Department of Education and Science. *Lighting in schools.* Building Bulletin No. 33. London: Her Majesty's Stationery Office, 1967.

Deutsch, M., Ellis, R., Nimnicht, G., & Covert, A. *A memorandum: Facilities for early childhood education.* New York: Educational Facilities Laboratories, 1900.

Educational Facilities Laboratories. *Schools for early childhood.* New York: Educational Facilities Laboratories, 1970.

Educational Facilities Laboratories. *The learning center.* New York: Educational Facilities Laboratories, 1970.

Educational Facilities Laboratories. *Instructional hardware: A guide to architectural requirements.* New York: Educational Facilities Laboratories, 1970.

Featherston, E. G. School transportation: The things a board should know. *American School Board Journal,* 1969, November.

Featherstone, J. The day care problem—Kentucky fried children. *The New Republic,* 1970, September.

Foster, J. C., & Mattson, M. L. *Nursery school education.* New York: Appleton-Century, 1948.

Gesell, A., & Ilg, F. *Child development—An introduction to the study of human growth.* New York: Harper & Row, 1949.

Goodman, P. Mini schools: A prescription for the reading problem. *New York Review,* 1968, January.

Osmon, F., 1966. Child Care Centers for Migrant Farm Labor Camps. Rosenburg Foundation, San Francisco (unpublished).

Pacific Training and Technical Assistance Corporation, 1970. Care for Our Children, a comprehensive plan for child care services. Berkeley, California.

Park Association of New York City, 1966. The Playground Revolution.

Pines, M., 1966. Revolution in Learning, The Years From Birth to Six. Harper and Row Publishers, Inc.

Powledge, F., 1967. To Change a Child, A Report on the Institute for Developmental Studies. Quadrangle Books.

Pragnell, P., 1969. The Friendly Object, in *Harvard Educational Review,* Vol. 39, No. 4.

Quail Roost Conference, 1965. Planning the Environment for Early Childhood Education. Educational Facilities Laboratories, New York.

Ramsey, C., and Sleeper, H., 1956. Architectural Graphics Standards, 5th ed., p. 437. Wiley and Sons.

Skutch, M., 1969. A Montessori School, Conference, Planning and Development of Facilities for Pre-Primary Education. Bureau of Educational Studies and Field Services, University of Georgia, Athens, Georgia.

Stanton, J., and Rudolph, M., Planning a Nursery School Building. Bank Street College of Education.

St. Louis City Art Museum, 1970. Product Environment (An Exhibition of New Furniture).

Stone, J., and Rudolph, N., 1970. Play and Playgrounds. National Association for the Education of Young Children, Washington, D.C.

Utzinger, R., 1970, Some European Nursery Schools and Playgrounds. Architectural Research Laboratory, University of Michigan, Ann Arbor, Michigan.
Van Der Eyken, W., 1968. The Pre-School Years. Penguin.
van Eyke, A., 1968A. Team Ten Primer, ed. by Smithson, P., and Smithson, A. MIT Press.
van Eyke, A., 1968B. The Child and the City, *Creative Playgrounds and Recreation Centers,* Praeger.
van Eyke, A., 1962. Place and Occasion, *Progressive Architecture,* September.
Waechter, H., and Waechter, E., 1951. Schools for the Very Young. F. W. Dodge.
Weber, L., 1970. Learning Readiness for Migrant Children. Grade Teacher, Dec.
Weikart, D., 1970A. Ypsilanti Preschool Curriculum. Demonstration Project, High Scope Educational Research Foundation, Ypsilanti, Michigan.
Weikart, D., 1970B. The Unit-Based Curriculum. High Scope Educational Research Foundation, Ypsilanti, Michigan.
Weikart, D., and Lambie, D., 1967. Preschool Intervention Through a Home Teaching Program. Special Child Publications, Vol. 2, Seattle, Washington.
Whitbread, J., A New Way to Raise Kids (Interview with Dr. B. Bettelheim). *Look Magazine,* February 24, 1970.

Chapter Thirteen

CREATING ENVIRONMENTS FOR PLAY

Jay Beckwith

Finding a market for sculpture is not easy today, especially if you're interested in doing work that has social significance. When I left college I had no illusions that I could make a living with my fine arts training. So I went on to Pacific Oaks College to study child development and to become a nursery school teacher. As a student at Pacific Oaks I not only came to appreciate the importance of the first 5 years of a person's life as the basis for all subsequent intellectual and personal growth, but I also began to see that nearly all environments for young children are completely inappropriate to their needs. While I loved working directly with the children, I felt that I could make a greater contribution by integrating my artistic abilities with the skills and understanding gained as a teacher.

When I left Los Angeles to move to San Francisco, I left behind the notion that one could meet the environmental needs of young children with any sort of commercially "merchandisable package," as they are called in the play equipment trade. Thus I began my work as a playground builder. I was rather naive at first, because I thought artistic ability and commitment would be enough to overcome the inadequacies I had observed in commercial products.

For the first 2 years I worked with a partner, Drew Langsner, in creating what we called "play sculpture." Our work was creative, solution-oriented, and energetically experimental. Not all of the work was tremendously successful in that the children did not use it as well as we had anticipated. But, on the other hand, we created no failures that broke down or were so dangerous or ugly that they had to be removed. Our willingness to stick our necks out with new materials and new ideas created the basis for an inventory of materials and designs which could not have been developed with a more conservative approach.

Drew decided that he wanted to travel and investigate provincial life styles in order to understand how various ethnic groups live in harmony with their environments. It was up to me then to decide to continue the work alone, to find another partner, or to get a regular job. I couldn't imagine another partner—Drew and I worked like a pair of hands together. The longest I had ever been able to tolerate a straight job was about a year. That left me alone with my ideas and the work. It was then that I made the commitment henceforth only to build playgrounds with the people from the community who would be using them.

The economic and social advantages of this method were clear. The problem was how to take a group of people who often had only a vague notion of child development theory, little artistic training, and generally no experience with construction tools, and somehow to create durable, aesthetic, functional play environments. The technique I have developed involves an initial meeting during which I show slides of creative children's environments and talk about safety, kids growing up, and people building their own playgrounds. This meeting is followed by a couple of rap sessions with the staff and/or parents, in which we assess the needs and potentials of the space to be developed.

Doing this kind of needs assessment requires some skill at leading group discussions. I generally structure the meeting so that the group interactions are positive, creative, and directly related to the solvable problems with which we are concerned. One way I do this is to make the rule that no one can raise an objection to an idea until he says three things good about that idea. Depending on the needs of the community, these rap sessions are followed by model building with parents and kids, field trips to good playgrounds, initial sketches for community consideration and evaluation, and construction plans.

I try to avoid any "final" plans in an effort to protect the spontaneity that can be developed on the work site. Even my most careful plans are intentionally vague and would be rejected by any contractor as impossible to build. I have gone so far as to lose plans and to let the models fall off my truck to overcome the creative stigma such "final" plans can impose. The real fun and creativity begins when the community and I meet on the site and start to build.

There is nothing more exciting, and at the same time more frightening, than a giant pile of lumber sitting on an empty expanse of asphalt. But once we begin, the fear that we can't do it, or that maybe it won't turn out well, evaporates in the joy of working together. When the process gets going it is less like a construction crew at work than like a bunch of kids at play. The element of fun and the excitement of spontaneously building an environment releases so much energy that we have built better playgrounds in less time with a dozen unskilled workers than could be duplicated by a professional contractor.

In these past 5 years I have seen the emergence of a new appreciation for the role of "free" play activities in the total development of each child. That play had a place in education was once a radical idea held by a few nursery school teachers. Now elementary and even secondary schools are demanding environments that facilitate and support play. Moreover, playgrounds are becoming more than organized game areas. Nature studies, construction and art projects, and other nonclassroom activities are being added to school curriculums.

It may only be a consequence of living in a civilized society, but many of us have lost touch with our childhood and feel unsure that what we choose for kids will really be enjoyed. Our first impulse when we set out to develop the playground is to open up the catalogs of commercial play equipment and select the best swing set and slide. Yet when we give the matter a moment's consideration, we remember playing in trees, holes in the ground, cardboard boxes, mud puddles, and under the kitchen table. A playground that offers these kinds of experiences for children is really what they want. How to provide such a playground in the crush of city life is a problem that can be solved to some degree with the help of an experienced designer.

If the problem were simply to make a playground that kids liked, the job would be comparatively easy. But the realities of our society are such that playgrounds are not created just for children and their enjoyment. Most playgrounds are designed to last for decades with no maintenance because labor costs are supposedly too high for even minimal ongoing repairs. Insurance restrictions require that play equipment be "absolutely" safe. Thus by the time grown-ups get done with their priorities for a playground, there is very little *fun* left.

Many of these difficulties are fictions that are more convenient than real. Safety is a good example. Fifteen minutes on a playground observing real kids at play will demolish the idea that a playground is a "safe" place. One of the major characteristics of play is that it involves risks. Children will go to incredible lengths to discover the risk potential of even the "safest" equipment. For a clear illustration of this principle, watch children playing with a traditional slide. The kids start off using the slide in the "proper" way, three, or maybe even a half dozen times. But soon they have exhausted the fun of that experience and they begin to invent new possibilities. a kid will go down backward, slide down with a friend, run up the slide, run up while a buddy is sliding down, slide down backward while somebody rides on his knees as a buddy runs up the slide. Often kids exceed the design limits of the "safe" slide in some extravagant way and an injury may result. When asked how the accident happened the child will respond, "Oh, we were just having fun." The child's answer is perfectly honest. He is not to blame for the injury. Adult ideas about how he *ought* to behave created a situation and a piece of equipment that was directly at odds with how children *do* behave.

KIDS RESPOND TO GOOD ENVIRONMENTS

The basic assumption motivating the designs I have been creating is that environments that promote spontaneous behavior reinforce a child's personal integrity. Such environments give him the nonverbal message that he is OK and that his natural behavior is good. Child-sized chairs, for example, let the child know that "here is a place for a little person," and if you're small that is good to know.

Children who get this sort of feedback from their environment are less likely to have the kind of accident described in our slide example, because the environment anticipates the child's behavior. A slide that is 4 feet wide and only 6 feet off the ground promotes many inventive variations, all of which are relatively safe because the slide is not too high.

The underlying assumption of the traditional one-way slide is that play is essentially entertainment. Hence it follows that children are entertained by slides. But entertainment and play are not the same thing. Children do not play with equipment as much as they play with each other. A child alone on a swing is somehow a melancholy sight. Anticipating the child's tendency for group play and exploratory behavior leads to new ways of making old designs that are as safe as life can ever be—that is, only relatively.

Environments that are designed with an understanding of the child's need for spontaneous behavior are not only better in the superficial sense that the kids are likely to have fewer accidents, they are also better in the sense that the children learn to know more about themselves and what they want. An environment that prescribes behavior into narrow channels, such as the one-way slide, deprives the child of the opportunity to make choices which can help him discover the basic mechanisms of his personal psychology. This may sound like a complicated process but to the child it is only "fun!"

Fun and spontaneous behavior are linked in the normal development of each child as nature's way of getting us to do what is best for us. This can be clearly seen in the play of young animals. A prime function of animal play is to rehearse later adult behavior. As serious and important to the animal's survival as these rehearsals may be, they are still great fun and pleasurable for the animals involved.

Building playgrounds in a spirit of fun insures that children will enjoy them. Most playgrounds are too formal and serious. They are built with consideration for what Saint-Exupery's Little Prince would call "matters of consequence," instead of joy. Joyless playgrounds are boring places. The feeling of boredom is the way the body signals its discomfort with being left out and turned off. Boredom is an early warning system that moves us away from situations where our bodies are neglected. One is seldom bored when body and senses are fully involved and active. A bored child is much more likely to have an accident because he becomes *careless,* whereas the child testing his abilities in a responsive environment is having fun and being *careful* because he knows he is taking a chance. The child's feeling about himself is related to the nonverbal message of the joyless playground: "We care most about having a nice, neat park and we couldn't *care less* about your fun!"

Much of our willingness to build joyless playgrounds stems from the fact that modern, complex society requires that childlike behavior be restricted to childhood. Most adults are really out of touch with their bodies and with any kind of spontaneous behavior. Thus we have difficulty seeing that a tidy playground might be a boring place for kids, who would prefer to play in a vacant lot or on the street. Part of the increased interest in building new playgrounds comes from the whole revolution now taking place in our society as people get "turned on" to their bodies and to the joy that comes from spontaneity.

HOW TO HELP MAKE PLAY HAPPEN

Children spend a great deal of time at school, and yet most schools are less like a home than like a jail. Many schools even look like "behavior correction facilities" built of concrete, painted institutional gray, and surrounded by an "exercise yard" and chain link fence. Movement of the children inmates is timed with bells and accompanied by guards. In contrast, some schools have "open classrooms" with "nature areas." Children are allowed freedom of movement to discover what is most interesting and valuable to them. Only by employing our great capacity to fool ourselves can we think that the education in these two settings is equivalent and that children are not greatly affected by the environments they encounter at school.

Children are attracted to, and feel comfortable in, an environment that has a sense of "place," a certain feeling that this space is special and unique. We have all experienced this quality in churches, old buildings, forest knolls, rock grottoes, and other unique environments. This quality of the environment can be designed into a playground, and children will naturally congregate there.

The importance of the sense of place can be easily observed in the places that children themselves select for their play. Child-chosen "playgrounds" are often found in unexpected locations. To the eye of the adult there may be little or nothing to play with—perhaps a tree, a hole in the ground, or a blanket and a few boards leaned against a fence. In these playgrounds there are no swings and slides, no merry-go-round or jungle gym, just the children and the place.

There is a certain tenderness and poignancy about this simple, unequipped play that seems inexhaustably satisfying to a child. Yet this kind of play is rarely seen on playgrounds. More often it occurs in back yards or vacant lots or other hidden corners that nobody owns. The child-selected play space is typically an abandoned area over which no one cares to exercise control. Even though the back yard is owned by the parents, for instance, they may rarely use it. Kids take over these spaces by default, and in the absence of restriction they begin to make them their own. If we are genuinely interested in promoting play, we can learn a lesson from this observation: playgrounds should really belong to children. Children should have the right and power to change the playground to suit their ideas and dreams.

The real value of well-designed equipment becomes apparent when kids return to it time and time again, discovering new games and creating ever more elaborate rules of play. Over a period of months a simple game of chase can evolve into regular teams with home bases, scouts, territories, and a complex system of law and justice. This kind of social development is greatly enhanced when the playground is rich in behavioral possibilities which support this natural tendency toward elaboration and repetition.

The traditional playground can be greatly improved by simply grouping and interrelating separate pieces into an organic whole. Thus instead of waiting in line for this ride and then waiting in line for the next, the child moves freely through the space, using the play equipment as an environment rather than an entertainment. This openness and interrelatedness of the equipment in the space encourages spontaneous interaction between children and matches the patterns to be seen in their games. Increased variety also enhances the playground's play potential. Instead of one narrow slide, a good playground will have, for example, a wide slide that encourages multiple use, a tunnel slide made of three barrels welded together, and an incline pole for a banister-type slide. Each play equipment idea can be expanded into many different designs which introduce a great deal of variety into the play space. Such a varied environment is not only more fun, it is also more challenging, because it provides a built-in test of skill as the child chooses which item to try next.

In contrast to the traditional playground with its isolated rides, this kind of "active play center" is safer because a child is seldom caught at a dead end. Have you ever seen a preschooler at the top of a one-way slide, afraid to take the risk and unable to back down? This problem would be avoided in a well-designed play environment. The active play center also requires less supervision; games like "king of the mountain" can't get started if there are three or four exits on each platform. What we are talking about here is simply maximizing the child's choices. The playground that allows for child experimentation puts control back into the hands of the child. By trusting in the child's ability to learn through free play, we allow natural testing to occur at the optimum moment, when the child is ready to learn and when recovery potential is at its maximum.

There is a surprisingly prevalent attitude that when children are permitted free play, chaos will result. Contrary to such expectations, play leads not to disorder, but to regularity. Children themselves limit their play, establishing all kinds of boundaries and rules. As with other animals, a basic function of children's play is to rehearse later adult behavior. This accounts for the repetitious quality of play, where spontaneous acts are elaborated and perfected. The initial rules or "pretends" are increasingly refined as play progresses and the players' skill increases. Thus what begins as free play becomes ritualized and situational; it moves from the emotional to the materialistic.

In 1944 Johan Huizinga published *Homo Ludens,* an exhaustive study of the play element in culture. This important study has recently been reprinted in paperback and is essential reading for those who are more interested in the philosophical aspects of play than can be covered in a short article like this. Much of what was academic speculation for Huizinga has gained scientific support from a new branch of biology that was fathered by Konrad Lorenz—ethology, the biology of behavior.

One of the most valuable lessons to be found in *Homo Ludens* is a better understanding of why playgrounds are more exciting when built by community people than when they are commercially installed. There is a quality of play itself that creates and supports a sense of community. When we play we enter into a special frame of mind in which we are "beside ourselves" and where make-believe borders on believing in a world that has been reshaped into our heart's desire by imagination. When we share this imaginary play world with others, it must become a magical and mysterious world protected by secrets. If we were to reveal our imaginary play world indiscriminately it would lose its credibility and revert to the commonplace.

This process can be observed when two or three children are pretending that a cardboard box is an airplane. The box is only an airplane as long as all the players agree to that imaginary reality. The more players involved in the fantasy, the less agreement there will be and the greater the risk that the entire game will collapse. Thus play draws people together in small groups and the players restrict their communications with people outside the fantasy world in order to protect its integrity.

Playgrounds that are built by community groups draw upon the mystery and magic intrinsic to play itself. When community volunteers get together to build a playground it quickly becomes a festival that combines work and play. Few social events generate so much good will and sense of community as these projects, and much of this energy comes from the magic of play itself.

KIDS CAN DO IT!

A successful project grows out of the realization that the most important ingredient of a playground is not equipment but people. The playground builder who concentrates on "innovative" play equipment may encounter the same disappointment as the parent who finds his children playing with the wrapping boxes on Christmas morning instead of the expensive gifts.

There are many manufacturers, designers, architects, and city planning departments which can supply you with "creative" playground equipment. Indeed, some of these people can supply equipment that is designed better than the traditional equipment. But none of these outside sources is going to be able to provide the qualities of a community-built playground. When your community works and plays spontaneously together, creating unique solutions to construction problems as they arise, they tap the energy that lies in play itself. A do-it-yourself playground may not be as neat as one done by "downtown" people, but it will be richer in texture, in color, in shape, and in play opportunities.

There are few playgrounds in America today that capture much of the joy of play. Few have been built by the people who will use them; few change as people use them. Playgrounds could be places where neighborhoods could express their individuality and where private citizens could exercise personal expression. Playgrounds could be places where children could build, paint, and have a substantial effect on their environment.

We are moving toward a society in which self-expression is a completely private matter. One can really only have an effect on his environment within the confines of his own home. That this is an unnatural and unhealthy situation can be seen in the effect it has on our children. The bulk of so-called vandalism is not wanton destruction but attempts by children to leave some mark of their existence on the environment.

We are producing a generation of children who not only lack the skills required to build a tree house, but who feel that such an activity would be somehow illegal, even if they could find a tree! In contrast, many British and European playgrounds are "adventure playgrounds." These are often simply dirt tracts with kid-built shanties where children are allowed to play with tools, animals, water, paint, mud, and even fire. In the 20 years since the first adventure playgrounds were started, much has been established about the value of putting children in control of their own environment. Adventure playgrounds may not be completely appropriate in this country, but certainly it is time that we took a look at the playground as a place for potential learning experiences through free play activities.

Perhaps we can begin to realize the social potential of community-built playgrounds. Perhaps it is time to become more sensitive to the environments we create for our children. It is even possible that we may join our children on the playground in a genuine celebration of life.

MATERIALS LIST FOR COMMUNITY-BUILT PLAYGROUNDS

WOOD PRODUCTS

Lumber:
- Recommended sizes: 6 X 6 posts, 3 X 6 safety rails, 3 X 8 beams, 3 X 6 decking for public elementary schools or parks
- 4 X 4 posts, 2 X 8 safety rails, 2 X 8 beams, 2 X 6 decking for nursery schools and semiprivate spaces

Railroad ties:
  6" X 8" 6 ft. and 8 ft. long. Use for sand retainer.
Telephone poles:
  Provide a place to unload and store poles, and someone to meet the delivery truck.
  5"-7" diameter, in 8-13 ft. lengths
  7"-9" diameter, in 8-13 ft. lengths
  8"-10" diameter, in 8-13 ft. lengths
Dowels (for ladders)
Peeler cores (logs 6" in diameter, 8 ft. long):
  Advisable to phone ahead. You'll need a truck (rental about $75). Price: $.75 per log.
Cable spools

METAL PRODUCTS

Sheet steel:
  22 gauge for slides over ¾" exterior plywood (have ends folded). An 8 ft. sheet, 4 X 8 with 6" lips on the 4 ft. ends, costs $20. 5 X 9 ft. is also possible. Stainless steel is better because it lasts longer and reflects heat, so it does not get too hot for kids. Cost of 4 X 9 stainless sheet, with 6" bends, is about $85.
Steel drums (55 gallon):
  Price: $7 each, cut and rolled on both ends. Ask for heavyweight barrel.
Pipe:
  Galvanized pipe recommended. 1" interior diameter, $.56/linear foot; 1¼" i.d., $.88 l.f.
Scrap steel:
  Steering wheels, other interesting metal salvage; about $.10 per pound.

HARDWARE

Hardware will cost from one-fourth to one-third of the materials budget. A significant savings is possible if you use threaded rod, with fender washers and nuts, cut to necessary length as used. This replaces conventional bolts, which are expensive and not as versatile as rod.

GOVERNMENT SURPLUS

Used rope, about $.10/foot; cargo nets, used, $15; new, $45. Also ship fittings, chain, other interesting stuff; fair prices.

BUILDING SUPPLIES

Redicrete:
Premixed cement, dry in 90 lb. bags, $1.52 each. One bag makes ¾ cubic foot.
Sand:
50 tons is about 800 square feet, about 12" deep (i.e., about 20 X 40 feet), $280.
Cobblestones:
Price: $.35 each.

SCROUNGABLE MATERIALS

Tires—tires stores.
Carpet tubes—carpet stores.
Tree stumps—city park and recreation department and tree service firms; stumps are cut-down trees, 8 to 12 ft high, 14" at base.
Cable spools—cablevision companies.
Also check with the city Department of Public Works and electric company.

DESCRIPTION OF THE MULTIUSE SCHOOLYARD

Play can be described in many ways. One useful method is to distinguish between activities that are directed by school staff members and those that are initiated by children, without direction. These types of play might be called staff-directed and free play; both are necessary parts of playground activity.

STAFF-DIRECTED PLAY

Hard-surface games	Kickball	Volleyball
	Basketball	Relays
Outdoor classroom		
Nature studies	Botany—planting areas	Astronomy—sundial
	Meteorology—weather observation	Biology—animals, birds, insects
	Physical geography—ponds, trees, rocks; water conservation	Topography—hills and valleys
		Ecology—natural relationships, cycles
Art	Painted murals	Banners, flags
	Mosaics	Supergraphics
	Sculpture	
Amphitheater	Drama, performances	Student assemblies

FREE PLAY

Hard-surface games	Tetherball	Four-square
	Jump rope	Hopscotch
Active play center/ related equipment	Low swings	Tunnels, tubes, holes
	Balance beams	Cargo net
	See-saws	Ropes
	Wide ladders	Towers
	Wide horizontal ladders	Ramps
	Monkey bars/climbers	Spring boards
	Fireman's poles	Arch climber
	Private spaces/hideouts	Peep holes
	Tire net	Rings
	Chinning and turning bars	Bridges

Table 13.1 Some Considerations for Playground Design

Goals

Maximize choice and diversity
- Grouping of equipment provides choices of activities
- Provide for active play, passive play, free play, and staff-directed activity
- Sensory stimulation—variety of textures, colors, shapes, sounds, smells
- Variety of scale suitable to children—spaces that are large, small, open, closed, private, public
- Range of challenge, difficulty, risk—giving child a choice to develop his own skills

Encourage individual development
- Building environment that encourages social interaction—such as development of elaborate games based on layout of equipment
- Sharing—such as cooperative play activities
- Large muscle development—stimulating sense of balance, coordination
- Use of imagination—such as building sand castles, inventing dramas
- Self-reliance—such as choosing degree of difficulty of play activities
- Social identity—sense that their school is special because it has a special space for kids

Relevance to curriculum
- Seeing playground as place that expands learning and teaching potential of school
- Ways schoolyard changes can have meaning to children
- Outdoor space as unique opportunity to involve kids who aren't comfortable in the classroom

Criteria

Safety—during construction
- Avoiding toxic characteristics of materials, such as mixing cement or using wood preservatives
- Using tools with proper safety instruction, such as power saws and drills
- Material handling, such as lifting correctly
- Removing all rough edges on playground structures

Safety—when in use	Structural strength—material of adequate size and strength; proper joining of materials; good design
	Protective surfacing—sand, tanbark, synthetic materials
	Avoiding situations that might result in serious accident or injury, such as falling from height onto object below
Ease of maintenance	Avoiding places that collect trash or are hard to clean
	Use of durable materials
	Adequate retaining of ground cover
Ease of construction	Planning each phase so that it can be built in a short time, with relatively unskilled labor
	Budgeting time as well as money
	Recognizing the importance of logistics of materials and people, such as enough people to hold heavy material while it is secured
	Concentrating work into the shortest possible number of days
Climate	Wind protection
	Sun and shade
	Drainage
	Corrosion resistance—use galvanized steel when using steel; use wood preservative whenever possible
Orientation to school buildings	Noise, distortion
	Window breakage—clean up loose rock after construction
	Visual impact
Separation of dissimilar activities	Separate kickball and planting areas; protect quiet play
Ability to be moved later	Relocation possibly required by earthquake-proofing of school
Expandability	Building so that additions are possible
	Construction that lends itself to creative change by children, such as the addition of mosaics, painting, flags
Lighting	If needed at night
Aesthetics	Theme—repetition of shapes or use of a motif
	Choice of materials
	Placement of objects and equipment for balance and scale
	Color and decoration

ADVENTURE PLAY

Another type of activity is adventure play, which combines responsible supervision with an environment where children have tools and materials to build and modify structures, or even tear them down and start over.

ENVIRONMENTAL IMPROVEMENTS DESIGNED TO ENHANCE PHYSICAL APPEARANCE AND SOCIAL INTERACTION

- Tables and benches—for children and adults
- Kiosk—for art and information
- Sheltered areas—trellis, windbreak
- Sand play area
- Water—stream, pond, water play area
- Storage for portable things—tricycles, costumes, balls, jump ropes, games, canvas, parachute, ropes
- Blackboards, mirrors
- Sound/music makers—gongs, whistles, drums, talking tubes

Figure 13.1a

This playground should cost less than $1000 and take no more than four Saturdays to construct.

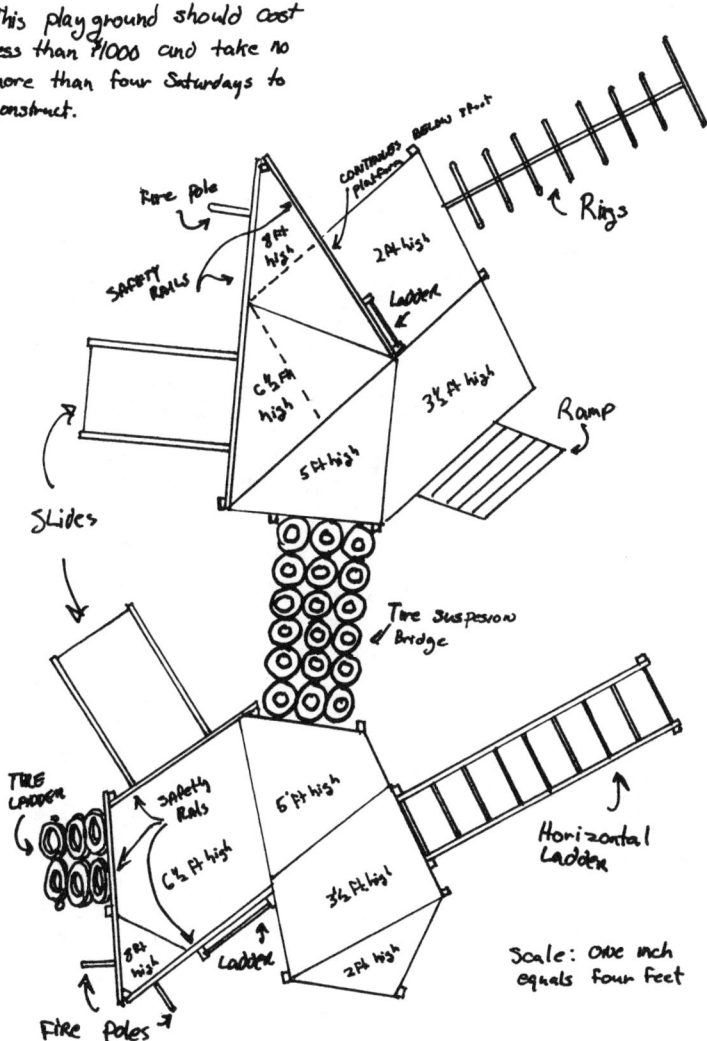

Figure 13.1b

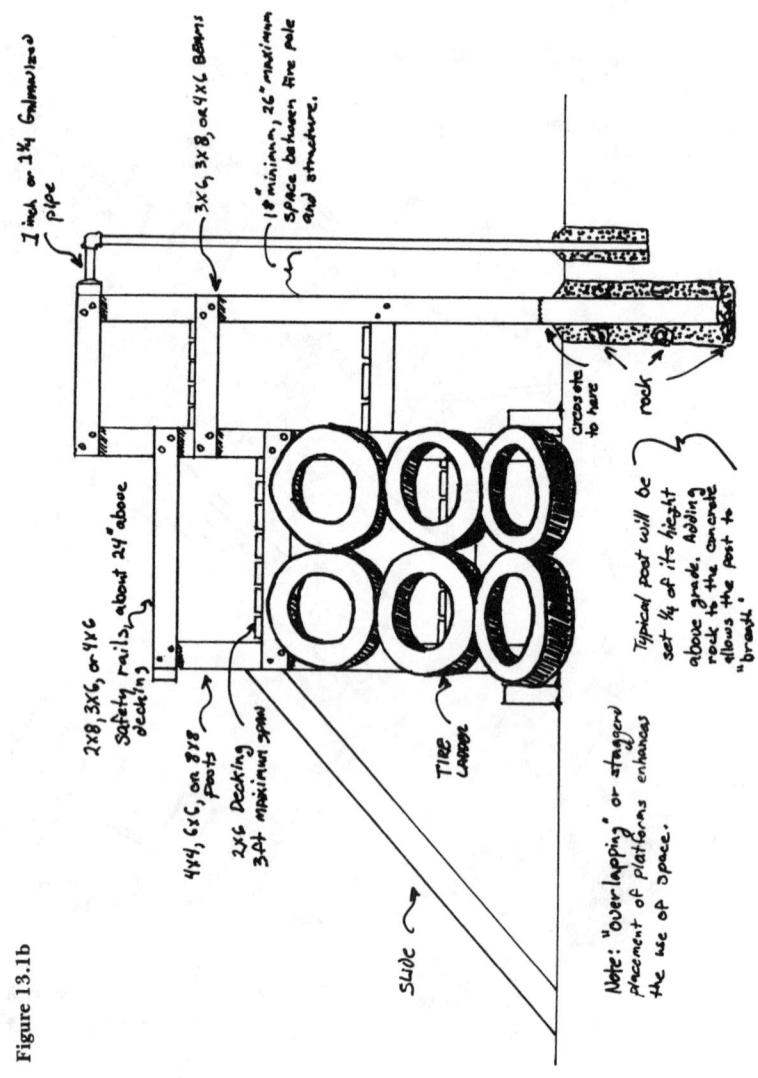

Figure 13.1c

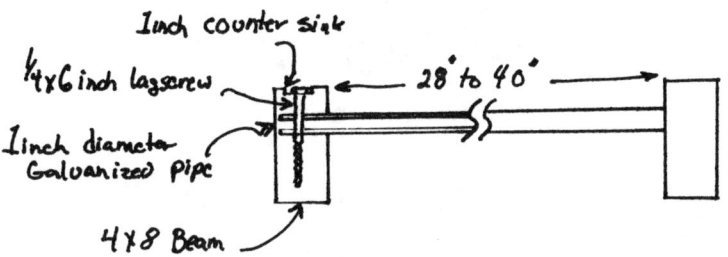

END VIEW OF A TYPICAL LADDER (HORIZONTAL + VERTICAL)

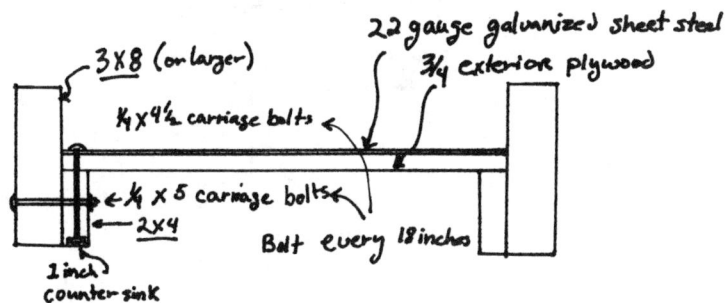

END VIEW OF A TYPICAL SLIDE

Figure 13.1d

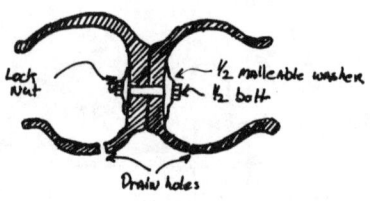

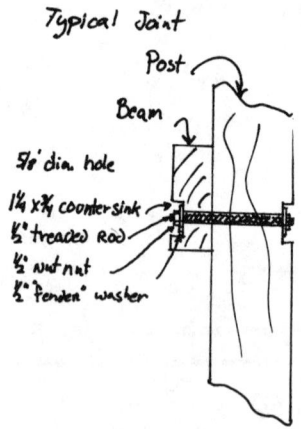

BIBLIOGRAPHY

PLAY

Aaron, D. *Child's play.* New York: Harper & Row, 1969.
Adventure playgrounds. *Education Digest,* 1962, March.
Allen, L. H. *Planning for play.* London: Thamass and Budson, 1968.
Bungtsson, A. *Adventure playgrounds.* New York: Praeger, 1972.

Cooper, C. C. Adventure playgrounds. *Landscape Architecture,* 1970, *61,* 18–29, 88–91.
Dattner, R. *Design for play.* New York: Van Nostrand Reinholt, 1969.
Freidberg, P. *Play and interplay.* New York: Macmillan, 1972.
Huizinga, J. *Homo ludens: A study of the play element in culture.* Boston: Beacon Press, 1970.
Lederman, A., & Trachsel, A. *Creative playgrounds and recreation centers.* New York: Praeger, 1968.
Linda Vista playground project poster. Lincoln Savings and Loan, P.O. Box 600038, Los Angeles, California 90060.
Murphy, L. B., & Leeper, E. M. *The ways children learn.* U.S. Department of Health, Education, and Welfare Publication No. 73–1026, 1970.
Osmon, F. *Patterns for designing children's centers.* New York: EFL, 447 Madison Avenue, New York, New York 10022.
Planning outdoor play (POP). Raleigh, North Carolina: North Carolina State University School of Design, 1971.
Sanoff, H. *Learning environments for children.* Raleigh, North Carolina: North Carolina State University School of Design, 1972.
Schoolworks, Inc. *Schoolworks primer.* 33 Union Square West, New York, New York 10003.
Special play. Reprint from *Natural History Magazine.* The American Museum of Natural History, Central Part West and 79th Street, New York, New York 10024.
Stone, J., & Rudolph, N. *Play and playgrounds.* National Association for the Education of Young Children, 1834 connecticut Avenue, N.W., Washington, D. C. 20009.

PLANTING NATURE AREAS

Gardens for All. Special edition of the *New Schools Exchange Letter,* July, 1973.

Gross, P., & Railton, E. *Teaching science in an outdoor environment.* University of California Press, 223 Fulton, Berkeley, California 94720.

Indoor-outdoor natural learning experiences. Sacramento County Office of Education, 6011 Folsom Boulevard, Sacramento, California 95819.

Project WEY—Washington Environmental Yard. Washington School, 2300 Grove Street, Berkeley, California 94704.

School nature areas in Sacramento county. Sacramento County Office of Education, 6011 Folsom Boulevard, Sacramento, California 95819

Appendix A

SELECTED RESOURCES FOR ADDITIONAL INFORMATION

American Academy of Pediatrics
   P.O. Box 1037
   Evanston, IL 60204

American Home Economics Association
   2010 Massachusetts Avenue NW
   Washington, DC 20016

American Nurses Association
   2420 Pershing Road
   Kansas City, MO 64108

   1030 15th Street NW
   Washington, DC 20005

American Psychological Association
   1947 Rosemary Hills Drive
   Silver Spring, MD 20910

Child Development Associate Consortium
   805 15th St NW, Suite 500
   Washington, DC 20005

Children's Defense Fund
1763 R Street NW
Washington, DC 20009

The Children's Foundation
1028 Connecticut Avenue NW, #614
Washington, DC 20036

Coalition for Children & Youth
1910 K St. NW
Washington, DC 20006

Council on Social Work Education
345 East 46th Street
New York, NY 10017

Educational Facilities Laboratory
477 Madison Avenue
New York, NY 10022

National Association of Social Workers
20 E Street NW
Washington, DC 20001

National Federation of Settlements and Neighborhood Centers
232 Madison Avenue
New York, NY 10016

National League for Nursing
10 Columbus Circle
New York, NY 10023

Appendix B

RESOURCES FOR INFANT EDUCATION PROGRAMS

Trudy Latzko, R.N., M.A.

The lists which follow are by no means exhaustive; rather, they represent resources which I have found particularly useful as Program Director of a center which serves infants of school age parents as well as handicapped infants. Staff training, parent participation and individualized programming for the children are among the primary components of the program. For this reason, the resources reflect the special needs encountered in these areas of activity. My personal bias toward theory and research as necessary foundations for the basic assumptions adopted in programming is also evident in the selection of references.

The film list is a result of over seven years experience in reviewing a wide variety of films. Although I have not had the opportunity to review the videotapes, they are the products of a high quality project and as such are valuable

Resources for Infant Programs, © Family Developmental Center, was developed as a product for dissemination under Grant #G007500329 from the Office of Education and appears in this publication with permission from the Family Developmental Center of the Family Service Agency of San Francisco.

adjuncts to infant program resources. The film strips are being produced at a rapid rate by Parents' Magazine Films, Inc.: the list reflects only those which are available as outlined in their 1976–77 catalog. The strips I have seen are short, usually 10 minutes and quite simplified. I have used them in a young parent group to promote discussion, but would advise previewing them before presentation to a professional audience.

Films are generally rented for a one to three day period. Some of the distributors, such as CRM Educational Films, encourage collect calls to order their films; whereas others, such as the University of California Extension Media Center, request orders well in advance to allow for confirmation or for any necessary changes. Many of the films listed as available through this university are also available through other sources such as Contemporary Films/McGraw Hill or New York University Film Library. Catalogs are available from all film distributors mentioned.

BOOKS AND ARTICLES

Ainsworth, M.D.S. et al. Deprivation of maternal care; a reassessment of its effects. *Public Health Papers, 14.* Geneva: World Health Organization, 1962.

Ainsworth, M.D.S., and Bell, S. M. Some contemporary patterns of mother infant interaction in the feeding situation. *Stimulation in Early Infancy.* Anthony Ambrose (Editor). London: Academic Press, 1969.

Allport, Gordon. *The Nature of Prejudice.* Garden City, N.Y.: Doubleday Anchor Books, 1958.

Als, Heidelise, and Brazelton, T. Berry. Comprehensive neonatal assessment. *Birth and the Family Journal. 2:1,* 1975.

American National Red Cross. *Basic First Aid.* Garden City, N.Y.: Doubleday & Co., Inc., 1971.

Bach, George, and Goldberg, Herb. *Creative Aggression.* New York: Avon Books, 1974.
Barnard, Kathryn. Trends in the care and prevention of developmental disabilities. *American Journal of Nursing.* 75:10, October, 1975.
Beadle, Muriel. *A Child's Mind.* Garden City, N.Y.: Doubleday and Co., Inc., 1970.
Berkowitz, Leonard (Editor). *The Roots of Aggression.* New York: Atherton Press, 1969.
Blumberg, Arthur, and Golumbewski, Robert T. *Learning and Change in Groups.* Hammonsworth, Middlesex, England: 1976.
Bobath, Karel. *The Motor Deficit in Patients With Cerebral Palsy.* England: The Lavenham Press, Ltd., 1969.
Boston Women's Health Collective. *Our Bodies, Ourselves.* New York: Simon and Schuster, 1973.
Bower, Eli M. *Mythologies, Realities and Possibilities in Primary Prevention.* Paper presented at the University of Vermont, Prevention of Psychopathology, June 27, 1975.
Bowlby, John. *Attachment and Loss, Vol. I Attachment. Vol. II Separation.* New York: Basic Books, 1973.
Bowlby, John. *Child Care and the Growth of Love.* Baltimore. Penguin Books, second ed., 1965.
Brazelton, T. Berry. *Neonatal Behavioral Assessment Scale.* London, Philadelphia: Spastics International Medical Publications, 1973.
Brazelton, T. Berry. *Infants and Mothers.* New York: Delacorte Press, 1972.
Brazelton, T. Berry. *Toddlers and Parents.* New York: Delacorte Press/Seymour Lawrence, 1974.
Bronfenbrenner, Urie. Is early intervention effective? *Day Care and Early Education.* November, 1974, 2, #2.
Bromwich, Rose M. Focus on maternal behavior in infant intervention. *American J. Orthopsychiat.* 46 (3), July, 1976.
Broussard, Elsie, and Hartner, Miriam. Further considerations regarding maternal perception. In *Exceptional*

Infant. Jerome Hellmuth (Editor). New York: Bruner/Mazel, 1971.

Caplan, Frank (Editor). *The First Twelve Months of Life.* New York: Grosset and Dunlap, 1973.

Center for Science in the Public Interest. *Nutrition Scoreboard.* Washington, D.C., 1974.

Chess, Stella; Thomas, Alexander, and Birch, Herbert. *Your Child is a Person.* New York: The Viking Press, 1965.

Chukovsky, Kornei. *From Two to Five.* Berkeley: University of California Press, 1968.

Elkind, David. Early childhood education in the seventies. What can we learn from past mistakes? *Contemporary Education.* Volume XLV, #4, Summer, 1974.

Erikson, Erik. *Childhood and Society.* New York: W. W. Norton & Co., 1950.

Fiorentino, Mary R. *Normal and Abnormal Development, the Influence of Primitive Reflexes on Motion Development.* Springfield, Illinois: Charles C. Thomas, 1972.

Fraiberg, Selma. *The Magic Years.* New York: Scribner and Sons, 1976.

Freud, Anna. *Normalcy and Pathology in Childhood.* New York: International Universities Press, Inc., 1965.

Freud, Anna, and Burlingham, Dorothy. *Infants Without Families.* New York: International Universities Press, 1944.

Freud, Sigmund. *The Sexual Enlightenment of Children.* New York: Basic Books, 1963.

Furman, Erna. *A Child's Parent Dies.* New Haven: Yale University Press, 1974.

Gersh, Marvin J., and Litt, Iris R. *The Handbook of Adolescence.* New York: Dell Publishing Co., 1971.

Ginsberg, H., and Oper, S. *Piaget's Theory of Intellectual Development.* Englewood Cliffs, New Jersey: Prentice Hall, 1969.

Gordon, Ira, Giunagh, Barry, and Jester, R. Emile. *Baby Learning Through Baby Play.* New York: St. Martin's, 1970.

Gordon, Thomas. *Parent Effectiveness Training.* New York: Peter Wyden Co., 1970.
Green, Morris, and Haggerty, Robert J. *Ambulatory Pediatrics.* Philadelphia: W. B. Saunders Co., 1968.
Grotberg, Edith H. (Editor). *Day Care Resources for Decisions.* Office of Economic Opportunity.
Hardy, Janet B., McCracken, George, Gilkeson, Mary Ruth, and Sever, John L. Adverse fetal outcome following maternal rubella after the first trimester of pregnancy. *J.A.M.A.,* March 31, 1969, Vol. 207, No. 13.
Harlow, Harry. The development of affectional patterns in infant monkeys. In *Determinants of Infant Behavior,* Vol. I. B. M. Foss (Editor). London: Wiley, 1961.
Haynes, Una. *A Developmental Approach to Casefinding.* Public Health Service Publication #2017, 1969.
Honig, Alice, and Lally, J. Ronald. *Infant Caregiving.* New York: Media Projects, Incorporated, 1972.
Jackson, Don D. (Editor). *Communication, Family and Marriage.* Palo Alto, California: Science and Behavior Books, Inc., 1970.
Johnson, Roger. *Aggression in Man and Animals.* Philadelphia: W. B. Saunders, 1972.
Kessler, Jane W. *Psychopathology of Childhood.* Englewood Cliffs, N.J.: Prentice-Hall, Inc., 1966.
Klaus, Marshall, and Fanaroff, Avroy A. *Care of the High Risk Neonate.* Philadelphia: W. B. Saunders, Co., 1973.
Latzko, Trudy. *Some Practical Aspects of Operating an Infant and Toddler Center.* San Francisco: Family Developmental Center, 1975.
Leboyer, Frederick. *Birth Without Violence.* New York: Borzai Book, 1975.
Lewis, Judith, et al. Infant Special Education Project. *Grant Proposal for Second Year Funding.* San Francisco, California: 1976–77.
Lewis, Michael, and Rosenblum, Leonard (Editors). *Friendship and Peer Relations.* New York: John Wiley and Sons, 1975.

Lewis, Michael, and Rosenblum, Leonard. *The Effect of the Infant on its Caregiver.* New York: John Wiley and Sons, 1974.

Lillie, David L., and Trohanes, Pascal L. (Editors). *Teaching Parents to Teach.* New York: Walker and Co., 1976.

Lyman, Patricia. *Growing With Your Baby.* San Francisco: Family Developmental Center, 1975.

Maier, Henry W. *Three Theories of Child Development.* New York: Harper & Row, 1965.

Maslow, Abraham. *Motivation and Personality.* New York: Harper, 1954.

Montague, Ashley. *Touching.* New York: Harper & Row, 1972.

Murray, Robert F. Jr., and Rosser, Pearl (Editors). *The Genetic, Metabolic and Developmental Aspects of Mental Retardation.* Springfield, Ill.: Charles C. Thomas, 1972.

Nilsson, Lennart (photographs). *A Child is Born.* New York: Delacorte Press, 1966.

Oglesby, Allan, and Sterling, Harold (Editors). *Bi-regional Institute on Earlier Recognition of Handicapping Conditions in Childhood.* Berkeley: University of California, Berkeley School of Public Health, May 3-7, 1970.

Parmelee, A. H., and Michaelis, R. Neurological examination of the newborn. In J. Hellmuth (Editor). *Exceptional Infant (Vol.) 2.* New York: Brunner/Mazel, 1971.

Patton, Robert, and Gardner, Lytt. *Growth Failure in Maternal Deprivation.* Springfield, Ill.: Charles C. Thomas, 1963.

Penrose, L. S., and Smith, G. F. *Down's Anomaly.* Boston: Little, Brown & Co., 1966.

Piaget, Jean. *The Origins of Intelligence.* New York: Norton.

Piaget, Jean. Piaget takes a teacher's look. *Learning.* 1975.

Prechtl, H. F. R. The short and longterm prognosis of perinatal complications. Survey lecture: Fourth European Congress of Perinatal Medicine, Prague, Czech., August 28-30, 1944.

Provence, Sally, and Lipton, Tose. *Infants in Institutions.* New York: International Universities Press, 1962.

Ramer, Cyril, and Lodge, Ann. Neonatal addiction: A two year study. *Addictive Diseases: An International Journal.* Spectrum Publications, 1975.

Raynor, Sherry, and Drouillard, Richard. *Get a Wiggle On.* Mason, Michigan: Ingham Intermediate School District, 1975.

Scherzer, Alfred L. Early diagnosis, management and treatment of cerebral palsy. *Rehabilitation Literature,* July, 1974.

Slobin, Dan I. They Learn the Same Way All Around the World. Psychology Today, June, 1972.

Spitz, Rene. *The First Year of Life.* New York: International Universities Press, 1965.

Spitz, Rene. Hospitalism: An inquiry into the genesis of psychiatric conditions of early childhood. *Psychoanalytic Study of the Child,* 1945.

Stone, L. Joseph, and Church, Joseph. *Childhood and Adolescence.* New York: Random House, 1973.

Stone, L. Joseph, Smith, Henrietta T., and Murphy, Lois B. *The Competent Infant.* New York: Basic Books, Inc., 1973.

Thorum, Arden R. *Instructional Materials for the Handicapped.* Salt Lake City: Olympus Publishing Co., 1976.

Tronick, Edward, and Greenfield, Patricia. *Infant Curriculum.* New York: Media Projects, Inc., 1973.

Uzgiris, Ina, and Hunt, J. McV. *Assessment in Infancy.* Urbana, Ill.: University of Illinois Press, 1975.

Vaughn, V. (Editor). *Nelson's Textbook of Pediatrics.* Philadelphia, Pennsylvania: W. B. Saunders, 1975.

Webb, Harold J. Pregnant schoolgirls and pregnant teachers: the policy problem school districts can sidestep no longer. *The American School Board Journal.* March, 1973.

White, R. A. Competence and the psychosexual stages of development. *Nebraska Symposium on Motivation,* 1965.

Wolff, Sula. *Children Under Stress.* Hammondsworth, Middlesex, England: Penguin Books, 1969.

Wright, L. The theoretical and research base for a program of early stimulation, care, and training of premature infants. In J. Hellmuth (Editor). *Exceptional Infant.* Vol. 2. New York: Brunner/Mazel, 1971.

Yarrow, L. J., Rubenstein, J., Pederson, F. A., and Jankowski, J. J. Dimensions of early stimulation and their differential effects on infant development. *Merrill Palmer Quarterly. 18,* 1972.

Yarrow, L. J., Rubenstein, J., and Pederson, Frank. *Infant and Environment.* New York: John Wiley and Sons, 1975.

JOURNALS AND MAGAZINES

American Journal of Orthopsychiatry, 1790 Broadway, New York, N.Y. 10019.
An interdisciplinary journal published five times a year.

Child Development, published by the Society for Research in Child Development, University of Chicago Press, 5750 Ellis Ave., Chicago, Ill. 60637.
One of three publications of the Society. The others are *Monographs of the Society for Research in Child Development* and *Child Development Abstracts and Bibliography.*

Children Today, published by the Children's Bureau, Office of Child Development, Office of Human Development six times a year. Available from the Superintendent of Documents, U.S. Government Printing Office, Washington, D.C. 20402.
An interdisciplinary journal which contains articles on topics of interest to those who work with both normal and handicapped children and their families.

Child Welfare, journal of the Child Welfare League of America, Inc., 44 East 23rd Street, New York, N.Y. 10010.

A professional journal concerned with the welfare of children, with practical methods as well as research and education, as they relate to child welfare services and with issues of public social policy that have a bearing on them. Published ten times a year.

Day Care and Early Education, published five times during the school year by Behavioral Publications, 72 Fifth Ave., New York, N.Y. 10011.

Although the primary focus is on day care issues, the magazine's articles and features are valuable for all those involved in the care of infants, toddlers and preschool children.

Exceptional Children, published by the Council for Exceptional Children, 1201 16th Street, NW, Washington, D.C., ten times a year. Also issued is a quarterly, *Education and Training of the Mentally Retarded.* Both are for professionals.

Young Children, issued six times a year by the National Association for the Education of Young Children, 1834 Connecticut Avenue, NW, Washington, D.C.

Articles of interest to teachers and others working with young children and their parents, in day care centers, camps, nursery schools and other settings. Members of NAEYC receive *Young Children* as part of their membership benefits.

CURRICULUM RESOURCES

Barnard, Kathryn E. and Powell, Marcene L. *Teaching the Mentally Retarded Child.* St. Louis: The C. V. Mosby Co., 1972.

Bluma, Susan M., Shearer, Marsha S., Frohman, Alma H. and Hilliard, Jean M. *The Portage Guide to Early Educa-*

tion. Portage, Wisconsin: Cooperative Educational Services Agency #12, 1975.

Finnie, Nancy R. *Handling the Cerebral Palsied Child at Home.* New York: E. P. Dutton & Co., 1975.

Gordon, Ira. *Baby Learning Through Baby Play.* New York: St. Martin's Press, 1970.

Gordon, Ira. *Child Learning Through Child Play.* New York: St. Martin's Press, 1972.

Karnes, Merle. *The Karnes Early Language Activities.* Champaign, Illinois: G.E.M., 1975.

Nisonger Center for Mental Retardation and Developmental Disabilities. *Infant Stimulation Curriculum.* Columbus, Ohio: The Nisonger Center, 1976.

Northcott, Winifred H. (Ed.). *Curriculum Guide: Hearing Impaired Children—Birth to Three Years—And Their Parents.* Washington, D.C.: The Alexander Graham Bell Association for the Deaf, Inc., 1972.

Painter, Genevieve. *Teach Your Baby.* New York: Simon and Schuster, 1971.

Preschool Special Education Project. *Curriculum Manual.* Rochester, N.Y.: Preschool Special Education Program, 1973.

San Juan Handicapped Infant Project. *The Developmental Interventions.* Carmichael, California: The San Juan Unified School District.

Tronick, Edward and Greenfield, Patricia Marks. *Infant Curriculum.* New York: Media Projects, Inc., 1973.

FILMS

Cognitive Development. CRM Educational Films, Del Mar, Ca., (714) 453-5000; rental cost $35; 20 minutes, color.

Piaget's maturational stages of development contrasted with behaviorist theory and practices. The film also uses children to explore this controversy.

Emotional Development Aggression. CRM Educational Films, Del Mar, Ca., (714) 453-5000; rental cost $35; 20 minutes, color.

Are we killer apes? Or do we learn to aggress? A nursery school provides the arena for exploring this question.

Everybody Rides a Carousel, Part I. Pyramid Films, Box 1048, Santa Monica, Ca. 90496, (213) 828-7577; 1975; rental cost $25; 24 minutes, color.

This series of films illustrates the view of the psychological stages of life, adapted from the works of Erik H. Erikson. Part I covers the Newborn, Toddler and Early Childhood periods.

Growth Failure and Maternal Deprivation. #7564, University of California Extension Media Center, Berkeley, Ca. 94720; 1967; rental cost $14; 25 minutes, black and white.

Effects of a stimulation program for two severely deprived children, aged 15 months and 4 years, in a Detroit hospital.

How Babies Learn. #8249, University of California Extension Media Center, Berkeley Ca. 94720; 1966; rental cost $17; 25 minutes, color.

Describes important developmental advances made by babies in their first year. Observes several babies to demonstrate how their type of care influences their learning.

I'm 17, Pregnant and Don't Know What to Do. Children's Home Society, 3000 California Street, San Francisco, Ca., (415) 922-2803; rental cost none, 25 minutes, color.

A poignant depiction of the dilemma faced by a young school age mother who must make painful decisions before and after her pregnancy.

Infancy. CRM Educational Films, Del Mar, Ca., (714) 453-5000; rental cost $35; 20 minutes, color.

Recreates the landmark experiment that demonstrated that human infants are born with very sophisticated mechanisms. One interesting sequence lets the camera follow an infant's exploring activity so that the viewer sees the world through the baby's eyes.

Language Development. CRM Educational Films, Del Mar, Ca., (714) 453-5000; rental cost $35; 20 minutes, color.

Stresses the universality of language development—they learn the same way all over the world. Illustration of a variety of beginning communication skills.

Learning to Learn in Infancy. Modern Talking Pictures, 2323 New Hyde Park Road, New Hyde Park, N.Y. 11040, (516) 437-6300; rental cost none.

Focuses on the experiences in the first year of life as they affect the baby's development.

Mother Love. #6661, University of California Extension Media Center, Berkeley, Ca. 94720; 1960; rental cost $11; 25 minutes, black and white.

Dr. Harry Harlow's now classic experiments with monkeys showing the effects of maternal deprivation and the importance of the comfort received from the mother figure.

Ordinal Scales of Infant Psychological Development. Psychological Development Lab, 1003 W. Nevada, Urbana, Illinois 61801, (217) 333-1000; six films are available: Object Permanence, Development of Schemas, Operational Causality, Object Relations in Space, Gestural Imitation and Verbal Imitation (black and white).

Demonstration of some procedures used to administer the scales developed by Ina Uzguris and J. McVicker Hunt and concrete illustrations of behavioral phenomena described by Piaget.

Person to Person in Infancy. Modern Talking Pictures; 1970; rental cost none.

The importance of personal interaction in infant development. One sequence depicts how a program in Greece allows for a child and his caregiver to live together, by themselves, in order to establish the attachment which is so important to the child's development.

Psychological Hazards in Infancy. Modern Talking Pictures, 2323 New Hyde Park Road, New Hyde Park, N.Y. 11040, (516) 437-6300; rental cost none.

How an infant's emotional as well as cognitive development is influenced by his caregiver's insensitivity to his needs.

Reward and Punishment. CRM Educational Films, Del Mar, Ca., (714) 453-5000; rental cost $35.

This film stresses the value of positive reinforcement in teaching and interacting with children. Although the film depicts pre-school and school age children, it is also applicable to infants and toddlers.

Rock-a-Bye Baby. #8507, University of California Extension Media Center, Berkeley, Ca. 94720; 1971; rental cost $19; 30 minutes, color.

Wide ranging examination of current research on the psychological and physical effects of the care children receive in the earliest period of their development. Award winning film which stresses the importance of kinesthetic and vestibular stimulation.

Tim: His Sensory Motor Development. UCLA Instructional Media Library, 405 Hilgard Avenue, Los Angeles, California 90024, (213) 825-0755; rental cost $29; 25 minutes, color.

Illustrates some concepts of cognitive development as described by Jean Piaget, starring the same child and his mother from infancy through toddlerhood.

Two Year Old Goes to Hospital. #3247, University of California Extension Media Center, Berkeley, Ca. 94720; 1952; rental cost $12; 50 minutes, black and white.

A moving film, part of the series, *Young Children in Brief Separation,* illustrating the effects of separation on a child. This is a British film in two parts, made by the Robertsons who have done much of their work at Tovistock clinic.

Other films in this series are: John 7 Months: Nine Days in a Residential Nursery #8310; Kate: A Two Year Old in Fostercare #8311; and Jane: Aged 17 Months in Fostercare for Ten Days #8309.

VIDEOTAPES

Available from:
High/Scope Educational Research Foundation, 600 North River Street, Ypsilante, Michigan 48197, (313) 485-2000; rental cost $30.

A Special Kind of Mother.
A special kind of mother is able to put herself in her baby's place and to respond in ways that meet cognitive as well as physical needs.
15 minutes, black and white.

Learning to Talk: An Introduction to Language in Infancy.
Beginning sounds, vocal responses, initiation and first words and phrases are the focus of examples used to demonstrate early steps in learning to communicate with words.
25 minutes, black and white.

Object Concept During Sensory Motor Stage III.
Key aspects of cognitive and perceptual growth demonstrated with a child from 5 - 8 months interacting with one toy.
19 minutes, black and white.

Visual Pursuit and Object Permanence.
The child's growing ability to recognize and distinguish objects and to remember and look for them when they are out of sight are shown in four sequences that occur during the sensore-motor period.
27 minutes, black and white.

FILMSTRIPS

Available from: Day Care and Child Development Council of America, 622 14th St. N.W., Washington, D.C. 20005, (202) 638-2316; rental cost: $7.50 non-members, $5.00 members.

Child Care: An Investment in the Community's Future. #AV53 Shows how parent, staff and community commitment have produced a developmental child care program for children of migrant families. Features the Parent-Child in Greeley, Colorado.

Day Care: Springboard for Migrants. #AV51

Parents and Staff Together. #AV52

A Rural Child Care Program. #AV50

Shiprock Day Care: Old Ways. #AV54

Available from:
Parent Magazine Films, Inc., 52 Vanderbilt Ave., New York, N.Y. 10017; purchase cost perset: $53 with record, $58. with cassettes. Each series contains 2 to 6 sound-color filmstrip sets. Each set contains: four to six color filmstrips, one 12" record or 2 to 3 cassettes, five audio script booklets and one discussion guide.

A Special Need, A Special Love: Children With Handicaps:
   Behavioral and Emotional Disabilities; Physical Disabilities; Intellectual Disabilities; and Educational and Language Disabilities.

Child Development and Child Health:
   Food and Nutrition; Health and Safety; Play and Self Expression; Love and Identity; How an Average Child Behaves—From Birth to Age Five; and The First 18 Months: From Infant to Toddler.

Children in Crisis:
   Child Abuse and Neglect; Death; Illness; and Divorce and Separation.

Even Love is Not Enough: Children With Handicaps:
   Behavioral and Emotional Disabilities; Physical Disabilities; Intellectual Disabilities; and Educational and Language Disabilities.

Forget Me, Forget Me Not: Parents and Teenagers, Portraits and Self Portraits:
   Portrait of Teenagers; Portrait of Parents; The Struggle for Independence; and Looking Toward Adulthood.

Understanding Early Childhood:
   The Child's Relationship with the Family; Preparing the Child for Learning; The Child's Point of View; and Development of Feelings in Children.

Understanding Parenthood:
   The Economics of Parenthood; The Growing Parent; Children and Family Relationships.

What Do I See When I See Me:
   I See Hope; I See Smiles, I See Frowns; I See Strength; and I See Love.

Will You Marry Me: Marriage and Creating a Successful Marriage:
Marriage: What is It All About; The Many Aspects of Love; Common Problems and Opportunities; and Looking Ahead and Looking Back: Four Marriages.

With Pride to Progress: The Minority Child:
The Black Child; The Puerto Rican Child; The Chicano Child; and the Indian Child.

BIBLIOGRAPHY

Atkinson, J. *Day care costs in Massachusetts.* Boston: State of Massachusetts, March 1973. 15 pp. [Office for Children, ATTN: Massachusetts State 4-C Committee, 120 Boylston Street, Room #246, Boston, MA 02116].

Bedger, J. E., Ehrlich, L. D., Zemont, D., Silhavy, C. K., & Weed, C. *Financial reporting and cost analysis manual for day care centers, head start, and other programs.* Chicago: Council for Community Services in Metropolitan Chicago, March 1973. 185 pp. $7.50. [64 East Jackson Boulevard, Chicago, IL 60604].

Bernstein, B. & Giacchino, P. Costs of day care: Implications for public policy, *City Almanac* (6:2). New York: New School for Social Research, August 1971.

Bikle, J. Social casework in a day care program, *Day care: An expanding resource for children.* New York: Child Welfare League of America, Inc., 1965. pp. 36–43. [67 Irving Place, New York, NY 10003].

Caldwell, B. M. What is the optimal learning environment for the young child? *American Journal of Orthopsychiatry,* 1967, *37,* 8–22.

Child care: Data and materials. Senate Committee on Finance (Russell B. Long, Chairman), 2nd Session of the 93rd Congress. Washington: U.S. Government Printing Office, October 1974. 258 pp. $2.55 [Superintendent of Documents, U.S. Government Printing Office, Washington, DC 20402].

Child care in Massachusetts: The public responsibility. Massachusetts Early Education Project. Washington: Day Care and Child Development Council of America, Inc., 1972. [1401 K Street NW, Washington, DC 20060].

Child welfare league of America standards for day care service. Child Welfare League of America, Inc. New York: Child Welfare League of America, Inc., 1969. 123 pp. $2.50 [67 Irving Place, New York, NY 10003].

Cohen, D. J. *Day care: 3: Serving preschool children.* Washington: U.S. Government Printing Office, 1974. 164 pp. [Superintendent of Documents, U.S. Government Printing Office, Washington, DC 20402].

Day care: An annotated bibliography. Educational Resources Information Center (ERIC). Urbana: ERIC, June 1971. [ERIC Clearinghouse on Early Childhood Education, University of Illinois at Urbana-Champaign, 805 West Pennsylvania Avenue, Urbana, IL 61801].

Day care: Who needs it. League of Women Voters. Washington: League of Women Voters, 1973.

Directory of resources on early childhood education. Educational Resources Information Center (ERIC). Washington: Day Care and Child Development Council of America, Inc., 1971. (Reprint). [1401 K Street NW, Washington, DC 20060].

Early childhood development in Texas: 1973–74. Texas Department of Community Affairs. Austin: Texas Department of Community Affairs, December 1973. 159 pp. [Jeannette Watson, Director, Office of Early Childhood Development, Texas Department of Community Affairs, P.O. Box 13166, Capitol Station, Austin, TX 78711].

Early childhood planning in the states: A handbook for gathering data and assessing needs. Early Childhood Task Force, Education Commission of the States. Denver: Education Commission of the States, 1973. 46 pp. $1.00 [300 Lincoln Tower, 1860 Lincoln Street, Denver, CO 80203].

Emlen, A. C., Donoghue, B. A. & LaForge, R. *Child care by kith: A study of the family day care relationships of working mothers and neighborhood caregivers.* Portland: Portland State University, 1971. 332 pp. [Field Study of the Neighborhood Family Day Care System, 2856 Northwest Savier, Portland, OR 97210].

Establishing a state office of early childhood development: Suggested legislative alternatives. Early Childhood Task Force, Education Commission of the States. Denver: Education Commission of the States, 1973. 48 pp. $1.00. [300 Lincoln Tower, 1860 Lincoln Street, Denver, CO 80203].

Farson, R. *Birthrights: A bill of rights for children.* New York: Macmillan Publishing Co., Inc., 1974. 248 pp. $6.95. [866 Third Avenue, New York, NY 10022.]

Goldsmith, C. A blueprint for a comprehensive community-wide day care program. *Child Welfare,* 1965, *44:* 501–503, 528.

Grosett, M. D., Simon, A. C., Stewart, N. B. *So you're going to run a day care service!* New York: Day Care Council of New York, Inc. Autumn 1971. 88 pp. [114 East 32nd Street, New York, NY 10016].

Growing up in Idaho: The needs of young children. Idaho Office of Child Development. Boise: State of Idaho. 17 pp.

A guide for planning: Food service in child care centers. Food and Nutrition Service, U.S. Department of Agriculture. Washington: U.S. Department of Agriculture, 1971. 22 pp. $.55. [Superintendent of Documents, U.S. Government Printing Office, Washington, DC 20402].

Harrell, J. A. (Ed.). *Selected readings in the issues of day care.* Washington: Day Care and Child Development Council of America, Inc., 1972. 85 pp. [1401 K Street NW, Washington, DC 20060].

Hest, M. S. A broad community approach to day care. *Child welfare,* 1960, *39,* 29–32.

Hoffman, L. W. & Nye, F. I. *Working mothers: An evaluative review of the consequences for wife, husband, and child.* San Francisco: Jossey-Bass, Inc., 1974. 272 pp. $12.50. [615 Montgomery Street, San Francisco, CA 94111].

An impact study of day care: Feasibility report and manual for community planners. Center for the Study of Public Policy. Cambridge: Center for the Study of Public Policy, February 1971. 198 pp. [56 Boylston Street, Cambridge, MA 02138].

Joint distribution committee guide for day care centers: A handbook to aid communities in developing day care center programs for pre-school children. American Joint Distribution Committee. Geneva: American Joint Distribution Committee, 1962. (ERIC Publication No. EDO 27961.) [ERIC Clearinghouse on Early Childhood Education, University of Illinois at Urbana-Champaign, 805 West Pennsylvania Avenue, Urbana, IL 61801].

Kiester, D. J. *Consultation in day care.* Chapel Hill, NC: Institute of Government, University of North Carolina at Chapel Hill, 1969. 72 pp.

Kitano, H. H. L. *The child-care center: A study of the interaction among one-parent children, parents, and school.* Berkeley and Los Angeles: University of California Press, 1963, 344 pp. $1.25.

Knight, E. V. *Serving the pre-school child: Day care as a service to the entire family.* New York: National Federation of Settlements and Neighborhood Centers, 1966. [232 Madison Avenue, New York, NY 10016].

Kraus, D., Beal, E., Taylor, R., & Blackford, L. *Survey of pre-school and day care needs and facilities in San Mateo county.* San Mateo County, CA: Office of San Mateo County Superintendent of Schools, San Mateo Board of Education, 1970. 50 pp.

Lewis, L. Broad community approach to day care. *Child Welfare*, 1960. *39*, 32–33.

Mattick, I. & Perkins, F. J. *Guidelines for observation and assessment: An approach to evaluating the learning environment of a day care center.* Washington: Day Care and Child Development Council of America, Inc., January 1973. 44 pp. [1401 K Street NW, Washington, DC 20060].

Morgan, G. G. *Regulation of early childhood programs.* Washington: Day Care and Child Development Council of America, Inc., January 1973. 130 pp. [1401 K Street NW, Washington, DC 20060].

Moss, M. A., Sullivan, R. J., & Pratt, E. *A menu planning guide for type A school lunches.* Washington: U.S. Department of Agriculture, 1974. 20 pp. and foldout worksheet. $1.00. [Superintendent of Documents, U.S. Government Printing Office, Washington, DC 20402].

Murphy, L. B., & Leeper, E. M. *Caring for children—No. 6: A setting for growth.* Washington: U.S. Department of Health, Education, and Welfare, 1973. 24 pp, (Illustrated). $.55. [Superintendent of Documents, U.S. Government Printing Office, Washington, DC 20402].

Murphy, L. B., & Leeper, E. M. *Caring for children—No. 7: The individual child.* Washington: U.S. Department of Health, Education, and Welfare, 1973. 24 pp. (Illustrated). $.55. [Superintendent of Documents, U.S. Government Printing Office, Washington, DC 20402].

Out to lunch: A study of USDA's day-care and summer feeding programs. The Food Research and Action Center. Yonkers, NY: Gazette Press, Inc., 1974. 94 pp. $2.00.

A plan for child care in Palo Alto. The Child Care Task Force Appointed by the City Council. Palo Alto, CA: City of Palo Alto, Division of Reproduction, April 1973. 83 pp.

Prescott, E. A comparison of three types of day care and nursery school—home care. Pasadena, CA, 1973. 11 pp. (Paper presented at the Biennial Meeting of Society for Research in Child Development, Philadelphia, PA. March 29–April 1, 1973). [Elizabeth Prescott, Pacific Oaks College, 714 West California Boulevard, Pasadena, CA 91107].

Project Head Start: Nutrition-staff training programs. U.S. Department of Health, Education, and Welfare. Washington: U.S. Department of Health, Education, and Welfare, 1969. 36 pp. [Superintendent of Documents, U.S. Government Printing Office, Washington, DC 20402.]

Recommendations for day care centers for infants and children. Committee on Infant and Preschool Child. Evanston: American Academy of Pediatrics, 1973. [P.O. Box 1037, Evanston, IL 60204].

Ruderman, F. A. Day care: A challenge to social work, *Child Welfare,* 1963, *43,* 117–123.

Ruffino, B. C., & Aitken, S. S. *Day care in Maryland: A study of child development needs and resources* (Summary Report). Washington: Maryland Child Development Planning Project, Maryland Office of Child Development, March 1972. 5 pp. [733 15th Street NW, Washington, DC 20005].

Ruopp, R. R. (Case study coordinator). *A study in child care, 1970–71.* Cambridge: ABT Associates, Inc.; Washington, DC: Office of Economic Opportunity, 1971. (Volume I—*Findings*; Volume II-A—*Center Case Studies;* Volume II-B—*System Case Studies;* Volume III—*Cost and Quality Issues for Operators*). [ABT Associates, Inc., 55 Wheeler Street, Cambridge, MA 02138].

Sauer, P. H., Hickey, M. F. Building a day care center: An introduction to planning and financing a day care center: What to look for and how to buy it or rent it with a city lease. New York: Bank Street Day Care Consultation Service, February 1970. [Bank Street College of Education, Day Care Consultation Service, 610 West 112th Street, New York, NY 10025].

Schultze, C. L., Fried, E. R., Rivlin, A. M. & Teeters, N. H. *Setting national priorities: The 1973 budget.* Washington: The Brookings Institution, 1972. 468 pp. [1775 Massachusetts Avenue, Washington, DC 20036].

Shannon, W. A radical, direct, simple, utopian alternative to day-care centers. *The New York Times Magazine,* April 30, 1972.

Siedman, E. *Day care in Vermont: An evaluation of the Vermont model FAP child care service system.* Washington: Leadership Institute for Community Development, 1972. 440 pp.

State and local day care licensing requirements. Office of Child Development, U.S. Department of Health, Education, and Welfare. Washington: U.S. Government Printing Office, August 1971. 52 pp. and appendices A-J. $1.75 domestic postpaid; $1.50 GPO bookstore. [Superintendent of Documents, U.S. Government Printing Office, Washington, DC 20402].

Swenson, J. P. *Alternatives in quality child care: A guide for thinking and planning.* Washington: Day Care and Child Development Council of America, Inc., 1972. 79 pp. [1401 K Street NW, Washington, DC 20060].

Zamoff, R. B. *Guide to the assessment of day care services and needs at the community level.* Washington: The Urban Institute, July 1971. 100 pp. $3.00 [Publications Office, The Urban Institute, 2100 M Street NW, Washington, DC 20037].

INDEX

Accountability in child care programs, 12
Adventure playgrounds, 226
Addison, Bertha, 16, 19, 83–92
Ainsworth, M. D. S., 8, 26
American Academy of Pediatrics, 69–70
Anixter, Valerie, 18–19, 163–183
Art activities, 151
Association for Regulatory Administration, 122
Auerbach, Stevanne, v–vi, xv–xx

Bayley Scales of Infant Development, 53
Baratz, J. C. & Baratz, S., 31
Beckwith, Jay, 19, 215–238
Billingsley, Andrew, 16–17, 30

Black children, Development Education Center, 16–17
 infant mortality rate, 19
 mental health, 20–23
 needs and rights, 21–28
 specific needs, 33–35
 and U.S. government, 17–21
Black families, maternal mortality rate, 19
 needs and rights, 28–33
 specific needs, 33–35
Boguslawski, D. B., 25
Boondoggle, 28
Bowlby, J., 8, 26
Bronfenbrenner, Urie Dr., 40
Brostrom, Margaret Ann, 16, 20, 93–107
Budget planning, 185
Bureau of Education for the Handicapped, 42

INDEX

Caldwell, Bettye M., 1–14, 20, 24, 26
California licensing, health offices, 95–102
Cattell Infant Intelligence Scale, 6
Ceilings, 168
Center for Early Development and Education, Little Rock, Arkansas, 5
Chapel Hill, North Carolina Frank Porter Graham Child Development Center, 5
Checklist for developing a facility, 158–162
Child abuse, 96, 118
Child advocacy, 26
Child Care, costs of, 11–13, 62, 68–69, 96–97
and industry, 104
Child development
associate, 11
effects of segregation, 15
evaluation, 53
intellectual, 6–7
measurement, 125–126
Child Welfare League of America, 24–25
Children's Bureau, H.E.W., 4, 11, 116
Children's Center, Syracuse, N.Y., 5–6, 7–9, 23–24, 27
Children's rights, 125
Closets, 183
Color, 187
Community Family Day Care Project, Pacific Oaks College, 15, 60–73
Community groups playgrounds, 224–232
Construction activities, 150–151
Cooking, 191–193

Dai, Bingham, 28–29
Day Care and Child Development Council of America, 99
Demonstration Nursery Center for Infants and Toddlers, University of North Carolina at Greensboro, 5
Desegregation, psychological impact of, 15
and social change, 16–17
Designing a children's center
art activities, 151
atmosphere, 163
book shelves, 173
ceilings, 140, 168
closets, 183
colors, 142, 187
construction activities, 150–151
defining activity areas, 141–143, 185
design procedures, 158–162, 184–185, 215–236
dramatic play, 152–153
entrance, 141, 164
floor, 141, 145–146, 168–170
food preparation, 148, 191–193
illness isolation, 155–156
indoor equipment, 171–183, 196–209
music, 154–155
outdoor play area, 141, 157–158, 216–236
quiet play areas, 143
relationship to program philosophy, 138–139
safety, 140, 218–219
sand play, 153–154
sinks, water play, 148, 149–150

INDEX

square footage requirements, 142
storage and presentation of play materials, 143–145, 146, 165–166, 167, 187–189
tables, 173–174
toilet areas, 146–147, 193–196
vandalism, 141
walls, coverings, 165–166
windows, 141, 166–167, 190
Dramatic play, 152–153

Economic Opportunities Council, 100
Entrance to center, 164
Environment, 140–142, 184, 185–187, 215–226
Equipment suggested, 171–172
ERIC Clearinghouse on Early Childhood Education, 57

Family day care, 60–73, 75–82
benefits, 61–63
services, 66–70
Family day care homes
characteristics of successful programs, 76–80
cooperative network, 99–100
licensing, 95, 97–98
starting a program, 101–102
Family Developmental Center, San Francisco, Calif., 41–57
Center Program for Children, 50–55
Infant Special Education Project, 47–50
School Age Parents Program, 44–47
services and goals, 41–44
teacher selection and training, 55–56
Family policy, 12

Family Services Agency, San Mateo, Calif., 100
Massachusetts, definition of, 124
program administration, 132–135
registration, 123–136
supportive services to, 130–132
Federal Interagency Day Care Requirements, 112
Film strips, resources, 255–257
Floors, 168–170
Food preparation, 148

"Gatekeeper" technique, 63
Graham, Frank Porter, Child Development Center, Chapel Hill, North Carolina, 5
Greensboro Project, 7
Group Day Care Home, California definition, 95

Handicapped children, 41–43, 47–50
Harvard Educational Review, 19
Head Start, 9, 112
funding standards, 112
Parent-Child Center Program, 5, 31
Health
effects of infant care, 2, 10
family day care homes, 62
non-white children, 19, 21
Hughes, Edna H., 16, 20, 108–122
Huizinga, Johan, 224

Infant Day Care, 1–13, 16, 42
Black children, 15–35
costs, 11–13
effects on health, 10

Infant Day Care (*cont.*)
  history, 4–5
  intellectual development, 6–7
  parents, 10–11
  social and emotional
    development, 7–10
Infant Education, 47–50
  program resources, 241–257
Infant rights, 22
Infants Special Education
  Project, San Francisco, Calif.,
  47–50
Intellectual development, 6–7

Joint Commission on Mental
  Health, 20, 21–23

Kagan, Jerome Dr., 144
Kuhn, Alyson, 18, 21, 163–183

Labor, U.S. Department of, 19
Latch key children, 10
Latzko, Trudy R.N., M.A.,
  241–257
Legislation, California, 99–100
Lewis, Judith, 14, 21, 39–59
Licensing, 94, 95–99, 101–102,
  108–122
  comparison to regulation,
    112–114, 126–127
  definition, 110
  Office of Educational Liaison
    of the Health and Welfare
    Agency, State of California
    Task Force, 1974, 98–99
  standards, 120–121
  theory of, 114–115
  See also Registration
Little Rock, Arkansas
  Center for Early Development
    and Education, 5
Lorenz, Konrad, 224

Massachusetts Office for
  Children, 123–136
Maternal attachment and
  deprivation, 2–3, 6, 24–25
Maternal-infant separation, 2
McCauley, Linda, 16, 21,
  123–136
Mental health
  of non-white children, 20–23
Mirrors, 187
Mothers' Club Cooperative
  Nursery School, 66
Music activities, 154–155

Naps and rest periods, 155,
  175
National Council of Jewish
  Women, 10
National Urban League, 29–30
Needs assessment, Texas, ix
  play space, 217
Neighborhood Day Care
  Program (NDCP), San
  Mateo County, Calif., 16,
  100–105
North Carolina, University of, at
  Greensboro
  Demonstration Nursery Center
    for Infants and Toddlers, 5, 7

Office of Child Development, 2,
  42, 115
Office of Educational Liaison of
  the Health and Welfare
  Agency, Calif., 98–99
Office of Management and
  Budget, 10
Osmon, Fred, 17, 22, 137–162
Outdoor play, 215–236
  materials for playground,
    226–228
  types of play, 228–232

Pacific Oaks College, 10
Painting, clay and plants, 189–191
Parent-Child Center Program, 5
Parent-Child Toy Lending Library, 16
Parents
 education, 33, 84
 effects of infant child care on, 10–11
 involvement in child care programs, 43–44, 103–104, 156
 School Age Parents' Program, San Francisco, Calif., 44–47
Piers, Maria W., 16, 22, 75–82
Placement service, 67–68
Play environments, 157–158, 215–236
 community-built playgrounds, 224–226
 designs for, 233–236
 materials for, 226–228
 "free" play activities, 217–221
 multiuse schoolyard, 228–232
 play sculpture, 216
 safety, 218–219, 223
 sense of "place", 221–222
Playground
 design considerations, 230–232
 materials list, 226–229
Poverty, 4, 15, 18–21
Powell, Gloria J., 15–38
Powell, Dr. Rodney N., 18–19
Private day care operators, 12
Private industry and day care, 104

Quality day care, 12, 129–130

Racism
 and economic status, 19–21
 and medical care, 21
 and mental health, 21–23
 in public schools, 19
Referrals, 67–68
Registration of family day care homes
 Massachusetts, 123–136
 self-evaluation by caregiver, 127–128
 technical assistance, 129
Report of Equality of Educational Opportunities, 19
Resources for infant education programs, 241–257
Responsibility of the state, parents, providers, 110–111
 of the child, 170–171
Richmond, Dr. Julius B., 33–34
Room dividers, 175

Safety, 218–220, 223
Sale, June Solnit, 22, 60–74
Sand play, 153–154
San Francisco Unified School District, 42, 44
San Mateo, California, 100
School age children, need care, 10
School Age Parents' Program, San Francisco, Calif., 44–47, 56
Schoolyard activities, 229
Segregation, effects on child development, 15, 31
Self-evaluation, 127
"Sequences of Development," 52–53
Sick child, 155–156

Single parents, 3, 40
Sinks, 148
Skolnick, Sharon, 163
Smith, L., 24
Staff
  family day care mothers, 63–64, 80–81, 83–92, 98
  salaries, 103
Staff and parent lounge, 156
Stanford-Binet Intelligence Test, 7
Stimulation program, 42
Storage units, 189
Supreme Court, 26

Tables, 173–174, 176, 178
Teenage mothers, 3, 32, 40, 42
  See Also School Age Parents' Program
Toilets, 147
Toy-Lending Library, 50, 66, 83–84, 89–92
Training, child care personnel, 55–56, 63–66, 67, 71, 79–80, 83–92, 98, 102–103, 116

Unwed mothers, 3
U.S. Department of Health, Education, and Welfare, 9
U.S. Government
  and the black child, 17–21
  response to family needs, ix–xiii

Videotapes, resource, 254–255

Wall space, 165–166
Wallach, Lorraine B., 16, 75–82
Water play, 149–150
Weissberg, Gloria M., 16, 23, 184–214
White House Conference on Children and Youth, ix, 18–19
Windows on Day Care, 10
Windows, uses and ideas, 166–168
Women's liberation, 3, 10, 33–34
"Work-fare" program, 20
Working mothers, 3–4, 23, 62, 94

Zigler, Edward P., ix–xiii